SANTA BARBARA'S ROYAL PRESIDIO

Artist Russell Antonio Ruiz provided this aerial view of the Presidio in the 1790s with the Mission visible toward the mountains. It is an accurate depiction missing only a two-story observation tower that was discovered later on a 1820s map and confirmed by archaeology. *Courtesy SBTHP*

Santa Barbara's Royal Presidio

The Rise, Fall, and Rebirth of Spain's Last Adobe Fortress

JARRELL C. JACKMAN

Foreword by Milford Wayne Donaldson, FAIA

Essex, Connecticut

An imprint of Globe Pequot, the trade division of
The Rowman & Littlefield Publishing Group, Inc.
4501 Forbes Blvd., Ste. 200
Lanham, MD 20706
www.rowman.com

Distributed by NATIONAL BOOK NETWORK

Copyright © 2022 by Jarrell C. Jackman.
Map on page 29 by The Rowman & Littlefield Publishing Group, Inc.

All rights reserved. No part of this book may be reproduced in any form or by any electronic or mechanical means, including information storage and retrieval systems, without written permission from the publisher, except by a reviewer who may quote passages in a review.

British Library Cataloguing-in-Publication Information available

Library of Congress Cataloging-in-Publication Data
Names: Jackman, Jarrell C., author.
Title: Santa Barbara's Royal Presidio : the rise, fall, and rebirth of Spain's last adobe fortress / Jarrell C. Jackman.
Other titles: Rise, fall, and rebirth of Spain's last adobe fortress
Description: Essex, Connecticut : Lyons Press, [2022] | Includes bibliographical references and index.
Summary: "Unique in California history—and beloved by visitors and residents alike—the city of Santa Barbara boasts three great historical properties: the Mission, the Courthouse, and the Presidio. Least known is the Presidio. This book corrects that vacuum, beginning with the story of its adobe construction between 1784 and 1790. . . ."— Provided by publisher.
Identifiers: LCCN 2022041186 (print) | LCCN 2022041187 (ebook) | ISBN 9781493067893 (hardcover) | ISBN 9781493070756 (epub)
Subjects: LCSH: Santa Barbara Presidio (Santa Barbara, Calif.)—History. | Fortification—California—Santa Barbara—History. | Architecture, Spanish—Conservation and restoration—California—Santa Barbara. | Santa Barbara Trust for Historic Preservation.
Classification: LCC UG412.S46 J33 2022 (print) | LCC UG412.S46 (ebook) | DDC 623.10979491—dc23/eng/20220826
LC record available at https://lccn.loc.gov/2022041186
LC ebook record available at https://lccn.loc.gov/2022041187

♾️ The paper used in this publication meets the minimum requirements of American National Standard for Information Sciences—Permanence of Paper for Printed Library Materials, ANSI/NISO Z39.48-1992.

Dedicated to Professor Harold C. Kirker

Photo of Patrick O'Dowd (left) Professor Harold Kirker and author Jackman. The photo from circa 1984 is in front of the Presidio chapel then under reconstruction. The book is dedicated to Kirker who served on the board of SBTHP, and chaired the doctoral committees of both O'Dowd and Jackman at University of California, Santa Barbara. *Author's Collection*

CONTENTS

FOREWORD BY MILFORD WAYNE DONALDSON..................ix

PROLOGUE: INTO THE MAELSTROM..........................xii

CHAPTER ONE:
The Presidio: The Birthplace of Santa Barbara.......................1

CHAPTER TWO:
Decline and Fall of the Presidio....................................31

CHAPTER THREE:
The Early Years of the Santa Barbara Trust for Historic Preservation....35

CHAPTER FOUR:
The Presidio Project: Peaks and Valleys of the 1980s.................51

CHAPTER FIVE:
Winning the Day...73

CHAPTER SIX:
Back to Adobe Mudslinging...91

CHAPTER SEVEN:
Making History Fun: Living History and Rewards of Research........101

CHAPTER EIGHT:
Creative Mudslinging in Full Swing................................113

CHAPTER NINE:
Some Amazing Presidio Real-Estate Stories........................143

CHAPTER TEN:
Pomp and Circumstance: Royalty Comes to the Presidio.............151

CHAPTER ELEVEN:
My First Twenty Years 157

CHAPTER TWELVE:
"We Are the Mud People" 161

CHAPTER THIRTEEN:
Some Outside Activities: Did These Benefit the Presidio Project? 175

CHAPTER FOURTEEN:
Surviving the Great Recession 183

CHAPTER FIFTEEN:
Santa Inés Mission Mills Takes Center Stage 195

CHAPTER SIXTEEN:
When Does an Interest Become a Distraction? 203

CHAPTER SEVENTEEN:
Casa de la Guerra: Profit Versus Interpretation 215

CHAPTER EIGHTEEN:
More Museum Space: More Exhibitions 223

CHAPTER NINETEEN:
Building a New Research Center 229

CHAPTER TWENTY:
Still Much to Celebrate 239

CHAPTER TWENTY-ONE:
Final Projects and Praises 247

CHAPTER TWENTY-TWO:
Why the Presidio Project Succeeded 259

ACKNOWLEDGMENTS 267

APPENDIX 269

BIBLIOGRAPHY 271

INDEX 275

Foreword

OVER the past sixty years, no organization has done more to preserve, advance, and promote the Hispanic-period historical resources and culture in the state of California than the Santa Barbara Trust for Historic Preservation (SBTHP). Dr. Jarrell Jackman, known as "Jerry" to many of his friends and colleagues, spent thirty-five years (1981–2016) at the SBTHP, and his personal account, *Santa Barbara's Royal Presidio: The Rise, Fall, and Rebirth of Spain's Last Adobe Fortress*, lays out the early history of the Presidio, and the efforts to preserve and rebuild the adobe fort over many decades in the twentieth century. His emphasis is on his years as projects administrator and CEO of SBTHP, but he makes the point strongly that he stands on the shoulders of giants who had advanced the Presidio project before his arrival. As the architect of record of various reconstruction and restoration projects of SBTHP, I experienced firsthand the outstanding work of Jerry and the SBTHP staff and volunteers. Rebuilding the Presidio was no easy task in modern California's regulatory environment—but with persistence and commitment, those individuals have succeeded against all odds.

To be sure, while *Santa Barbara's Royal Presidio* reads like a very personal story, Jerry's reflections capture the challenges, political maneuverings, and negotiations along the way that led to the rebirth of the Presidio. We readers learn what it took to create and advance El Presidio de Santa Bárbara State Historic Park—the complex real-estate transactions and the research and archaeology required to carry out actual reconstruction and restoration projects. "Creative mudslinging" is Jerry's unique way of describing the massive number of adobe bricks that had to be made on site. We learn how the Presidio project was funded. We learn too that SBTHP's interests tied to the Presidio other historical resources such as Casa de la Guerra, the El Paseo shopping complex, and the Santa Inés Mission Mills. We learn of the publications, living-history events (including reintroducing the Japanese history of the Presidio site), and royal visits, many of which Jerry initiated. Dr. Jackman in his full Don Quixote mode takes us on his research trips to Mexico and Spain. We gallop along as he visits all two hundred eighty California state parks and as he becomes involved with the California League of Park Associations. It was not accidental that at his decoration ceremony as a knight in the Order of Isabel la Católica in 2016, he had opera baritone Eduardo Villa sing "The Impossible Dream."

Architectural historian Dr. David Gebhard once remarked:

> If we glance back into Santa Barbara's history, especially that of the late nineteenth and early twentieth centuries, it should not be a surprise that the Spanish/Mediterranean tradition of architecture was seized upon as the image which would provide a linkage between the past, present, and future. The community had been one of the principal early Spanish towns of Alta California and, like Monterey, the town possessed several renowned and striking examples of early nineteenth century Spanish and Mexican architecture. The Mission Church overlooking the city and the adobe dwellings clustered around the former Presidio lent a sense of old world age which was unusual for an American community west of the Mississippi.

Jerry and the SBTHP built on this heritage in reconstructing the Presidio in a town that had already established its Hispanic roots by promoting and implementing a Spanish colonial style of architecture after the 1925 earthquake. In fact, civic activist Pearl Chase, who had been a key member of the planning committee of Santa Barbara's downtown core post-earthquake, was also the founder of the SBTHP whose primary project from the start was rebuilding the adobe fort that represented the founding of the town in 1782.

Santa Barbara's Royal Presidio is an important chronicle of the Spanish beginnings of Santa Barbara, of SBTHP's commitment to preserving that history, and of Jerry's legacy in being a person who was instrumental in the success of the Presidio project. It pays fitting homage to Santa Barbara's early settlers and their descendants who participated over the years in keeping alive the Hispanic heritage of the town. *Santa Barbara's Royal Presidio* also is an important documentation of how a state historic park was formed and grew to its current stature as a site of not only local but also statewide and international significance. SBTHP and Jerry have received many awards over the years for their efforts and these were indeed well deserved. Dr. Jarrell Jackman's personal account should be read widely as one of the great examples not only of his sound leadership practices but also of the team effort that has preserved and developed a major historic site—at the center of one of the most beautiful coastal cities in America.

Milford Wayne Donaldson, FAIA
California State Historic Preservation Officer (2004–12)
Chairman Advisory Council of Historic Preservation (2010–19)

Wayne Donaldson at work at the Casa de la Guerra. *Author's Collection*

PROLOGUE

INTO THE MAELSTROM

"Adobe. Add water to earth and let it dry in the air. But no fire! Three out of the four elements: that's what we're all about at the Santa Barbara Trust for Historic Preservation. A few years back it was the search for roots. But today, humanity, it seems, wants to get back in touch with Mother Earth. . . . I've observed a true esprit de corps, a real sense of accomplishment among Trust volunteers making adobe bricks. It's more than romance. I detect a deep, almost unconscious feeling associated with molding earth into blocks. In this basic building process, terra firma has a grip on our souls. As we look for answers away from the high tech complexities of modern life, what could be more consoling than finding meaning in mud?"
　—A quotation from one of my reports to the SBTHP membership.

I could have never guessed as I began my career as a historian that it would be defined by one hundred thousand adobe bricks. My world was *echt* German back in the 1970s—German literature, German history, German food, studying in Germany, teaching in Germany, all of which culminated in a dissertation on German intellectuals who escaped the Nazis and ended up in Southern California. But after four-plus years in the Fatherland and two in Washington, D.C., due to my wife, Michele, working in the Pentagon, I landed back in Santa Barbara and was hired as the lead administrator in charge of rebuilding El Real Presidio de Santa Bárbara, an eighteenth-century Spanish adobe fort. Mud was to be my future. I was to lead a pack of "creative adobe mudslingers," as I came to call those of us who dedicated ourselves to rebuilding an adobe fortress.

　In retrospect it was a harbinger of things to come that I used to take my university students in Germany to see Saalburg, the rebuilt Roman fort near Bad Homburg. The site has in recent years been designated a UNESCO World Heritage Site, and perhaps someday El Real Presidio de Santa Bárbara will attain such a high status

Volunteers at the California League of Park Associations annual conference at the Presidio make adobe bricks. Tim Aguilar, master adobero (adobe maker), who oversaw much of the adobe making, is in the foreground. Jackman describes the ongoing adobe making as "creative mudslinging." *Author's Collection*

as well. Founded April 21, 1782, the Presidio was the last Spanish presidio built in North America—during the reign of King Carlos III, one of Europe's best known enlightened despots. The Presidio marked the beginning of the town of Santa Barbara, which has grown into one of the most famous resorts on the coast of California.

The original adobe fort was built over a period of about five years, with extensions and other changes taking place into the 1790s. It took around three hundred thousand to four hundred thousand adobe bricks to build the fort. These bricks weighed 55 pounds each and were made by the paid labor of around twenty to thirty local Indians and a near-equal number of Spanish soldiers and sailors. The size of the rectangular fort was about that of a typical modern city block. Unfortunately, as Santa Barbara expanded outward from the Presidio in the nineteenth century, an American grid was laid over the city, and streets crossed over the footprint of the fort. This meant that to rebuild it, modern city streets would have to be closed. Trouble ahead.

Lined up bricks at the site. More than 100,000 bricks were made for the Presidio reconstruction and Casa de la Guerra Restoration during the author's tenure at SBTHP. *Courtesy SBTHP*

Fast forward to the 1950s—as a result of earthquakes and neglect, only two rooms from the original fort survived. Enter Pearl Chase, a leading citizen of Santa Barbara in the twentieth century, by many described as a force of nature. She began to organize the men of the town as well as some women, under the aegis of a nonprofit called the Santa Barbara Trust for Historic Preservation (hereafter SBTHP). The organization was founded in 1963 and shortly thereafter the Presidio site was designated a state historic park.

Besides being crisscrossed with streets, the remaining fort foundations were overlaid with later construction. Most striking was the twentieth-century wood-framed Japanese Buddhist church built on top of the eighteenth-century Presidio Chapel foundations. The original Hispanic settlers had spread throughout the community and were replaced by newcomers, among whom were Japanese and Chinese Americans.

It is one thing to rebuild a historic fort, such as has been done at places like Vancouver, Washington. There at least the fort lay outside of town, unlike the Santa Barbara Presidio, which became and remained in the center of the city. Thus, there was the formidable task of trying to acquire expensive commercial real estate. And the later residents of the site were not too happy that someone was going to take away their businesses and domiciles. But first let us briefly survey the history of the Santa Barbara Presidio, the last Spanish fort built in North America.

CHAPTER ONE

The Presidio: The Birthplace of Santa Barbara

TWO HUNDRED YEARS after laying claim to California in 1542, Spain finally sent the so-called Sacred Expedition, led by Gaspar de Portolá and Father Junípero Serra, to take possession of the region in founding ceremonies in San Diego on July 13, 1769, and in Monterey on June 3, 1770. During this pre-Presidio period, Spanish soldiers passed through the Santa Barbara region along with the padres, including Father Serra, recently named a saint by Pope Francis. Spanish settlements to the north in San Francisco and Monterey were connected to the south in San Diego by the original El Camino Real, the so-called Royal Highway that passed through the Santa Barbara region. Truth be told, most travel and communication took place by ship between ports, and the Royal Highway served more as a trunk line for delivering goods to the missions, presidios, and pueblos. More on that later.

Serra had wanted since his arrival in 1769 to have a mission in the area of today's city of Ventura, and this was finally granted by the Spanish viceroy in Mexico City—the mission was founded March 31, 1782. Because of an Indian uprising at the Colorado River, it was felt that a presidio was needed to protect the mission, and so the Santa Barbara Presidio was founded April 21, 1782, at its present location. Present at the founding were Governor Felipe de Neve and Father Serra, who said the founding mass. Santa Barbara became the fourth military district of Alta

Because the Presidio was founded during the reign of Charles III, this statue of the king is located in the outdoor cemetery next to the Presidio Chapel. It was donated to Santa Barbara by King Juan Carlos of Spain in 1982 in recognition of the two hundredth anniversary of the founding of the Presidio. *Courtesy SBTHP*

The founding of the Presidio on April 21, 1782, as depicted by artist and Presidio descendant Russell Ruiz. *Courtesy SBTHP*

California, covering the area that extended to the Santa Maria River in the north to the Pueblo de Los Ángeles to the south. The pueblo had been founded September 4, 1781. The last Spanish adobe fort built in North America, the Santa Barbara Presidio, provides a window into the three-hundred-year Spanish presence in North America (1520–1820). This empire extended at one time all the way to the Mississippi River and into Florida. Its influence on the American southwest and California was profound. Alta California's colonization came late in the history of the Spanish empire in North America—in large part due to the growing Spanish fear of English and Russian encroachment in the region. The Presidio served two main purposes: to protect the coast from this encroachment and to pacify the indigenous population by providing military support to the mission system. A by-product of these purposes was to establish the first permanent and lasting European settlement of California. In fact, the town and now-modern city of Santa Barbara can trace it roots directly to the founding of the Santa Barbara Presidio.

Building the Presidio

The years 1784 to 1790 were when the Presidio's adobe construction took place and two missions, Santa Barbara (1786) and Mission La Purisima (1787) near modern-day Lompoc, were established. Serra had died in 1784 so these missions were founded under the leadership of Serra's successor, Fermín de Lasuén.

There were two original fort structures: a palisade version (built 1782–3) and an adobe version that superseded the palisade version. The palisade structure was made of timbers and was built during the tenure of the first comandante, José Francisco Ortega, most famous for being the pathfinder who discovered San Francisco Bay in 1769 as the lead scout of Portolá's Sacred Expedition. During the early phase of the construction, Serra, who had celebrated the founding mass April 21, stayed for over a month, probably living in a tent as the soldiers began their work. Also, by late 1783, an aqueduct had been built bringing water to the Presidio from the creek near where Mission Santa Barbara would be built later. Remains of the aqueduct were uncovered behind the comandancia during an archaeological investigation in the 1980s but the aqueduct has never been traced from the Presidio to the exact site of its origin. In the event, it was quite a feat to have built the aqueduct in a relatively short period of time. The section uncovered indicates it was built of stone and tile, and was plastered and covered to keep debris from getting into the water. The SBTHP came up with a project to try to trace the likely course of the aqueduct following the landform leading to Pedrogosa Creek (as Mission Creek was called then). However, no one responded to the Trust's inquiries of landowners of any possible remnants on their properties, and it is not difficult to conclude that these people were not too excited about finding something that might impact their control over their properties.

The year 1784 marked the arrival of one of the most important historical figures in Spanish Santa Barbara history, Felipe Antonio de Goicoechea (1747–1814). Unlike some of the other well known historical personages such as José de la Guerra, José Francisco Ortega, Pablo Cota, and José Raimundo Carrillo, Goicoechea does not have a street in the city named after him. One person suggested to me half-jokingly that the reason Goicoechea hasn't been honored with a street name is that it is so hard to pronounce his name. Goicoechea is a Basque name, in fact a fairly common Basque name, and not surprisingly he was born in a Basque region of Mexico near the present-day Mexican state of Durango. His mother's lineage dated back to sixteenth-century Durango, in that same region. Goicoechea was in charge of building the adobe fort, then later remained as comandante, making him the chief military officer of the Santa Barbara Presidio district, overseeing all the political, legal, and business affairs of the region. He spent eighteen years in Santa Barbara before leaving for Mexico City and Loreto in Baja California. At the latter, he served as governor and died there in 1814. I make the case for his importance in several articles I have published on him. Most important was his overseeing and guiding construction of the last Spanish adobe fort built in North America.

Spanish Adobe Building Techniques

Building an adobe fort on the frontier was no small task, and Goicoechea commenced construction as soon as he arrived. The quadrangle foundations were laid out outside the original palisade construction and the first foundations were installed at the southwest corner. Apparently, a ceremony took place at the southwest corner of the foundation, because when it was uncovered in the 1970s, one of the stones on top looked to have been carved out for placing something in it, but no relic or the like was found.

There were various phases to the construction of each room. First came the foundations that had to be excavated. Stones and boulders had to be gathered at the local creeks and beach and carted over on wagons called *carretas*. Foundations that went into the ground several feet were filled in with the boulders, and were finished aboveground about a foot to protect against moisture. While this was going on, adobe brickmaking was taking place, and eventually bricks were laid on the foundations that had been leveled; the walls were raised to a certain height, beams were installed to form a pitched roof, and Rhonda reed plants retrieved from local streams were tied to the beams with leather straps, after which fired roof tiles were fastened to the reeds with mud. Mud was the essence of just about all aspects of the construction. Floors consisted of hardened adobe and the blocks themselves were almost exclusively mud, with straw and other natural binders used. Mortar consisted entirely of mud as well. Thus, the world of mud is the main reason I came to call those of us involved with the Presidio project "creative mudslingers."

There were four fronts to the rectangular fort and each front required seventy thousand to ninety thousand adobe bricks, which had to be laid out to dry for about three weeks before they could be installed in the walls.

The last phase of the construction was whitewashing the walls with a lime plaster. The lime was obtained from seashells and lime deposits in the area. The walls had to be whitewashed annually to protect them from damage from rain.

Labor for the work was drawn from local Chumash Indians, sailors who were in port, and local soldiers. Later, Indians also were recruited from Mission San Gabriel, and why this recruitment took place is not explained in any documents. Indians were paid for their labor. There was no forced labor. Very physical labor, yes, but it is interesting to contrast this with the curiosity that this must have engendered in the Chumash, who were spending days tramping mud with their feet.

Construction proceeded in a direction toward the southeast corner, where a bastion was to be located. This section contained a sergeant's quarters, barracks for single soldiers, a jail, and the front gate, and on the other side of the gate was a storage area. Between the defense wall and the buildings were the corrals for the horses. This section of the Presidio no longer exists but the State general plan for the park calls for much of it to be reconstructed. There is so much to be interpreted in this section that it is indeed important that it be rebuilt.

The idea was to complete one of the four fronts of the Presidio per year. This made sense since adobe is sensitive to moisture. It was important to begin making bricks as the rainy season ended and then try to finish a whole section, especially completing roofing in advance of the oncoming winter rains. Thus each year a front about four hundred feet in length was completed—this included rooms for soldiers and their families on the second and forth fronts. The third front was the location of the comandancia and the chapel, which were completed between the years 1786 and 1787. These rooms had flat-planked ceilings and the floors were covered with fired tiles made on site.

Most of the adobe work had been completed by 1788, but there were some additions after that: The chapel was lengthened, additional work on the defense wall was required after the lengthening, and a two-story observation tower was constructed on the second front. When all is said and done, one cannot help but appreciate the more than three hundred thousand adobe bricks that had to be made and laid to create the fort. Fifty-five pounds each times three hundred thousand equals 15 million pounds or 7,500 tons of earth. The right soil had to be found, which consists of a blend of clay, sand, and silt. The soil had to be put into a pit and stirred by mostly the bare feet of the workers. Then it was poured into forms about the length of a *vara* (slightly less than a yard), 4 inches thick and 12 inches wide. Loading the mud into the forms was one of the more strenuous activities as one had to bend over and knead the mud into the corners of the forms.

Also, not usually mentioned in the building of the Presidio were the efforts that had to go into making the large roof and floor tiles that had to be fired in a kiln. At least fifty thousand tiles had to be made, fired, stored, and then moved to the buildings, where they were lifted up to the roofs. All this was hard work. Wood beams had to be harvested from the local forest or sailed down from Monterey. Adzing, the method used to square the timbers, also was strenuous work. The Presidio was in essence an adobe factory with many of these activities going on simultaneously.

It appears, though not confirmed archaeologically, that the staging area for the construction was somewhere near the present-day Alhecama Theatre. The aforementioned kiln was likely in this area. Needless to say, there were no tractors, backhoes, or forklifts to dig trenches or move and lift materials around the site. The work was done primarily with the physical labor of the Indians and the soldiers. Yet there is no record of harsh treatment of laborers. The only incident I found in the historical records was when Comandante Goicoechea had a soldier pulled down from the wall for disobeying his orders. The man was tried, convicted, and sentenced to jail time. Convicted criminals were sent away to another presidio to serve time. This is what happened to the soldier who served his term at the Monterey presidio. Later records show that after release he married and spent the rest of his life in Alta California without incident.

It is a story often told that Indians were flogged at the missions for misbehaving. Since the Indians were being paid, it would have been counterproductive to flog them for not working hard enough at the Presidio, also considering the large potential replacement labor pool. As previously mentioned, records show that about twenty or so Indians were working at one time along with a similar number of Spanish soldiers and sailors. Perhaps a thorough scouring of the historical records will uncover more evidence of labor relations. There is so far no evidence of flogging of Indians at the Presidio during construction or afterward for slouching on the job. There were whippings as punishment for crimes, but that is another subject. In fact, Indians were hired away from the missions, including women to card and spin wool at the Presidio and men and women to tend the Presidio fields; Indians were hired by soldiers to build soldiers' personal residences in later years outside the walls of the fort.

In fact, the Chumash were among the most skilled Indians in California, known for their basketry, cave paintings, and boats that they rowed to the islands. In short, they were a sophisticated people who engaged in trade with one another, onshore and offshore on the main islands off the coast. Chumash resided on these islands, especially the two main islands of Santa Cruz and Santa Rosa. Many of them adapted their skills to work on the Presidio, and its completion and the quality of work certainly were attributable to these skills. In fact, Captain George Vancouver reported that the Santa Barbara Presidio on his visit to Alta California had the appearance of being in the best condition of all the presidios in California. In contrast, apparently the construction of the presidio in San Francisco in the 1770s faced repeated problems, in part because the soldiers tried to use only unskilled Indian labor and there was resistance among the native people to the backbreaking work. There were other factors that resulted in a less-than-satisfactory result, including ongoing wet, foggy weather that was not conducive to adobe construction.

Previously, presidios had been built of adobe in San Francisco (1776), San Diego (1774), and Monterey (1770). The San Diego Presidio was built on a hillside overlooking the San Diego Bay and present-day Old Town San Diego. It went through various building phases. There are some excellent renderings of the Monterey presidio dating from the 1790s drawn by a man named Cardero, who was part of the Spanish Malaspina Expedition. The images show the adobe fort with its high defense walls and buttresses and a chapel currently being enlarged. There are multiple images that show the fort from different angles, and in one are shown kilns for making the tile for the new roof of the church. Another detail actually includes laundry hanging from a wash line.

Dr. Jack Williams has done a detailed study of the construction of the four presidios of Alta California (see the bibliography), from which one can deduce who was in charge, the labor used, and how the respective projects were carried out. We know that Santa Barbara learned from the challenges that San Francisco had faced, and thus opted to use a combination of Indian and soldier labor.

Historical Significance of Presidios

These adobe citadels came and went due in large part to the forces of nature (storms and earthquakes, and in one instance Monterey was burned down by the insurgent Hippolyte Bouchard), but in their day presidios were equal in importance to missions. Besides the one in Santa Barbara, there is little left today of the physical remains of the presidios—a few rooms in San Francisco, the beautiful presidio church in Monterey, and nothing but foundations in San Diego. The latter is in a park setting and is on a site where some reconstruction could take place most easily. The local will seems to be lacking.

In Santa Barbara, the early years were consumed by the fort construction and negotiating with the local indigenous population. Spanish Governor Felipe de Neve and original Presidio Comandante José Francisco Ortega had paved the way by establishing relations with the local Chumash chieftain Yanonali, who lived in a large Indian village near the harbor about a mile away from the site of the fort. On his arrival in 1784, Goicoechea continued harmonious relations with Yanonali.

At this time there was no mission in Santa Barbara; the mission would not arrive until its founding on December 6, 1786, under the Serra successor Lasuén. Thus Santa Barbara became the first place where the soldier went it alone in working with the local Indians. At this time in Europe and in Spain, the Enlightenment movement was dominating the intellectual climate, and that movement spread to New Spain (Mexico) and manifested in Santa Barbara in the relations with Indians. Priests coming up from Ventura were to preach to the Indians in their villages, and

The plaque listing burials in Presidio Chapel that identify early Spanish settlers and, at the bottom of the left column, Juan Bautista, the five-year-old son of Chumash Chieftain Yanonali. *Author's Collection*

it was intended that even after Mission Santa Barbara was founded, Indians would be converted to Catholicism while still living in their villages. They could later go to the mission for services but would not reside there. This method of conversion stayed more or less intact until Goicoechea was transferred to Mexico City and later became governor of Baja California. Eventually the villages of the region would empty completely into the missions of the Santa Barbara Presidio district, two of which were founded during the Presidio construction work—Santa Barbara (1786) and Mission La Purísima (1787) near present-day Lompoc.

Burial of Chieftain Yanonali's Son in the Presidio Chapel

Before moving on to the 1790s, one event stands out in my mind that captures Spanish relations with the Chumash on the most human level. In 1788, one of the sons of Chieftain Yanonali died. This five-year-old boy, given the Christian name Juan Bautista, was buried in the Presidio Chapel September 6, 1788. This is the only record of an Indian burial in Santa Barbara during the Spanish period. Yanonali himself had declined entering the mission at this time, albeit he would later join the mission after Goicoechea's departure and ironically would be buried in a common unmarked grave. Clearly there were some politics involved with this singular burial

of a local Indian, scion of the most important leader of the Chumash at that time. It is a testimony to the positive relationship between the two leaders.

A number of years back, I taught an adult-education course at the Presidio and walked the senior students to the site of the former front gate of the Presidio, and we then turned around from there and returned up Santa Barbara Street to the rebuilt Presidio Chapel. I asked the students to imagine what the dirge must have been like walking to the Chapel and there burying the young child in the Chapel floor. Present at this event must have been the two leaders, soldiers, and Indians, including perhaps the wife of Yanonali. Goicoechea was unmarried. How the child died is not known but this sad event indicates the possibility of a mutuality developing between the Spanish and the Chumash. And a whole different cultural, political, and social evolution seemed to be unfolding as the Spanish continued to develop their California colony. The next two decades were in a way the Halcyon Days of the Santa Barbara Presidio.

Heyday of the Santa Barbara Presidio

This two-decade time period between 1790 and 1810 represents the prime period when the Presidio was a fully functioning Spanish fort, carrying out military oversight of the Santa Barbara region. Also during this time frame, two more missions were founded under the aegis of the Santa Barbara military district—Mission San Fernando Rey de España (1797) and Mission Santa Inés (1804) near present-day Solvang. With the three other missions founded earlier, one each in Ventura and Santa Barbara and Mission La Purísima near Lompoc, there were five missions in total in the district. Each one of these missions had an *escolta* or mission guard that presidio soldados were assigned to. These mission guard soldados actually lived at the missions, with their families if they were married or in separate barracks if single.

This is an important point to remember as it meant that at any one time there were many of the soldiers on assignment and not living in the Presidio. Usually the number of soldiers living with their families in the fort was in the range of only fifty to one hundred people. The precise numbers have not been determined, but this could be a nice research project, listing all the soldiers at the missions over time and deducting that total from the master list of soldiers on the roster. Many of these documents are currently available in the Santa Barbara Presidio Research Center and at the Bancroft Library at UC Berkeley. A great deal of interesting genealogical history can be derived from these records of people, who represented the early colonists of Alta California.

The Presidio's Ethnic Brew

Perhaps more important than raw numbers was the racial and ethnic makeup of the soldiers. An Alta California Census of 1790 indicated California's early colonists were not quite what some might have thought. The notion of the conquistador outfitted in a metal helmet and chain mail arriving from Spain had been tempered by two hundred fifty years of the Spanish frontier that moved gradually northward from Mexico City. The "new" Spanish soldier who arrived in Alta California and thus Santa Barbara was called a *Soldado de Cuera,* or leather-jacket soldier, because his outfit was made of layers of leather, usually deer skin. This uniform was found to protect one against the arrows of Indians. The soldier did have a musket, broadsword, and lance, the latter the weapon of choice in encounters with Native peoples elsewhere. More on the ethnic background of the soldiers will be discussed later.

It has been put forth in various accounts that the Indians with their bows and arrows were not at that great a disadvantage in opposing soldiers as it took time for a soldier to reload, that is, loading the ball and ramming and priming. That may have been the case when there were only a few soldiers firing at one time, but there was an incident in Santa Barbara in which the soldiers with their muskets facing Indians had several men become wounded but they clearly won out against the Indians with their bows and arrows.

While the Presidio housed families, that is, women and children in the quarters in the second and fourth fronts of the fort, the Presidio's main function remained military. The fort usually had two officers; Goicoechea served as comandante longer than anyone else (1784–1802). Under him over time were Cota and Carrillo, both of whom, as previously mentioned, have streets named after them in modern-day Santa Barbara. Noncommissioned officers included sergeants but they usually were stationed at the missions. Normally, only the officers and noncommissioned officers could read or write: the enlisted men were illiterate. Also serving at the Presidio was an armorer whose job was to take care of the weaponry, and supposedly a trained cannoneer but that position was not always filled. Research has determined that four-pound (caliber) cannons were available at the Presidio for the bastions, but a bastion has yet to be found archaeologically at the Santa Bárbara Presidio. There were frequent inspections, sometimes several times yearly, and reports pointed out many deficiencies. Powder, always important, was kept in a casemate, under double lock and key. There was frequent target practice, and even fireworks were available for special events, especially saints days.

At the coast to protect the forts, each presidio, including Santa Bárbara, apparently had a *castillo* (gun emplacement) but Santa Bárbara's has never been found. If it existed and foundations remain in the ground, it will be somewhere on the campus at Santa Barbara City College. Those in Monterey, San Diego, and San Francisco have been located and at least two of them saw action during the Spanish period. All the foregoing information on artillery is a sampling from a marvelous unpublished study by longtime SBTHP volunteer Michael Hardwick titled "Arms and Armament: Presidios of California." (See the bibliography.)

The Santa Barbara soldiers were recruited from the northern provinces of New Spain, mostly from Sonora, Sinaloa, and Baja California. Earlier, unmarried soldiers

A Chumash dancer of the Santa Ynez Reservation performs at the Presidio in 1988. According to Fernando Librado, Indians danced in front of the Chapel during the Hispanic period. Paid Indians, mostly Chumash. and Spanish soldiers and navy crews did the hard labor of making adobes and building the walls of the fort. *Author's Collection*

A Presidio soldier based on an original drawing of a Soldado de Cuera (leather-jacket soldier), typical of soldiers who manned the Presidio, an ethnically mixed troop that evolved over two hundred years on the Spanish frontier.
Courtesy Harry and Ellen Knill

who had come to California with Portolá brought resultant problems with native women. Serra urged the viceroy that only soldiers be sent to California who were married. This was the situation at the Santa Barbara Presidio—almost all the soldiers were married, except for Goicoechea, who came and left unmarried, but he did leave behind a love child, born to a woman whose husband had been killed by Chumash Indians. She was a young woman of mixed Indian blood (*mestiza*) from Cosalá, a town in Sinaloa where Goicoechea had been born. Illegitimate birth rates were very high on the Spanish frontier.

The Spanish in Santa Barbara adhered to what looked like a strict racial structure that left Indians, Blacks, and those of mixed race technically on the bottom social rung. However, over time a person in a particular racial category might move up in social rank. After almost three centuries of frontier encounters, the soldiers and their families were a mixed people so that a census in 1790 indicated about half were of Spanish origin. That meant of the Spanish born in the New World, a quarter were mestizos, of mixed blood, and about a quarter were registered as non-California Indians, mulattos or mixed Black and Indian. About 12 percent of the Santa Barbara soldiers were of African origin. The 1790 census shows only two Santa Barbara persons born in Spain—a servant of Goicoechea who was from Catalonia and a soldier from Cádiz. It is worth noting that Goicoechea, with Spanish Basque roots, had a Catalan servant. In addition, there were seventeen interracial marriages, including, for example, an Indian soldier to a Spanish woman, a Black soldier to a Spanish woman, and a Spanish soldier to a Black woman. Thus from its beginning, Santa Barbara was a pluralistic, multiethnic society, and since most of the soldiers had wives and children, they perpetuated this original society. Many of this society's members became the first citizens of Spanish Santa Barbara, and their ancestry has come down to today as descendants of the Presidio. Many of these people's genealogical charts are on display in the Santa Barbara Presidio museum. While the Chumash as a distinct genetic people no longer exist, there are a number of individuals still extant who proudly carry a mixture of their Chumash and Hispanic ethnicities.

The Spanish Transform the California Environment

Between 1790 and 1810, Santa Barbara grew to be the most populous area of non-native residents of Alta California, but that still meant only a population of less than five hundred. At the same time, Spanish ships made periodic stops to deliver needed goods that were not available in the new Spanish province. Two hundred years after this period, the SBTHP commenced a major research project to translate and publish all the goods ordered and received as part of this trade at the Santa Barbara Presidio. Coordinated by Dr. Giorgio Perissinotto, a Spanish linguist from UCSB, and Cathy Rudolph, then director of the Santa Barbara Presidio Research Center, with the help of UCSB graduate students, this material was published in 1998 under the title *Documenting Everyday Life in Early Spanish California* and reveals an eighteenth-century California more connected to the world at large than expected. One invoice alone from 1796 listed the delivery of earthen dinnerware, hats, cloth from various places in New Spain, yarn, 75 pounds of cocoa and 300 pounds of ordinary and "good gift" chocolate, 80 bundles of glass beads, fabric for clothing from Spain and France, thread, blankets, candles, 3 barrels of Catalan *aguardiente*, 1 barrel of Málaga wine, and 7 pounds of mixed white sugar.

Clearly clothing and material for sewing came by ship in the 1790s. But as the sheep industry in California developed, some of the material for clothing came from the wool from sheepshearing. By the end of the Spanish period in Santa Barbara, there were at the missions and the Presidio more than fifty thousand sheep. More will be discussed later on how this sheep industry can be connected to interpretation at El Presidio de Santa Bárbara State Historic Park.

A fact that is well discussed and written about is the impact of Spanish agriculture and livestock on remaking the landscape of California, especially at the missions. Besides sheep, the animals introduced were pigs, horses, mules, and cattle. Crops took over thousands of acres of land. Presidios were dependent on this introduced farming and Indians provided the labor. Soldiers also raised some of their own crops. Goicoechea had his own vineyard for raising grapes, and local legend points to modern-day De La Vina Street as the location of this vineyard site. Also, Olive Street once had olive trees near the Presidio.

Horse breeding and raising was nearly the exclusive domain of the soldiers, and there was a corral at the front gate of the fort where these animals were kept. Donkeys and mules were also raised, and mules were especially prized for their surefootedness and were often preferred as soldiers' mounts, especially when traveling to and through areas that did not have trails and were rocky and hilly and had loose footing. Horses had since the time of Cortés and the Aztecs provided an advantage in conflicts with indigenous peoples, and soldiers were reluctant to share this riding skill with the Chumash. Much later, in the 1830s after the secularization of the missions, Indians became skilled horsemen. An important historical fact sometimes forgotten is that the Spanish were responsible for the introduction of horses to North America as early as the sixteenth century on the Great Plains but in large numbers in the seventeenth century. Eighteenth-century California was another example of this happening with the result that after the Spanish rule in California was overturned in 1820, a strong ranching tradition emerged that continued into the Mexican period and remained well after the United States annexed Alta California after the 1840s Mexican War.

Goicoechea and Bodega Bay

Two events stand out from the 1790s portion of the so-called heyday period of the Santa Barbara Presidio (1790 to 1810), not surprisingly both involved Goicoechea. The first event involved an expedition that Goicoechea was ordered to organize to reconnoiter an area north of San Francisco previously named Bodega Bay after Spanish naval officer Bodega y Quadra. With a dozen men, and with a supply of horses and mules, he crossed over from the San Francisco Presidio to the peninsula on the other side of the bay, proceeded after a few missteps to locate Bodega Bay, then continued northward for a short while. Several years ago I traced this trek by car using the measurements and distances he provided in his report and determined that it was likely he and his men made it to what is today the Russian River, but because it was late summer, the river probably had stopped running to the coast and he didn't recognize his discovery. Basically what this event demonstrates is that the Spanish were still, late in the eighteenth century, in an expansionist mode and attempting to secure their claims to the Pacific Northwest against the geopolitical incursions of the Russians and British. Little old Santa Barbara at the far reaches of the Spanish empire still found itself with its men and its operations connected to international events of the time. The idea of colonizing Bodega Bay was abandoned and the historical record does not tell us why—at least so far it hasn't.

Vancouver Visits Santa Barbara

The second related event took place when Goicoechea, back from his trip to Bodega Bay, greeted British Navy Captain George Vancouver, who, in October of the same

A painting by Oswald Brett re-creating the Vancouver expedition laying anchor in Santa Barbara in 1793. Vancouver reprovisioned his ships in Santa Barbara with the cooperation of Presidio Comandante Felipe de Goicoechea. *Courtesy Harry and Ellen Knill*

year, anchored his three ships, including the *Discovery*, in Santa Barbara Harbor, where he asked to provision his ships. Goicoechea not only gave him permission to do this, but also invited him to dinner in the comandancia. Among the officers in attendance were lieutenants Peter Puget and Joseph Whidbey, who would have a sound and an island named after them, respectively. Vancouver also hosted Goicoechea for dinner aboard the *Discovery*. However, the Spanish comandante returned from the dinner seasick. Vancouver had previously been to the Pacific Northwest to negotiate an agreement with Spain over disputed lands and incidents in the Nootka Sound area. Eventually Spain ceded the area to the British and ended its ventures in that area; its other claims south of the modern-day Canadian border were ceded to the United States by treaty in 1819.

Goicoechea most likely would have had some knowledge of the foregoing political events surrounding the controversy, but playing the friendly host was a reflection of his demeanor as he was known as being "affable to his men." But he received a reprimand from his superiors for allowing Vancouver to stay as long as he did—eight days. In fact, Goicoechea had a habit of getting in hot water with his superiors, a behavioral pattern that followed him in his career to Mexico City and as governor of Baja California.

That said, he was highly respected by his men—elected as *habilitado* (paymaster) to handle their individual accounts. He was also respected enough that he was named in 1802 habilitado general (general paymaster) of the Californias in Mexico City.

The Spanish Legal System

In addition to CFO duties, Goicoechea had responsibility for handling all local legal matters of the Santa Barbara district. Some of the most fascinating social history of the period comes out in the many court cases he oversaw. Many of the cases dealt with capital crimes: murder of one soldier by another, murder of Indians by another Indian, murder of Spanish soldiers by Indians, commitment of bestiality, sexual assault of two Indian women, a sexual assault of a soldier by his wife. In one case the testimony came to ninety pages. During Goicoechea's tenure, two people were executed for their crimes, the one in 1794 the first in Spanish California. There were small civil cases, such as one Los Angeles settler accusing another of stealing his sheep. These cases took place over a period of a decade and more, so that the amount of criminal activity should not be exaggerated. But while I have described this period as the heyday of the Presidio, it would not be fair to call it halcyon. Goicoechea may have been generally friendly with his men, but at the same time there were a few who complained about him including one who said Goicoechea had cheated him in his accounts. It is probably best to conclude that the Presidio was very much where human nature was on display. The high illegitimacy rate is further testimony to another human weakness.

Presidio Relations with the Chumash

Perhaps it would be best to sum up Indian relations, since this is a topic of great interest these days. There was a spirit of cooperation that I mentioned in the building of the Presidio, but there were also incidents of soldier-and-Indian violence. Indians in the mountains above Santa Barbara ambushed and riddled two soldiers with arrows, explaining after their capture that they killed the soldiers because they were traveling with Indian enemies of the perpetrators. Another time soldiers pursued a chronic Indian fugitive from the mission and became embroiled with Indians who were with him, who shot arrows and wounded soldiers, and in turn the soldiers killed three Indians. It is important to add that soldiers did not often pursue individual neophyte fugitives from the missions. Padres created Indian auxiliaries whom they would send out in most instances to bring back Indians who had fled the missions. According to one source, padres sent soldiers after Indians only if they thought the Indians were a physical threat to the mission.

At the missions themselves during the Spanish period, where soldiers were stationed, padres did not want soldiers in charge of punishing Indians—they wanted that to be solely the padres' responsibility. Soldiers were there to protect the padres from attacks and outsiders, whether Indians or non-Indians. In the early years of Alta California, there were incidents of violence against Indians. Those numbers declined as soldiers arrived with families, and there were cases in Santa Barbara during Goicoechea's time when soldiers were put on trial for abusing Indians. In today's climate of opinion, Spanish soldiers are given a bad rap as violent rapists and as people who committed atrocities against Indians. Needless to say, there were abusers in Alta California, but nothing to the magnitude some today would have it. There are many thousands alive today who are descendants of these soldiers and they have every reason to be proud of their heritage.

Comandantes after Goicoechea

When Goicoechea departed in 1802, he was replaced by José Raimundo Carrillo, who had served under him as an officer. Carrillo would remain in that position until 1807, after which José Darío Argüello served until 1815, and finally José de la Guerra served as the last Spanish comandante into the Mexican period to 1820. De la Guerra would marry Carrillo's daughter María and start Santa Barbara's most prominent Hispanic family. In a search I have done in documents of Baja California, from 1802 until Goicoechea's death in Loreto, Baja California, Goicoechea, Carrillo, and de la Guerra became close friends corresponding with one another in most amiable terms. The connections between the latter were solidified when José de la Guerra married the daughter María of José Raimundo Carrillo. De la Guerra had status having been born in Spain and thus was a so-called Peninsular, and he was the nephew of one of the wealthiest men in Mexico City, Pedro González de Noriega. Carrillo himself had had a significant, successful career that economic historian Marie Duggan summarizes as follows: At age 24, he assisted in putting down the 1775 Kumeyaay revolt in San Diego and was made corporal. From 1783 to 1795, Carrillo served as sergeant at Santa Barbara. He was commander at Monterey in 1800, then at Santa Barbara from 1802 to 1807, and finally at San Diego, where he died 1809.

Importance of Research

So far most of the history I have written on the Presidio heyday period from 1790 to 1812 has reached only to the time of Goicoechea's transfer. The reason is simple: I have done most of my research on his life and times. My administrative responsibilities limited the time I could spend on research and thus I did most of the research while on vacation. I began working through some of the materials that one of the great SBTHP volunteers, Richard Whitehead, had collected and then donated to the Santa Barbara Presidio Research Center. These materials included translations of Spanish documents related to the history of the Santa Barbara Presidio. I also took time to go to the Bancroft Library at UC Berkeley, which has a major collection of Spanish documents on microfilm now gradually being transferred to CDs from the Archivo General de la Nación in Mexico City and the Archivo General de Indias in Seville, Spain. I made trips to Cosalá in Sinaloa, Mexico, where Goicoechea was born, and to Álamos in Sonora, Mexico, where he spent more than twenty-five years of his life. Next, my wife, Michele, and I spent ten days in the special collections department at New Mexico State University in Las Cruces, which has a huge collection of Spanish documents related to the history of Durango, Mexico. Here we uncovered the family heritage of Goicoechea. Lastly, I received a grant from the Spanish government to do research in Spain, where I spent a month in Spanish military archives and in the Archivo General de Indias. That said, there is still much more research that can be done on Goicoechea and his time period. And of course the world is wide open to looking into the years from 1802 to 1812. Ships were still coming to deliver supplies, and the commandants' lives and actions at this time bear uncovering and comparing with Goicoechea's.

A major issue to be researched is the Chumash migration to the missions after Goicoechea left for Mexico City. By 1810 most of the Indian villages in the region had been abandoned, including those on the islands. Why that happened so quickly is an open question. I asked anthropologist Dr. John Johnson, the leading expert on the Chumash, his take on why this happened. He said that around 1803, the viceroy in Mexico City had issued a change in policy that Indians would no longer be Christianized in their villages and that this was to be done at the missions instead. I posed the question to various scholars in the field why this new policy had been instituted. Various responses were proffered. One historian said that somehow Napoleon's takeover of Spain had affected this policy. Another historian said it probably had to do with Bourbon reformers and those opposed to these reforms. And another historian said that they doubted an issue like this was paid much attention by the higher-ups. In short, the answers were ambiguous and it would be valuable to do research on the subject to obtain a more definitive answer. From 1800 onward the Indians all across Alta California would swell the population of the missions, and that would in essence be the beginning of the end of an independent cultural and political world for them. Their fate would henceforth be inextricably bound to the Spanish and their resultant political, social, and economic institutions.

El Camino Real and Santa Barbara

Before moving to the years after 1812, this is an appropriate time to bring up the famous El Camino Real, or the Royal Highway. Today, El Camino Real is identified with historical markers along Highway 101 from San Diego to San Francisco. The highway actually evolved over time as missions were founded along it that changed the course of it. In the Santa Barbara military region, the first site to be founded was not a mission, however, but the Pueblo de Los Ángeles in 1781. Next came Mission San Buenaventura in March 1782 and El Real Presidio de Santa Bárbara in April 1782. Four years were to pass before Mission Santa Barbara was founded in December 1786. Later came Mission La Purísima in 1787, Mission San Fernando Rey de España in 1797, and the last mission, Santa Inés, in 1804. After each founding, the Royal Highway had to be relocated. A similar evolution followed for the development of the highway in the other military districts of Alta California. By 1804, one might say the final route of the Royal Highway during the Spanish period had been established in the Santa Barbara Presidio military district. Or had it?

Historically, the highway led from Pueblo de Los Ángeles via Mission San Gabriel to the east and outside the Santa Barbara district, then back northwest to Mission San Fernando. From there, it took a route still somewhat in question today to Mission San Buenaventura. Then it went along the coast to Santa Barbara, which, depending on the tide, could cause problems. After the Presidio and Mission Santa Barbara, the route continued up to the Refugio beach, passing by the original Ortega Rancho over the Refugio Pass until it went down toward the Santa Ynez River. There it crossed to Mission Santa Inés, then followed the river to the northwest, and crossed again to arrive at Mission La Purísima. If traveling north to Mission San Luis Obispo, one would cross the river one more time. Clearly this was a circuitous route and was not conducive to wagon or mule-train pack travel. It raises the question of how often the trail was deviated from depending on the mode of travel: horseback, wagon, or mule train. In the 1770s Governor Fages had a mule pack train sent from San Diego to Monterey. The highway itself was graded in a way that wagons could travel up and down for hundreds of miles without breaking down.

The answer to the question of how El Camino Real was used was broached at a symposium held at the Santa Barbara Presidio May 6–7, 2012. Leading scholars of the history of early California were invited and most attended. The symposium was titled "Presidio, Ports, Pueblos and Caminos," and its primary goal was to begin discussions of the possibility of having El Camino Real listed as a UNESCO World Heritage Site (WHS). Funded by grants from the California Office of Historic Preservation and the John and Beverly Stauffer Foundation, the symposium laid out a plan for a phased research process for determining the eligibility of the highway for WHS designation. One of the major outcomes of the symposium was the conclusion that El Camino Real needed to include the sea lane along the California coast, because so much of the shipping of goods and travel took place on ships that stopped

The author at a rest stop with a bell marking Historic El Camino Real that ran through before, during, and after the Spanish settlement of Santa Barbara. *Photo by Michele Jackman*

at ports all along the coast. In the Santa Barbara district, that included deliveries to the Presidio, but also to Cojo and Refugio Bays to the north. In short, the land version of El Camino Real was used more for trunk lines delivering goods and providing travelers from the ships access to the missions in the area.

For various reasons, the initial symposium study of El Camino Real has not advanced in recent years, but its recommendation of breaking down the research into the four Spanish Alta California military districts still has great merit, for it could serve as a tool for the study of early California in a way that would provide a more integrated history of the era. In fact, one of my last acts at the SBTHP was to create a detailed timeline of the history of the Santa Barbara military district. Also, Janet Dowling Sands recently published her book *On a Mission: The Real Story of the California Missions* (2019) telling her story of the missions in the context of the four California military districts—San Diego, Santa Barbara, Monterey, and San Francisco.

Dr. Julianne Burton-Carvajal, who coordinated the symposium with me, compiled all the pertinent materials, many of which she personally gathered, and then had them printed in a detailed report under the title "Year One Overview: El Camino Real de California Initiative" (2013); a copy of the report is available for review in the Santa Barbara Presidio Research Center.

Interestingly, Dr. Joseph P. Sánchez, keynote speaker at the symposium, was inspired by his participation in this event, followed up with his own research, and published in 2019 *El Camino Real de California: From Ancient Pathways to Modern Byways*. The book takes the tack that a first step is to authenticate the first camino established by Portolá, then follow the evolution of a braided version of the camino over time as it found new directions to connect ports, missions, presidios, and ranchos. Sánchez brings forth various sources to begin this process by tracing back the Camino Real concept to Greco-Roman times, and forward to the road system developed during the fifteenth- and early-sixteenth-century reign of Queen Isabel that was codified in the Spanish "Laws of the Indies" published in 1573. Even more ancient are the prehistoric Native American trails that Spanish followed in many instances in developing their Royal Highway. This made sense because missions were sited in areas near Indian villages.

The topic of El Camino Real is pertinent for California State Parks for many of its parks run along and through this famous highway in Santa Barbara and elsewhere in California; in Santa Barbara it is also relevant for California State Parks and the SBTHP, which manages El Presidio de Santa Bárbara State Historic Park and the Santa Inés Mission Mills state property. In fact, El Camino Real was redirected over Refugio Pass to connect with Mission Santa Inés on the other side of the mountain across the Santa Ynez River. Thus these two historic parks are made to be connected with one another, a matter that will be taken up in a later section on future interpretation of these important historic places.

Spain Leaves Santa Barbara

Two seismic events changed the course of history at the Santa Barbara Presidio, one human and the other geologic. Napoleon Bonaparte was the human cause and two mammoth earthquakes the geologic cause. Let's start with the earthquakes of 1812. Prior to 1812, Carrillo reported damage to the chapel by an earthquake in 1806 and requested materials from the mission to make the repairs. Then came the two seismic events in December 1812. Seismologists believe that both of them were over 7 on the Richter scale. Again, speculating, the seismologists believe the epicenter of one was near Wrightwood and its most serious impact was the collapse of the church in San Juan Capistrano as a service was taking place—Indians and priests were killed. The epicenter of the second temblor may have been in the Santa Barbara Channel and wreaked havoc on Mission Santa Barbara and especially Mission La Purísima, which was so damaged that it had to be completely abandoned. By 1813, the mission moved across the Santa Ynez River, where a new church and mission complex were built. This later version was restored and rebuilt in the 1930s by the Civilian Conservation Corps with the assistance of the National Park Service. Today it is one of the historical treasures of the California state park system.

The Santa Barbara Presidio was also severely damaged, although it is not known the total extent of the damage. The chapel was damaged, as records show, and buttresses were added after the repair, an interesting story that spills over into the later restoration that will be discussed in a future chapter. The comandancia was damaged and apparently no longer suitable for occupancy. It was repaired enough to be converted into a storage facility, as described on an 1820s ground plan. The commandant's quarters were moved into the east wing, according to this ground plan. Other soldier-family quarters in both wings also were damaged and residents were forced to live in the courtyard in tents as aftershocks continued off and on, causing fear and anxiety. It is not known how much damage was done to the defense walls, but the damage was probably considerable as the walls likely had not been buttressed. Vancouver recorded after his visit to the Presidio in 1793 that it was the cleanest and in the best condition of the California presidios. Things clearly changed after 1812, and there was to be a gradual decline in the Presidio's situation from then on. This is in contrast to Mission Santa Barbara, which had been totally destroyed and then completely rebuilt in the 1820s to its present structure. One-story adobe buildings tend to survive quakes, and that may be the reason the Presidio came through only partially damaged.

The upshot of the earthquakes was a tsunami that was recorded at Refugio Beach, supposedly carrying an anchored ship in the harbor up the valley a mile and back down again. Also, there has been an undocumented urban legend that the tsunami came all the way up to the gate of the Presidio. Local artist Russell Ruiz did a painting of the wave breaking just in front of the Presidio. But documentary evidence is lacking so far confirming the veracity of the painting.

The second seismic event, the human one, took place in Europe with the ascendancy of Napoleon to power in France: this had a huge political and economic impact on Spain, which had a longtime Bourbon connection with France. While Spain had the good fortune of having one of its best kings in Charles III, his successors after his death in 1788 were two of the least talented, his son Charles IV and his grandson Ferdinand VII. Charles and Ferdinand vied for power with one another, both then fled the country to France and abandoned it to Joseph Bonaparte, who was placed on the throne by his brother Napoleon. What followed was the bloody

Peninsular War, eventually leading to expulsion of the invading French. All of this meant that New Spain (Mexico) and much of the remainder of the Spanish empire was neglected. This had a ripple effect all the way to Alta California as the ships with supplies stopped coming from New Spain, and funds to pay the military dried up after 1810. Bancroft's *History of California* (1884) reports that various individuals in these faraway lands took sides supporting or opposing King Ferdinand VII. Had Spain not been engaged in various conflicts in Europe, it likely would have made more of an effort to hold onto New Spain. However, some of the Spaniards themselves seeking constitutional government and engaged in defending their homeland felt a certain sympathy for the New World rebels seeking freedom from the Spanish royalty.

Insurgency in Mexico began in the decade of the 1810s and continued with Mexico eventually gaining its independence in September 1821. Yet even while this rebellion was going on, the Spanish viceroyalty deployed more soldiers to Alta California in response to the Russian incursion at Fort Ross in northern California. Some of these soldiers were assigned to the Santa Barbara Presidio. This part of the military history of Santa Barbara needs to be better understood, but as the arrival of the Argentine insurgent Hippolyte Bouchard in 1818 would reveal, the military presence of the Spanish in Alta California was hardly formidable.

Before delving into Bouchard's attack on Alta California in 1818, I turn back for the moment to an earlier time, 1813, and the economic and political state of things in Alta California and in Santa Barbara. The fate of the American ship *Mercury* and its captain, George Washington Eayrs, demonstrates well the history of the Santa Barbara Presidio from 1800 to 1820 and even into the 1820s. The Spanish capture of the *Mercury* in Refugio Harbor took place June 2, 1813. The captain of the Spanish ship was Nicolás Noé sailing out of Peru, who claimed to be a privateer and forced the *Mercury* to the Santa Barbara Presidio, where he confiscated its cargo and charged Eayrs with smuggling. Spain was still practicing mercantilist economics and was actively trying to stop contraband from being traded in Alta California.

A previously mentioned volume published by the SBTHP in 1998 and edited by UCSB Professor Giorgio Perissinotto and Cathy Rudolph, *Documenting Everyday Life in Early Spanish California*, enumerated the goods and necessities ordered and delivered to Santa Barbara from Mexico from the 1780s to 1810. These supply ships stopped coming from San Blas in 1810 and were replaced by Spanish merchant ships sailing out of Lima, Peru, and by American ships such as the *Mercury*. Warfare in Europe before and after Napoleon had a huge impact on international mercantile shipping. In Alta California, American ships kept out of Europe by decrees and blockades sought new markets around the world in Asia and in Alta California. The *Mercury* has a particular Santa Barbara twist to it and was the reason the SBTHP published Robert Ryal Miller's *A Yankee Smuggler on the Spanish California Coast: George Washington Eayrs and the Ship* Mercury (2001). Eayrs and his wife were held at the Presidio and he had his cargo confiscated. This is not the place to tell his full story of the years he spent with the Spanish and Mexican governments trying to retrieve his lost cargo, valued at five thousand dollars. But his case was typical of many American ships sailing around the horn directly to Alta California and on to the Pacific Northwest engaging in the otter trade, which included sailing on to Canton, China, where the otter skins were highly valued. Much of the history of this period involved American ships smuggling contraband in and out of various ports, avoiding anchoring in areas near the presidios, where ships, crews, and cargo would have had to deal with the military enforcers who supposedly would intercept this illegal trading. But some of the officers were in fact engaging in this trade, and even some of the padres. Scarcity was a problem, and there were even some like de la Guerra and others who built financial wealth from this putative illegal activity.

José de la Guerra

Without question, de la Guerra was the most important and powerful Santa Barbara individual from his becoming comandante in 1815 well into the 1820s. His growing wealth was manifested with the construction of his mansion (today called Casa de la Guerra), which began in the Spanish period in 1819 and finished in 1826. De la Guerra and his large family relocated to this thirteen-room adobe from the Presidio. It is not common knowledge that de la Guerra and his family spent the first ten-plus years living inside the Presidio. His son Pablo, who became a prominent politician when California became part of the United States, was born at the Presidio. The

An 1850 painting of Don José de la Guerra by Leonardo Barbiera. Born in Novales, Spain, de La Guerra eventually arrived in California as a junior Spanish officer, and in 1815 became the last Spanish Comandante of the Santa Barbara Presidio. *Courtesy Santa Barbara Historical Museum*

story of de la Guerra and his family became more important to the SBTHP when the large family adobe was donated to the organization in 1971. The story of its restoration will be detailed in a future chapter.

With the breakdown of Spanish mercantilism, the relationship between the local Chumash and the soldiers and the padres also was changing. After the 1802 departure of Goicoechea, the notion of Christianizing the Indians in their villages was pretty much abandoned, both on the coast and on the islands, and by 1810, Indians had moved to the four regional missions of Santa Barbara, La Purísima, Buenaventura, and Santa Inés. The change of this relationship might have taken a more positive direction had the collapse of the Spanish control in Mexico not taken place at the same time. One of the severest consequences was the Chumash revolt in 1824, which will be discussed shortly.

Bouchard Invades Santa Barbara

Preceding the revolt was one of the more fascinating incidents in Spanish California history, which took place in 1818. This was the arrival of the insurgent Bouchard with his two ships and crew of more than four hundred men, who were Argentines, Americans, and Hawaiians. Bouchard's actual first name was André-Paul, and for unknown reasons he took the name of his brother Hippolyte upon arriving in the New World. Born in 1780, he started his radical career under Napoleon aboard a ship that went to Egypt. He eventually made his way to America imbued with a revolutionary spirit, first stopping for a time in Baltimore, Maryland. Then he made his way to Argentina, which, by the 1810s, was under insurgency like most of Latin America. As an insurgent, he is today seen as a hero in Argentina, with a plaza named after him and a statue of him in Buenos Aires. Also, he is recognized in France with a statue in his hometown of Bormes-les-Mimosas. Much of what we know of Bouchard's early life is thanks to the research of historian Patrick O'Dowd. More will be discussed about Patrick as the manager of the SBTHP restoration of Casa de la Guerra in the 1990s.

Bouchard's arrival in California was, in his mind, to create revolutionary upheaval, starting with sacking the capitol in Monterey, then drifting down the coast to Refugio Cove, where he burned the rancho of the Ortegas and set sail to Santa Barbara. At the Santa Barbara Presidio, de la Guerra negotiated an exchange of prisoners. After committing the ruse of having his soldiers march behind a hill to give the impression that there were more men than he actually had, Bouchard sailed away, after negotiating an exchange of prisoners. He burned buildings at San Juan Capistrano before he returned to South America, where he was later murdered by one of his servants.

Had Bouchard decided to send his men ashore at the Santa Barbara Presidio, he would have likely received limited resistance. Interestingly, among de la Guerra's troops were Indian auxiliaries, who had been trained in the use of arms. This provides an interesting transition to the Chumash revolt of 1824. The training of Indians to be soldiers gave the Chumash the ability to take up arms, as they did at Mission Santa Inés during the largest Indian revolt in early California history. But we will never know how effective they might have been against Bouchard's marauders.

This brief encounter brings us full circle. We started this section of history with how Napoleon's rise to power disrupted Europe in ways that contributed to the rise of the independence movements in Latin America, including Mexico. Napoleon was finally defeated and permanently exiled by 1815, yet in faraway Alta California, one of Bonaparte's acolytes showed up on the coast wreaking revolutionary havoc. This really brings home the impact that one person can have on history. On the positive side, one can point out that one man, King Charles III, provided leadership that brought the Enlightenment movement to Spain, which spread to the New World and Alta California through personages like Visitador Generál (Inspector General) José de Gálvez and California Governor de Neve, who was decorated with the Order of Charles III for his efforts in bringing the Enlightenment movement to California. How quickly this leadership was reversed with Charles IV and Ferdinand VII. The nadir, one might say, was reached with the Chumash revolt, which resulted from the political and economic collapse of the Bourbon system.

The Chumash Revolt

It is important to emphasize that the 1824 Chumash revolt took place after New Spain had achieved its independence and officially become the Empire of Mexico and then shortly thereafter the Republic of Mexico in 1824. The republic abolished the racial categories and the system of castes. But from 1820 on, the Spanish Laws of the Indies were no longer enforced, and the rank-and-file soldiers were left to deal directly with the Indians. Unrestrained by an orderly legal system, the common soldiers were feeling their oats. In an oral history that I translated and that was published by Bellerophon Books in 1987 (see the bibliography), soldado Rafael Gonzalez complained how the common soldier was looked down upon by the officer class, and this changed once Alta California came under the flag of the Republic of Mexico. This resentment may have carried forth in relations with the Indians, now that the soldiers in many cases dealt directly with them rather than through the officers or the padres.

In fact, the revolt began at Mission Santa Inés after a soldier had whipped an Indian. Earlier, the padres had prohibited soldiers from engaging in this form of punishment, reserving it to being doled out themselves. They were concerned it would have negative consequences, which indeed it did in this instance. After forty-plus years of relative peace, the Indians and the soldiers were suddenly at one another's throats. After setting the mission on fire, the rebels retreated to Mission La Purísima, which is about twenty miles from Mission Santa Inés. Neophytes from that mission joined the insurrection, and one of the outcomes was the capture of Mexican settlers who just happened to be passing through when this was transpiring. A Mexican woman was murdered, and that was to have significant ramifications for the Indians.

Soldiers arrived from the north, and also came up from the Presidio. At Mission Santa Barbara, Indians learned of the uprising, and many of them joined the resistance. Eventually Indians at both Mission La Purísima and Mission Santa Barbara were overwhelmed by the soldier onslaught, and both contingents fled to Tulare in the present-day San Joaquin Valley, where other Indians over time had taken refuge. Not long after their flight, a group of soldiers was sent to retrieve the Indians. While there was some mercy shown as requested by the padres, there was also some harsh treatment meted out: According to historian Bancroft, six Indians were executed for killing the woman at Mission La Purísima and a half dozen others were given jail sentences of ten years for leading the rebellion. They were incarcerated in the presidio jails.

This sad story in some ways overshadows the overall picture of the relationship between the Chumash and the soldiers, but it must be added that it is only part of the story. A unique relationship had been formed between these two peoples that led to unique outcomes in Santa Barbara but was cut short by the collapse of the Spanish empire in North America after 1820. Also, some of the Chumash rebels went on to become upright Mexican citizens.

More Than a Sliver of History

The last of the Spanish provinces settled in North America was California, and the last Spanish fort established in North America was the Santa Barbara Presidio. As the last, this province and the Santa Barbara Presidio manifested unique characteristics of the Spanish experience in the New World, not least of which were relations with Indians and the incredible remaking of the physical environment of the region that came with the Spanish settlement in forty short years; its components in Santa Barbara included missions, a rancho, and Pueblo de Los Ángeles, whose impact spread across the Santa Barbara military district. By 1820, the nonindigenous population of Santa Barbara barely exceeded one thousand, with soldiers spread across the area on assignment, but that small number leaves the wrong impression as to their impact. More than one hundred thousand livestock now roamed the land, including thousands of cattle, horses, mules, donkeys, pigs, and sheep. Thousands of acres were now growing wheat, grapes, and other crops, ghhand orchards grew olive and citrus trees, figs, and other fruits. While much of this new life was introduced at the missions and their lands, the Presidio had its own crops and livestock, especially sheep and horses.

The soldiers called *soldados de cuera* (because of the leather jackets they wore) were primarily cavalrymen and thus their horses were a huge part of their culture, which would be passed down through many generations into the Mexican and

American periods. Any meaningful interpretation of Presidio history must incorporate this equestrian world—each soldier having at least three horses and possibly a mule, the mule more valuable because of its surefootedness.

The soldiers and their families were Santa Barbara's founding colonists, and their descendants of mixed ethnic ancestry take pride today in their heritage. Presidio

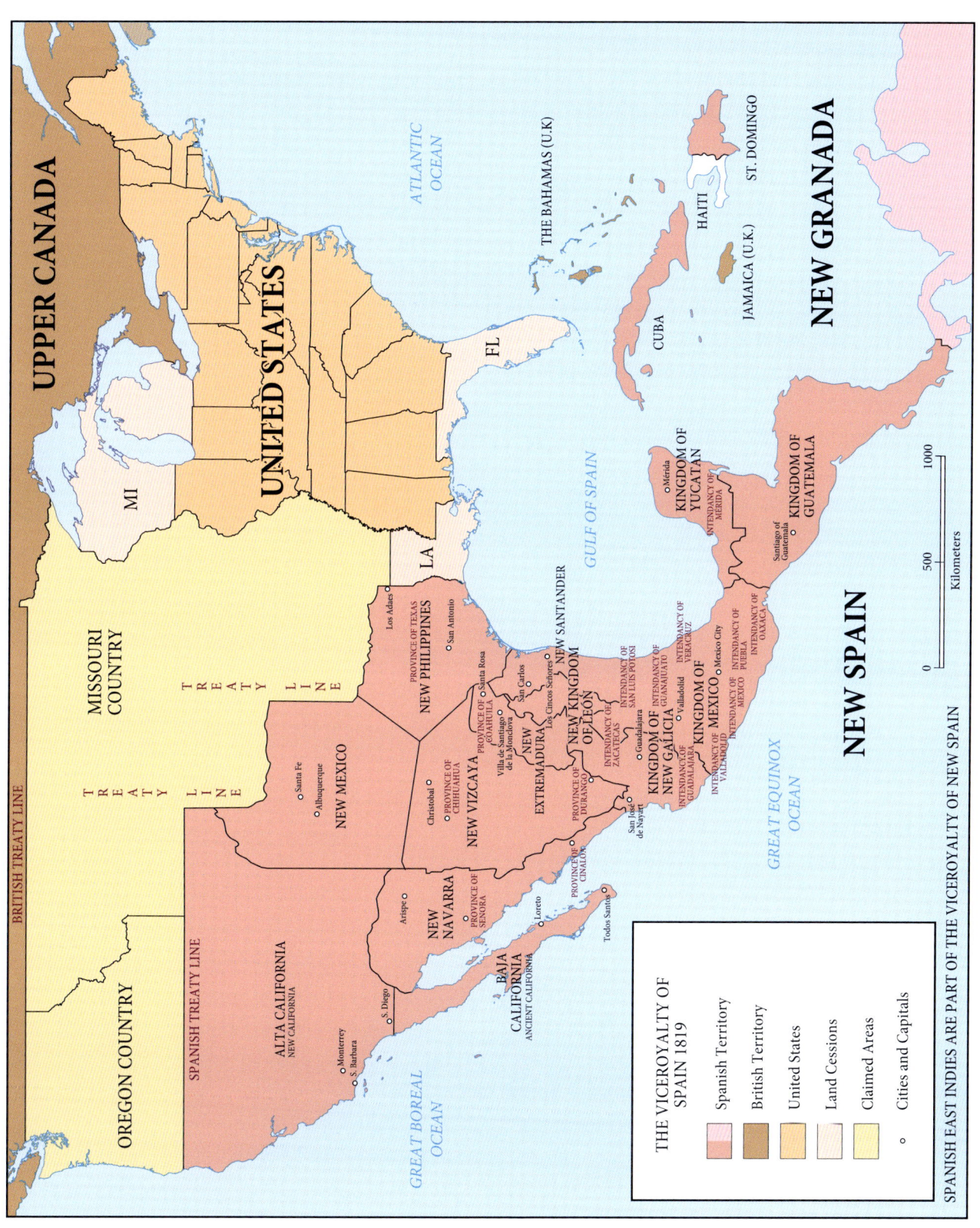

A map of the extent of Spanish empire in North America at the time of its collapse.

descendant Russell Antonio Ruiz once estimated that at least ten thousand Santa Barbara residents could trace their roots to the Presidio; that coincides with estimates that as many as one hundred thousand Californians could trace their roots to the early Spanish settlements. One of the complaints against the soldiers has been that they were responsible for retrieving fugitive Indians trying to return to their previous village lives. With their villages no longer available, many of the fugitives headed to the Central Valley and an area called Los Tulares. According to the research of Marie Duggan, most of the time Indian auxiliaries, rather than Spanish soldiers, were sent to retrieve the Indians. Soldiers were used when Indians threatened the mission itself.

The history of Indian auxiliaries is a topic that needs further research and interpretation: Historian Jack Williams has been collecting data on them for years. Before Bouchard, the emphasis was on defense against potential Indian attacks—e.g., attacks from Indians in the Central Valley and from Mojaves from the Colorado River. After Bouchard, Williams points to examples in Santa Barbara of development of regular lancer units. His research indicates that despite government prohibitions, Indians were given horses and some of the most assimilated may have been trained in the use of arms. In the event, the role of these Indian auxiliaries and their relationship to Presidio soldiers is an important story that needs further elucidation to provide proper perspective of soldier-Indian relations in Santa Barbara.

As mentioned, the total Spanish population of the Santa Barbara military district including the Pueblo de Los Ángeles, the missions, and the ranchos at the end of the Spanish period in 1820 was barely over one thousand. The total Spanish population of Alta California at this time was about three thousand. I cannot emphasize enough how this small number hardly reflects the impact of these recent settlers to Santa Barbara. Spread across this region were thousands of acres of land that had been transformed into agriculture and pasturage. In 1820, Santa Barbara produced more than 25,000 bushels of wheat and 10,000 bushels of maize; at the same time, there were more than 50,000 sheep and 40,000 cattle roaming the hillsides, and at least several thousand horses, donkeys, and mules kept in corrals and also left out to pasture. The environment of Santa Barbara had been transformed in forty short years of Spanish settlement, Indians were now in the missions, and a new world had taken hold that had changed the land the Native peoples had lived on for millennia. Europe in essence had taken over this far corner of North America and there was to be no turning back. While the Spanish in Europe migrating to New Spain drew from various ethnic identities (e.g., Catalan and Basque), the Spanish settlers in Mexico developed their own identity—a racial and ethnic mixture of European, African, and Native peoples. That heritage took hold in California and Santa Barbara and its impact is manifested in the history of the Santa Barbara Presidio. A commentator disparaging the impact of the Spanish in Santa Barbara has called it a "sliver of history." Actually, the contrary is the case—its impact was profound and echoed over time in local interest in this history that still survives into our time.

CHAPTER TWO

Decline and Fall of the Presidio

From 1820 to 1846, the Presidio served as a fort for the nascent Mexican government. With passage of time, even before the Spanish period ended, various adobes began to appear outside the Presidio walls. We do not know to what extent the exterior defense walls survived: additional gates had been cut through the fort, on the west and east sides. JoséDe la Guerra and his family still lived in the fort until 1826, awaiting the completion of their large adobe residence. The adobe was enormous in size (the interior and exterior space totaled more than fifteen thousand square feet) for a frontier residence and was worthy of being considered a mansion as it contained thirteen large rooms, with a porch on all three sides and outbuildings. The history of the house is connected to the Presidio due to the fact that it belonged to the Presidio comandante and today is in the ownership of the SBTHP. It took at least twenty-five thousand adobe bricks and ten thousand roof tiles to complete the construction, which was done primarily with paid Indian labor.

With de la Guerra taking up residence there, one can make the case that the political power of Santa Barbara had shifted to this residence. In fact, in later years, when Santa Barbara became part of the United States after the Mexican–American War, the first town council met in the de la Guerra adobe. During the Mexican period, a town council called *ayuntamiento* was put in place so that the military authority no longer had total political control. The fort itself continued to drift into decline, and as it did, town residents scavenged bricks from the fort walls to build their houses. These houses included the Rochin Adobe, built around 1856 and still in existence today inside El Presidio de Santa Bárbara State Historic Park and owned by the State of California. Another residence in the Park is the Pico Adobe, whose construction date is not known but may be as early as 1820.

The Presidio Chapel was still in use into the 1850s but was destroyed beyond repair by the 1857 Fort Tejon earthquake. Interestingly, the porch of the de la Guerra house was destroyed by this earthquake, but the main structure survived. By this time locals knew about earthquakes, and de la Guerra himself knew that wall thickness had to be increased in anticipation of future temblors. The house would also survive the 1925 earthquake that crumbled so many of the downtown-area buildings.

As the American period in Santa Barbara unfolded after 1846 following the Mexican-American War, what remained of the Presidio was used as residences. A section of the comandancia was still occupied and there were a few other rooms that were literally in the way of the wheels of progress—that is, an American grid was laid out to cut streets right through the adobe fortress, and these streets were actually plowed through in the 1880s, resulting in the demolition of some of the original adobe rooms in the way. A classic example of this destruction was taking half of one of the rooms and then sealing up the wall facing the street. This left the half room attached to a full room that eventually was called the Valenzuela Adobe and was to become known as El Cuartel, one of the two remaining buildings surviving into the 1950s. The 1925 earthquake destroyed what remained of the comandancia, and a row of Presidio adobes behind El Cuartel was demolished for a parking lot for the new post office built in 1937. A story I have heard often is that some of the citizens welcomed this "improvement" as those adobes were supposedly the red-light district of the town.

The 1925 Earthquake and the Rebirth of the Santa Barbara Presidio

The 1925 earthquake was a critical event for the future of the Presidio. With many of the State Street buildings leveled, leaders in the town decided to rebuild the downtown in the Spanish Colonial–Mediterranean style. This is a well known story told in scholarly detail in architectural historian David Gebhard's catalog for the exhibition he curated at the UCSB Art, Design & Architecture Museum in 1982 titled *Santa Barbara: The Creation of a New Spain in America*. Among the leaders involved in this architectural rebirth was Santa Barbara's leading citizen, Pearl Chase, who through the Plans and Planting Committee helped guide Santa Barbara through this unique process of city planning. As Gebhard pointed out, the culmination of this turn back to its architectural past was the rebuilding of the Presidio, and it was going to be Pearl Chase who spearheaded the project. I submit that without her, the project likely would have gone nowhere: as one of her admirers told me, she was a "force of nature." There had been talk of preserving and rebuilding the Presidio over many decades in the twentieth century, with plaques laid in the sidewalk around various locations identifying the area as the former site of the fort. But as we close in on the founding of the SBTHP, I don't think there were many in the city who, deep inside, felt that the Presidio would ever be rebuilt. There was one man who had been studying the Presidio and was promoting it, and his name was Russell Antonio Ruiz. Mentioned already for his valuable artwork, Russell was a direct descendant of various Presidio soldiers, the most important being Goicoechea. Russell even went so far as to propose that Pershing Park be renamed after Goicoechea, which obviously never happened. His voice would become more prominent after the SBTHP was founded in 1963.

Pearl Chase, a Force of Nature

It was Chase, however, who knew what it would take to get the Presidio reconstruction off the ground, an interesting turn of phrase since the project is grounded in the earth, as it were. But the task was daunting. By the 1950s, to continue the airplane metaphor, the Presidio had come in for a hard landing. Only two separate buildings remained intact, the previously mentioned El Cuartel, and the Cañedo Adobe across Canon Perdido Street. The situation, however, was not much different from that of the other three presidios in California. In San Francisco, the Spanish presidio had been incorporated into the American military fort and there was a small row of adobe buildings whose construction date was uncertain; they were possibly built in the Mexican period rather than the Spanish period. At Monterey, the presidio was completely gone except for the original chapel, the version there dating from its extension and roof replacement with fired tiles. In San Diego, nothing remained but foundations in a park above Old Town San Diego. This presidio could be much more easily rebuilt because the city owned that land and no buildings are

SBTHP Pearl Chase in front of El Cuartel, original soldier family quarters. This is the oldest building in the state park system, dating from 1788. *Courtesy SBTHP*

in the way of reconstruction. But San Diego has lacked one thing: a Pearl Chase—that is, the will to make it happen. But in fairness, I do not want to diminish the efforts and commitment of others—nor myself—to the Presidio project who have made this project happen. As many as I can remember will be given their full credit.

This brief overview of the other California presidios serves to bring home the fact that this important part of the physical heritage of the Spanish Colonial history of the state has been more or less lost in contrast to the missions, all twenty-one of which are major historical tourist sites today. This point became apparent to me when I first was hired by the SBTHP. The Presidio project is grounded in the special commitment of Santa Barbara to preserve and interpret its birthplace, but its significance transcends our town: It is a key part of our early state history, and has national connections as part of Spain's expansion into California, Arizona, New Mexico, Texas, Mississippi, and Florida—not to mention its international ties to the history of Mexico and Spain.

What follows is the fascinating story of the SBTHP and the Presidio reconstruction, with very vital sidebars into the worlds of Casa de la Guerra, the historic El Paseo Complex, and the Santa Inés Mission Mills state property. *Siempre adelante*.

CHAPTER THREE

THE EARLY YEARS OF THE SANTA BARBARA TRUST FOR HISTORIC PRESERVATION

AS BECAME APPARENT in the last chapter of this history of the Santa Barbara Presidio, there were two key factors that separated Santa Barbara from the other California coastal urban towns: One was an idea and the other was leadership. Santa Barbara had committed to the idea of returning to its Spanish past, rebuilding its town after the 1925 earthquake in a Spanish Colonial style. Plus, it had the leadership of Pearl Chase to carry out the idea. She and others would use their political connections and provide the financial support needed to get the Santa Barbara Presidio project off the ground.

But that leadership was more than just the elite of the town. Russell Antonio Ruiz, confined to a wheelchair due to suffering from muscular dystrophy, inspired a whole group of volunteers who became the heart and soul of the Presidio project during the 1960s. As a Presidio descendant himself, he knew there were many people in the town who were direct descendants of the Presidio, and he became the person who told many of them that they had a proud heritage being the founders of the town. Thus many of these people and others became involved with the Presidio project, coming out on weekends to participate in archaeology and learn more about Santa Barbara's early history.

I do not pretend that the story that follows regarding the early years of the Presidio project is in any way comprehensive. But I feel it is important to make sure these early years are acknowledged because they laid the foundation for the project that made it possible for those who came after, including me, to advance the reconstruction and interpretation of this important international site. The emphasis from my view must always be on the fact that our efforts had not just a local but international impact. These so-called early years span from 1958 to 1981.

As with any timeline, there are historical moments that often extend beyond themselves in both directions. As a result, a number of people who were in at the founding of the SBTHP were still there when I arrived January 1, 1981, and continued to have an impact on the project. While the SBTHP would not be founded until 1963, Pearl Chase, behind the scenes as early as 1958, was in contact with officials of the state, looking into the possibility of having the Presidio designated a state historic park.

Chase early on learned that what was needed was a feasibility study identifying the site as historically significant and worthy of becoming a historic park. She convinced the California Division of Beaches and Parks Department, later to be California State Parks (hereafter CSP), to assign a historian to undertake the study. His name was Dr. Glenn Price, at the time a park historian who later would become a professor of history at Sonoma State University. The title of this document, completed in 1959, was *The Santa Barbara Presidio: A Report on the Presidio of Santa Barbara*. This document turned out to be just what the doctor ordered for the enthusiasts desiring to rebuild the Presidio. It gave a glowing review of the site and acknowledged the fact that Presidio history was an under-interpreted part of California's early Spanish heritage of the state. I certainly would be curious to know if Chase was looking over Price's shoulder during this process of determining the feasibility of rebuilding the Presidio. Basically, Chase now had what she needed to convince park department administrators and legislators that the Presidio should be declared a historic park. In a typical bureaucratic time frame, the Presidio and its supporters would have to wait until 1963 before the Park became official with a vote of the California State Park and Recreation Commission. Years later, SBTHP volunteers would prepare an acquisition-and-development plan for the Park in 1979, which would be followed by an official State Park General Plan in 1988 and an official department Interpretation Master Plan in 2012. In terms of influence on the development of the state park, clearly Price's report was the most important.

Thus, one can imagine my surprise when one day in 2008, I was in my office in the Park and the front-desk person came into my office to say there was an elderly gentleman with his daughter looking at the exhibits, who identified himself as "Glenn Price." I knew immediately who that was and went out to meet him. He was in his eighties, very cordial, and he said this was the first time he had been to the Presidio since finishing his report in 1959—almost fifty years ago. I then had a conversation with him about the report and asked if he remembered Chase. "Absolutely," he responded. "She was a force of nature." Thus he was the source of this description of Chase that I previously alluded to. I took down his address, and then went to the board to tell the story of his visit. I suggested that he be given the Pearl Chase Preservation Award that the SBTHP gives out at its annual meetings. Price was presented the award at the SBTHP meeting in January 2009, which was then fifty years after its creation. I love this story of continuity with SBTHP's past.

The Creation of the Santa Barbara Trust for Historic Preservation

The next step for the advancement of the Presidio project was creating a nonprofit organization to support the Park. The nonprofit was to be the SBTHP. Chase had articles of incorporation and bylaws prepared, and officially declared a nonprofit in 1963. Among the signers of the document were leading citizens of Santa Barbara—these included bankers, a few wealthy people, and Thomas Storke, the publisher of the local *Santa Barbara News-Press* who also happened to be descended from the first comandante of the Presidio, Ortega. The first president of the SBTHP was Judge John Rickard, former city attorney and mayor who just happened to be a descendant

El Cuartel, original soldier's family quarters rooms dating from 1788. Purchased and donated to the State by SBTHP in 1964, it became El Presidio de Santa Barbara State Historic Park, the smallest park in the state park system. *Author's Collection*

of de la Guerra. Part of the Santa Barbara elite, these founders were important in advancing the Presidio reconstruction project, but equally important were the Presidio volunteers who were more of the hoi polloi, one might say, coming out on weekends to give the project a positive public face. Their impact in advancing the project was at least equal to that of the so-called elite.

Not to say that the project could have made it with only grassroots support. These elites did light the fire, with Chase always behind the scenes pulling the strings, as it were. Their first major act was to buy El Cuartel from the local Boy Scouts. One of the two original adobe buildings, El Cuartel was restored by the SBTHP. The organization made some mistakes in that process, including installing a heated concrete floor that damaged the adobe walls. All these mistakes were reversed later.

To seal the deal with the state, the SBTHP donated the property to the state to form the first park property of El Presidio. It became the smallest park in the state park system.

Land Acquisition Advances the Presidio Project

These early years of SBTHP were devoted primarily to gradually purchasing parcels of land that made up the original footprint of the Presidio. There were many people involved in this process, but besides Chase, two of the most important were Bill Luton and Jeremy Hass. Very quietly, as properties became available, the SBTHP would approach owners and make offers on purchases of the properties. Bill, who owned the KEYT-TV station and also was a descendant of the Presidio's first comandante, José Francisco Ortega, would at his own expense service the mortgages of properties SBTHP acquired. Jeremy Hass, then a young attorney, became involved with SBTHP in 1964 and researched deeds to help locate properties that contained foundations of the original Presidio buildings. He would then go out and help develop real-estate deals, some of which were complex, involving exchanges.

At the same time, the state, if slowly at first, would acquire certain SBTHP-owned properties, proceeds from which were used to buy other properties. Many of these transactions took place in the 1960s and included purchase of the site of the original Chapel. Over time, the SBTHP purchased the Moullet property, Cota-Knox House, Pico Adobe, Cañedo Adobe, Bonilla House, and the old city-college site. All these properties had been acquired before I arrived on the scene in 1981. All told, nearly half of the Presidio footprint had been acquired from willing sellers by 1981. Also, a right of refusal to purchase the Rochin Adobe was obtained thanks to Hass. In my mind, this was a monumental achievement. From my first days, I soon came to be a Presidio enthusiast. So much had been achieved through volunteer effort—Bill and Jeremy were two model citizens devoted to the project. Major factors in this success were the political connections Jeremy's father, John, had in

Photo of Governor Ronald Reagan with local Santa Barbara attorney John Hass. Hass's political connections helped advance state acquisition of available parcels in the Presidio area in downtown Santa Barbara. *Courtesy Michael Hass*

Sacramento—Hass was a confidante of Governors Pat Brown and Ronald Reagan, both of whom would contact him regarding political issues related to Santa Barbara.

An anecdote sums up perfectly Hass's enthusiasm. There are various versions of this story but the one I recollect from Jeremy is as follows: His research had indicated where the Presidio Chapel foundations were likely located, at an address on Canon Perdido Street. He obtained permission from the owner of the property, a Mr. Nixon, to go out on the lot, and dig down where he thought the foundations were. He had with him an archaeologist, Lewis Binford, who was to become a famous scholar in the field. While they were digging around the site, night fell, and still they found no foundations. They ended the evening shining the car headlights on the site, without results. They were in the right area, however, and further archaeology uncovered the foundations upon which the Chapel would be reconstructed later. Afterward, the state would acquire the property with Hass helping arrange the transaction. This early excavation anecdote was the beginning of archaeology at the site that dates back to 1965, with even earlier efforts by property owner Elmer Whittaker to locate foundations on his property next to the Chapel. From this time well into the 1970s, various phases of excavation took place with too many names to mention here but all of which contributed to moving the Presidio project gradually forward—many were amateurs but others, like Professors James Deetz, Michael Glassow, and Brian Fagan, were well known professional archaeologists and anthropologists. More information on these people is available in a report Michael Imwalle prepared in 2010, "El Presidio de Santa Barbara State Historic Park: Acquisition and Development History." Other reports in the Santa Barbara Presidio Research Center lay out in more detail each of the excavations. Over the years, the SBTHP has done a reasonable amount of documentation of work undertaken at the site. Most of this initial archaeology was done on a volunteer basis.

Presidio Volunteers Provide Spark to the Presidio Project

These early volunteers had an admirable dedication to the Presidio project. I remember years later after I arrived in 1981, Bill Luton was still on the board, and still owned the TV station. He had Gene Forrsell, who had a weekend talk show, interview me numerous times to promote the Presidio project. Plus, one of my favorite memories of Bill was his showing up one day at the Presidio in his beat-up yellow Ford Fiesta. I happened to be outside and he called me over as he opened the hatchback. He reached in and pulled out a statue that he told me his parents had bought in Spain years ago. He said, "It is for the Chapel if you want it." I confirmed with art historian Norman Neuerburg that it was a sixteenth-century Spanish wooden sculpture of Mary and Jesus. That statue has been in the center niche of the rebuilt Presidio Chapel since 1988. It was only a month or so later that I opened a morning edition of the *Santa Barbara News-Press* and learned that Bill had died suddenly of a heart attack—a true Presidio hero lost.

Another Presidio hero, who arrived at the SBTHP in 1969, was Richard Whitehead; he had recently retired as the planning director of the county of Santa Barbara. He had been in that position since shortly after World War II and he brought to the SBTHP his scientific training from the Massachusetts Institute of Technology, where he had earned an MS in engineering. He became fascinated with the Presidio project and joined the Presidio volunteers, but also served on the board of the SBTHP, including two terms as president. By the 1970s, most of the foundations of the Presidio footprint had been located but not accurately recorded on a map. Whitehead took on this task, using his own personal surveying equipment, and created a map with the Presidio foundations laid over the modern streets. This accurate map is still used today in all Park materials.

The Presidio Research Center Created in 1982

His interest piqued, Whitehead also decided to take on documenting the original construction of the Presidio and set about collecting Spanish documents from the eighteenth century, which were available on microfilm at the Bancroft Library. He had hundreds of pages printed from the microfilm, then enlisted a stable of people who translated them. These documents are now in three-ring binders in the Santa Barbara Presidio Research Center in the Park. Whitehead also prepared a manuscript on the history of the Presidio, which the SBTHP published in 1996 under the title *Citadel on the Channel: The Royal Presidio of Santa Barbara, Its Founding and Construction, 1782-1798*. He published other works related to the Presidio's history, and gifted to the Research Center all of his papers.

This collection contains research materials, drafts, and published writings; facsimiles, transcriptions, and translations of historic documents; correspondence; and deeds, maps, and plans that document the history and reconstruction of El Real Presidio de Santa Bárbara and other organizations in Santa Barbara related to history and preservation. His book collection also formed the basis for the Research Center that officially came into being shortly after I began at the SBTHP in 1982. Thus I had the privilege of knowing and working with Richard.

He came to me when I first started and asked to have one of the rooms in the reconstructed padre's quarters as a research center. We soon settled on something better—converting a garage and living quarters behind the Cañedo Adobe into the research center. He died in 1988, happy that we had created the Center, but he was not with us when the SBTHP decided to take the Center several steps further rehabilitating a 1920s Spanish colonial building outside the Presidio walls, albeit still within the boundaries of the Park. At one point, several people suggested naming the Center after him: he said absolutely not! His ego was not of the type that needed that kind of glory. Advancing the Presidio reconstruction was his passion—a passion that I came to embrace myself.

At the opening of the Research Center, I made the following remarks: "This research center has been created in the spirit of Don Quixote—and the vision and commitment of Richard Whitehead, Russell Antonio Ruiz, and many others who paved the way for those of us here today. They were 'idealists working in matter'—individuals who dreamed and also cared about details. They knew, as we know, that the Presidio Project is an act of the imagination built on a solid foundation of research."

Other Stars in the SBTHP Volunteer Firmament

To continue this initial identification of some major contributors to the Presidio project, I return to Russell Antonio Ruiz. Having served in the Navy as an aerial photographer, Ruiz, whose DNA was connected to the founders of the Presidio, retired to Santa Barbara, where he reignited his fascination with early Spanish history of his town. Mention of his work as an aerial photographer relates to the wonderful artwork Russell created of conjectural images of the Presidio. He also did paintings of Chumash Indian villages in the area. Almost all the images are done from an aerial perspective. Had he done nothing else, these creations alone would have secured him a place as a major contributor to interpretation of the Presidio.

Yet there was more: his research and storytelling to the Presidio volunteers, whose numbers swelled, and who came out weekends to celebrate at the Presidio Chapel site. But the volunteers also did work, starting an archaeological program that was overseen by a team of amateurs, who did their best to undertake archaeology that would eventually be picked up by professionals during my time in the 1980s. I can't possibly name all of the people from these days starting in the late 1960s. But I will name a few whom I came to know as they were still involved during my tenure. Bud Decker, a World War II veteran, organized one of the digs and later became a member of the Presidio soldiers group. Eventually the SBTHP would purchase replica cannons and Decker made the carriages for these cannons. Another volunteer was Mike Hardwick, whose wife, Paula, also gave many hours of her time. In 1969, Mike had just retired from the Navy and was about to begin his studies in anthropology at UCSB, where he would eventually earn his BA. He caught the Presidio bug, befriending Russell and carrying his interest to help start in the 1990s a soldier reenactment group. He also undertook a major study of the arms and armament of the Presidio soldiers and has produced an important document on this subject that I previously mentioned. He further chose to re-enact the eighteenth century governor of Alta California, Felipe de Neve, studied his life, had his uniform accurately created, and even went so far as to obtain in Spain an actual medal of the Order of Charles III, the same decoration that Neve had received from the king for his good works in Alta California. There is something very inveterate about each and every one of these early-Presidio-project people.

Another of my favorite early-Presidio-project volunteers was Virginia Scott. I got to know her also in the 1980s. Originally from the Midwest, she and her husband came west after World War II. Her husband had served in postwar Japan, and when they landed in Santa Barbara, she became a history teacher at Santa Barbara High School. She brought many of her classes to do research and help with archaeology; her students helped make soldier uniforms that were used in living-history activities and parades. One of her students was Eric Hvolboll, who was descended from a Presidio soldier. He later went to Stanford University and wrote a senior paper on the Ortega rancho, which is at Refugio Beach and next to his family's ranch. After graduating from Stanford Law School, he became the youngest board member of the SBTHP at age 28. Keeping it all in the family, as it were, his mother, Elizabeth, later became a board member of the SBTHP. Trained in opera in her younger days by the world-famous diva Lotte Lehmann at the Music Academy of the West, she, along

Prior to the author's arrival at the Trust in 1981, key volunteers of the Presidio project included, left to right: Russell Clay Ruiz and his mother, Alice Ruth Ruiz; artist, historian, and descendant Russell Antonio Ruiz (in wheelchair); attorney Jeremy Hass (seated on ground); Michael Hardwick, cofounder of the Presidio Soldados group (standing with camera); and retired County Planning Director Richard Whitehead. *Courtesy Michael Hardwick*

with local musicians Luis Moreno and Francisco Gonzalez, sang and helped preserve early-California music at numerous Presidio events over the years.

The connection to Lotte Lehmann was interesting to me as it related to my previous doctoral research on German exiles from the Nazis who ended up in Southern California and of which she was one. Before I left that world for my new Spanish world, I was asked to edit for publication the papers from a colloquium I had participated in at the Smithsonian in February 1980, titled "The Muses Flee Hitler." With the help of Carla Borden, who then worked in the Office of Smithsonian Symposia and Seminars, those papers were published in 1983 and the book was reviewed in many major newspapers, including the *New York Times*, the *Washington Post*, and the *Los Angeles Times*. My fifteen minutes of fame.

But the new world I was in had its own fascination and the people I met at the Presidio were a unique group—Presidio zealots, as I liked to call them. To wit, another transgenerational example of dedicated Presidio enthusiasm is Russell Clay Ruiz, the son of Russell Antonio and Alice Ruth Ruiz. From his teenage years in the 1970s, he was at his parents' sides helping on various projects while serving as a caregiver for his father, who was wheelchair bound. He always participated in re-enactments in period dress and helped make signs with his father that were placed on the Presidio site. When the SBTHP finally decided to try for the first time in the 1970s to rebuild a Presidio adobe, they chose the padre's quarters. A well known adobe maker, Ben Aguilar, was brought on board and Russell Ruiz led the volunteers in making about two thousand bricks. We will learn much more about this Presidio-adobe world in the pages ahead.

After a tour of duty in the Navy that ended in the early 1980s, Russell returned to Santa Barbara, and has been an active volunteer at the Presidio to this day. He and others mentioned so far have been designated by the SBTHP board as either Life Honorary Members or Life Honorary Directors of the organization. This grassroots energy sustained the Presidio project in these decades before I arrived and should not be underestimated.

Two Critical Decisions

On the other hand, some very significant board decisions were made that propelled the SBTHP onto an entirely different management level. It was not possible to know at that moment just how important these management decisions were to be in the future of the Presidio project. The two decisions were to accept the gift of the historic El Paseo, a fifty-thousand-plus square foot complex of shops and offices, and to enter into a concession agreement with the state to manage El Presidio de Santa Bárbara State Historic Park.

THE GIFT OF EL PASEO

Both these decisions were made possible in large part due to the law firm before Weldon and Hass, where John Hass worked with his son Jeremy, one of the previously mentioned major players in the history of the Presidio project. Jeremy's brother, Michael, told me the following when I interviewed him in June 2020: Jeremy came to know Irene Suski Fendon, the owner of El Paseo, under circumstances Michael could not recall. Irene, a former Broadway actress, had inherited from her deceased husband, successful Broadway producer Thaddeus Suski, various properties in the downtown Santa Barbara business district. The properties included a multistory building containing a major store and offices, another office complex, parking lots in the Presidio neighborhood, and El Paseo. In short, she and her family and her second husband, Ron Fendon, were major commercial property owners in Santa Barbara.

El Paseo, built before the 1925 earthquake, became the model for rebuilding the town after the temblor. It was donated to the SBTHP on December 4, 1971. *Photo by Michele Jackman*

Clearly Jeremy Hass was at the center of discussions with the family to consider donating El Paseo to the SBTHP as a tax offset for income from their other properties. These negotiations were taking place around 1970 and culminated in the donation of the property on the feast day of Saint Barbara, December 4, 1971. In a June 15, 2020, conversation I had with Ron Fendon of these goings-on regarding El Paseo, he mentioned to me that his memory was somewhat vague of events, but he said he definitely remembered dozens of meetings between Jeremy and his wife. Fendon said he and Irene had their separate businesses and estates, so he was not directly involved in the negotiations that led to the donation, but he heard about it in conversations after the fact. Constructed in the Spanish Colonial style in 1924 and surrounding and including the famous de la Guerra Adobe, El Paseo was received as a gift in honor of Pearl Chase, and all surplus proceeds from income generated on the property were to go toward the restoration of Casa de la Guerra and the reconstruction of the Santa Barbara Presidio.

In a follow-up story, I heard from Richard Berti, the present managing partner of the Presidio properties across Anacapa Street from El Paseo, that he had met Irene after the gift of El Paseo. She had set up a meeting at the Elephant Garden at the Presidio properties. She arrived with Ron in their Rolls-Royce, Ron opened the door for her, and she walked over by herself to meet with Berti. She queried him about his background, and an outcome of this meeting was she sold the Presidio properties to him and a partnership. This was a property the SBTHP had been interested in because the parking lot contained the foundations of the front gate of the Presidio. Whatever the reason for the sale to Berti, that property would become an issue when the SBTHP decided to dispose of the El Paseo property. Real estate hijinks to come.

The proposed El Paseo gift had unleashed a torrent of debate among SBTHP board members, especially from bankers who were wary of a nonprofit organization managing a commercial property. Several resigned when the majority of voters agreed to accept the gift. One of the issues was that the gift came with a mortgage that would likely not be retired until the 1980s, and that turned out to be the case. In addition, after almost fifty years, the complex was in need of major renovation. As a result, for the next eighteen years, El Paseo would dominate the attention of the board, and I recall that during my first years at the SBTHP, more than two thirds of the time of board meetings was taken up by El Paseo business matters.

To be honest, El Paseo seemed for the longest time to be a white elephant. The gift could well be justified under the broad historical-preservation articles of corporation of the SBTHP that Pearl Chase had wisely adopted. The El Paseo complex had served as a model for rebuilding Santa Barbara after the 1925 earthquake, and Casa de la Guerra was connected to Presidio history not to mention being the home of the most prominent family of nineteenth-century Santa Barbara. Nevertheless, for over a decade and a half, El Paseo was to be a financial drag on the SBTHP. The story did have a happy, albeit controversial, ending that would unfold during the latter part of the 1980s.

PRESIDIO CONCESSION AGREEMENT

The second critical decision the board made was to enter in 1966 into a concession agreement with the California State Parks Department to operate and develop El Presidio de Santa Bárbara State Historic Park. A key factor in effectuating this agreement was the Weldon and Hass Law Office, again especially through the work of Jeremy Hass. The Hasses were prominent Republicans in town, and John served several years as chair of the Republican Party in Santa Barbara. In a conversation with Michael Hass, I learned that his father was also very close to Governor Pat Brown, who Michael remembered called his dad a lot for advice, especially related to any appointments he might want to make in the Santa Barbara area. Those were the days when there was collegiality between the parties.

With the election of Republican Ronald Reagan in 1966 and the appointment of William Penn Mott as his parks director, the door, as it were, was opened for the Hasses to promote the Presidio project. The project also had a friend in Robert Lagomarsino, who at the time was the Republican state senator from the Ventura/Santa Barbara district. It was a bit odd to sign a concession agreement with the SBTHP as these were usually done for for-profit businesses to operate sales of goods and services at the parks. But it somehow was the only vehicle the SBTHP could come up with, as the only other operator could have been a county or municipal governmental entity. Eventually an operating agreement would take its place, but that would be much later, in 1989.

On paper, at least, it was starting to look like the Presidio project might zoom ahead, with the SBTHP at the helm and a potential future income stream available from El Paseo. But that was not all; Chase was not done. She brought together four parties—the California State Parks Department, the county and city governments of Santa Barbara, and the SBTHP—to form a joint powers agreement for depositing funds for acquisition of the properties needed to purchase the footprint of the Presidio. Thus there were to be multiple sources of funding—bond money from the state, budgeted annual amounts from the local government, and the private sources from the SBTHP. In actuality, it was solely money deposited from the city and the county: Each contributed $10,000 annually, and that money was used to help purchase real estate in the Presidio area. The county ceased its funding after the 1974 passage of Proposition 13, which lowered statewide property taxes—the city, however, did continue to deposit its $10,000 through the end of the century. I would tap into that fund to help rebuild the Presidio in later years.

The stage seemed set for the SBTHP to advance with its financial and institutional toolbox filled to overflowing, which had the organization operating at two levels. The board had been at work evolving itself into an economic and political force, while the public face of the organization was being put forth through the Presidio volunteers, who had become an official committee of the SBTHP. As with just about every nonprofit that springs from nonpaid volunteers, egos began to play a part, and very smart businesspeople sometimes deal with matters in a very unbusinesslike manner. Needless to say, one could also not expect that a small nonprofit could sneak into town, with the force of government behind it, and buy up valuable real estate, close city streets, tear down some buildings, and thereby alter the town—all this without a whimper from the townspeople. I will try to explain the ups and downs of this story in the pages ahead.

I have already alluded to the many behind-the-scenes events regarding property acquisitions. Some of these acquisitions had rental properties on them and thus provided an income stream to help operate the park, but these also included El Cuartel, with its two original presidio adobe rooms. The state expected the SBTHP to manage and operate the Park at no cost to the state. But the state did contribute bond funds that helped the SBTHP purchase the Presidio Chapel site, the Cañedo

Adobe, the so-called Shalhoob building, and other properties. All totaled, between 1971 and 1975, seven properties were acquired: all the properties (except for one to be acquired later, thanks to John Hass) fronted Canon Perdido Street on the north side between Anacapa and Santa Barbara Streets. The SBTHP in its turn picked up some properties already mentioned that would be conveyed to the state after I arrived. Things were definitely moving along.

A Bump in the Road

Unfortunately, a nasty conflict began in 1979 between the board's management committee and the manager the SBTHP had hired to oversee operations of El Paseo and its Presidio rental properties. The manager had been in the position since 1971, and the brouhaha had been brewing for quite a while. I think it would be inappropriate to name names in this matter, which really upset the comity of the organization for over a year. It involved stacking the board, which led to the hiring of a lawyer, ending up in court, and a judge restoring the original slate of candidates the board had put forth. It wasn't pretty and it got into the press, with a reporter from a local newspaper attending board meetings. I am not sure why the board didn't call executive sessions: part of it might have had to do with the SBTHP's contract with a public agency, the California State Parks Department.

In some ways, this was the beginning of a decade of challenges for the SBTHP. The noble preservation cause had been sullied by this internecine battle, but I give the board credit for course-correcting and planning for rehiring and redirecting the organization. Were it not for this, I would never have been hired by the SBTHP. I was interviewed by a committee of five, three of who are now deceased—these three, in my opinion, contributed mightily to progress made on the Presidio project, and you know their names already and you will hear more about them later. Apparently, there were dozens of candidates, and I earned an interview likely because one of the people on the committee had been on my doctoral committee at UCSB. Also, I expect my doctoral chair, Harold Kirker, one way or another influenced my eventual choice as the new administrator of the SBTHP.

We Return *to* California

When I told my wife Michele that I thought we should move back to California from Washington, D.C., she was in the midst of a powerful career working as a civilian employee for the Army in the Pentagon. Her response was she was willing only if we moved to Santa Barbara. Thus in the summer of 1980, we packed up and vacated the row house we were sharing with another family in Alexandria, Virginia, and headed west by car during one of the hottest summers on record. We did not have a day under 100 degrees until we got to Flagstaff, Arizona. Neither of the two VWs we were driving had air-conditioning. During our time in Alexandria, I had worked for six months as a public historian for the Alexandria Archaeology Research Museum, reviewing historical documents, working with volunteers, and reviewing grant proposals. This at least gave me some experience to talk about related to the Presidio when I was interviewed for the position at the SBTHP in fall 1980. I was told later that I was the second choice of each person on the committee, each who had a different first choice. Because I did not have property-management experience, the committee and the board hired a person with that experience to oversee all the business operations of the SBTHP. My job, in essence, was to build the Presidio. Simple enough, until I began to realize that it was not all that simple for a person without a construction background. The skill I did have was knowing how to go about doing historical research, and that was to be a significant part of this job. To engage in restoration work, one has to have a good knowledge of the history behind it.

I could not start officially until January 1, 1981, because I had set up teaching in Los Angeles at three schools: Occidental College; California State University, Los Angeles; and Santa Monica College. We had taken up residence in Santa Barbara, so I traveled around Los Angeles, crisscrossing the city, to meet my teaching obligations. An anecdote worth relating regarding this experience is that while I was teaching a freshman class at Occidental College, Barry Obama was a student there. Another Oxy student was Ruth Coleman, who would later become director of California State Parks and a personal friend. She also was one of the most important directors in advancing El Presidio de Santa Bárbara State Historic Park. Another supportive director earlier was William Penn Mott, who has already been mentioned.

Mott had supported funding to acquire the property on which the original foundations of the Chapel were located. During the period of the Reagan governorship, much property was acquired, and perhaps this is the moment to summarize what had been accomplished from 1963 to the time I arrived in 1981. The real estate acquired was in itself a major achievement—about half of the footprint, that is, original foundations of the fort had been acquired. A number of phases of archaeology had been undertaken with the help of the Presidio volunteers—exposing the foundations of the Chapel and of the adjoining padre's quarters. Richard Whitehead had also tracked the location of other sections of the foundations, including opening a small trench that revealed the southwest corner of the Presidio.

The SBTHP published a number of books that provided background of the Spanish history of Santa Barbara. Richard Whitehead also edited and the SBTHP published *California's Mission La Purísima Concepción: The Hageman and Ewing Reports* in hardcover and later in paperback. This in-depth analysis of the archaeological excavations and documentary and photographic record of the site of the mission in Lompoc had been drafted by National Park Service staff Fred Hageman and Russell Ewing in 1939 in conjunction with the reconstruction of the mission by the Civilian Conservation Corps. Besides being an important documentation of the restoration, Whitehead and others perceived it as a potential source and guide for the reconstruction of the Presidio. It turned out that there were significant differences between the later-built mission and the earlier-built Presidio, but that was all part of the research that makes the Presidio project so interesting.

Lastly, among the earlier progress made by the SBTHP was rebuilding the padre's quarters, whose three rooms were nearly completed when I came on the scene. Roof tiles had been ordered, and building was completed in late 1981. In addition, the SBTHP restoration committee had hired architect Gil Sanchez to create architectural plans to rebuild the Presidio Chapel. Indeed altogether, with the gift of El Paseo, the organization was on the verge of greatness. That may sound a bit hyperbolic, but my observation was there was a lot of diverse talent committed to the SBTHP and the Presidio, and while there were for certain some major stumbling blocks ahead, I was about to ride a wave that others had created. I wanted in this introduction to make sure that, first of all, the historical significance of the project was established and that those who came before me shared the glory of what has been achieved over the years.

Not that every day for me was to be totally happy, and I certainly asked myself many times if the stresses and strains were worth it. I got a clue of the human side I was about to encounter on the very first night I was introduced to the SBTHP board and others in the Red Room of the El Paseo Restaurant in December 1980. Executive Director Bob Cleveland and I, as the new employees, made some remarks, followed by comments from two board members who seemed to go on and on and whose comments seemed more a dialogue between them than addressed to us. I found out later that one had been the head of the Democratic Party in Santa Barbara and the other the head of the Republican Party. One thing I learned from this was to keep my mouth shut and listen. These were not shy retiring people. One other thing I think back to from the beginning of my tenure was my fortitude. I stayed with it, and the motivation for me was the Presidio project was utterly fascinating from a political, intellectual, and just plain human perspective. A special brand of person is drawn to nonprofits and to projects based on the study and interpretation of history. Those people became an essential part of the story of the Santa Barbara Presidio reconstruction and interpretation.

CHAPTER FOUR

The Presidio Project: Peaks and Valleys of the 1980s

I MAKE NO CLAIMS that my version of the years as projects administrator and executive director of the SBTHP is an objective account and that all the pertinent facts are covered in my version of the history of the Presidio project during my years. It is best to lay out my main prejudice—I think the Presidio reconstruction project is of major historical importance and its proponents are my heroes. Their commitment helped win the day against political and financial challenges in the 1980s, and was capped by rebuilding the Presidio Chapel, one of the great achievements of the organization to this day.

I was from early on totally committed to rebuilding the entire Presidio and that passion still is very much alive to this day. On the other hand, I did not have a problem with settling for a limited Presidio in the short run, which turned out to be longer than I might have hoped. Thus over time, there have been some people, like myself, totally committed to the full rebuilding, such as local dentist Garvan Kuskey and pharmacist and environmentalist James Mills, now both deceased. Others helped the Presidio project's cause but didn't believe in the full vision. Then some on the board just came along for the ride without any commitment to the big dream of rebuilding the fort. People join nonprofit boards for various reasons and those who have participated in this world know what I mean. The motives are not always pure. But at their core, the board and Presidio volunteers believed in the vision of preserving and rebuilding the mud fort that marked the beginning of the city of Santa Barbara. Added to this is the international nature of the project—it is inextricably connected to the history of Spain and Mexico.

Inside the Political Maelstrom

I remember my first week on the job—starting January 1, 1981. I was given an office in the Cañedo Adobe and was about to settle in by moving a desk around, bringing in a few other things, and setting up the telephone when a man came in whom I met for the first time. His name was Vince Pownall and he was in charge of construction of the padre's quarters. He stated abruptly that he had to cut through the window of my office that connected with the recently reconstructed padre's quarters. He had a concrete saw cutter in hand. Fine, I said and vacated the office. When I came back later, he had finished the job and left. The entire office, including my desk, was covered with a layer of concrete dust. Vince saw me as one of those neck-up guys, and I decided that, well, that's okay. I had to prove that I belonged and was not one of those people I alluded to as just taking up space. Admittedly, I had a lot to learn by the seat of my pants.

I don't think it hurt that I was the son of an electrician of the old school, pulling wires through flex tubing, learning how electricity was brought to one's home and workplace. I had been around construction people a lot and I would identify with hands-on people I would encounter on the SBTHP's many building projects. Vince was my first encounter with such a person.

I also count as valuable experience working full-time as a dishwasher for a summer during my high-school years. After attending the University of California, Los Angeles, I had more than a year of experience selling advertising for the *Los Angeles Times*. That job, in some ways, best prepared me for being the administrator for the Presidio project. I would have to raise money for the Presidio reconstruction, which meant I would have to sell the project to potential donors.

My public-history experience was limited to a brief stint at the Alexandria Archaeology Research Center in Virginia. It was the first time I worked directly with archaeologists who primarily were excavating privies of the eighteenth- and nineteenth-century town of Alexandria, where George Washington spent many a day. Historians and archaeologists are dealing with the same subject of history, but the historian's world is based in documents, most often the printed word. The archives are where we are at home. The archaeologist obviously worships the objects excavated and other features, such as burials and foundations of structures. There is a basic difference between each's thinking, and I will delve into that as we discuss the excavations at the Presidio and the aboveground archaeology of the walls of the Casa de la Guerra. One might say that together, however, the two disciplines provide a fuller picture of the past.

Nonprofit as a Business Entity

What I learned pretty early on is that one had to view the SBTHP as more than a public-service organization: It was a business, only different from a regular, for-profit business in that all the profits were reinvested into the business. Like a business, the nonprofit has to do a business plan, often called a strategic plan, that covers defining, planning, raising money from investors (donors), and then executing the project or multiple projects. Once you realize that nonprofits fall under the same corporate codes as for-profit businesses, with certain differences, then you begin to understand my point.

This might be obvious to some, but I was surprised that the perfectly good businesspeople in the SBTHP would not always demonstrate the best business behavior. As the nonprofit owners of the El Paseo shopping, office, and apartment complex, the SBTHP had a volunteer management committee that made decisions on the day-to-day operations, including rent rates. I remember from attending many of these meetings that members on occasion would make decisions to keep rents below market rates for various reasons. Since these decisions did not affect these people's personal finances, they were easier to make. On the other hand, over the years, the SBTHP was quite a responsible group in budgeting and spending conservatively. From 1981 to 2016, we weathered three recessions, including the Great Recession of 2008–9 with investments intact and zero layoffs. Part of this success was based on successful fundraising as well.

Bob Cleveland was in charge of property management and overseeing the budgets of the SBTHP and the Park in the early 1980s. He had previous real-estate experience and was named executive director at the same time that I was appointed projects administrator. My responsibilities were focused on the Presidio project, which included growing the SBTHP into a more viable organization. With the public-relations committee headed by a local woman named Heather Bryden, we upgraded the SBTHP's newsletter, *La Campana*. When I started, membership had shrunk to eighty due to the internal conflict that had leaked to the press. Within a year, the committee increased membership to more than three hundred. We also began putting on public events to promote the SBTHP, including the proverbial wine tastings aiming toward the then-upcoming two hundredth anniversary of the Spanish founding of the Presidio on April 21, 1982. The SBTHP also participated in community events such as Old Spanish Days, held each year in early August.

The padre's quarters were more or less completed when roof tiles made by an Indian tribe north of San Luis Obispo were installed in 1982. My attention then turned to advancing the plans for rebuilding the Presidio Chapel. I was unfamiliar with the state's rules and regulations: I knew nothing about the Public Resources Code, under which the Presidio fell as a state park. That code was important because a careful reading of it mentioned that major projects were not to proceed at parks before completion of a State Park's Commission–endorsed general plan.

Art Historian Provides Expertise

For whatever reason, the California State Parks Department allowed the SBTHP to proceed with the Chapel project without a completed general plan. Architectural drawings were just beginning when I arrived. Restoration architect Gil Sanchez was hired and I remember the early meetings when the restoration committee asked questions such as whether the Chapel had a choir loft and if the floor sloped down away from the altar as archaeology seemed to show. Brought in to try to answer these questions was mission-period art historian Norman Neuerburg.

This Saint Barbara painting by José de Alcíbar, who resided in Mexico City and was of Basque origin, hung in the Presidio Chapel from the 1790s on. Art historian Neuerburg discovered it in the Our Lady of Sorrows Church in damaged condition. It is restored and hangs in the reconstructed Chapel. *Courtesy SBTHP*

Art Historian Neuerburg designed the chapel interior and with volunteers painted the interior decorations. *Courtesy SBTHP*

Sanctuary of the rebuilt Chapel. *Author's Collection*

Thus began a long friendship between Norman and myself. We particularly bonded when I learned that in a previous life he had been the historical-design consultant for the Getty Villa, one of my favorite museum sites in the world! Norman answered the question about the choir loft by pointing out that in an original painting of the Chapel from the nineteenth century, there was a window. In every instance he knew of, there was a choir loft whenever such a window existed. On the second question, he pointed out that a number of California mission churches had floors sloping away from the altar, and if archaeology indicated such at the Presidio, then it should be left as found. Later, we would hire Norman to design the interior of the Chapel, which was so well done that an author who wrote a history of the missions of California used an image of Norman's interior design on the cover of his book. During the process of researching the Presidio Chapel, Norman found a painting of Saint Barbara in the basement of Our Lady of Sorrows Church, the successor church of the Presidio after the Fort Tejon earthquake destroyed the Chapel in the 1850s. More research determined that this painting originally hung in the Chapel and was painted by Mexican artist Alcibar in the 1790s. After the painting was restored, the church gave it to the SBTHP on permanent loan to hang in the Chapel. Today, that painting is the most valuable artifact in the Park, with the statue of Spanish King Charles III outdoors at the site a close second in importance.

Rebuilding Santa Barbara's First Christian Church

The reconstruction was based on a painting of the Chapel exterior from the 1850s, archaeology, and various historical documents including surviving ground plans of the Presidio. Besides research, there were many details that had to be dealt with before construction actually began. One of the most important questions was where the labor was to come from. SBTHP volunteer Richard Whitehead had arranged a meeting with the California Conservation Corps (CCC), a state agency created by Governor Jerry Brown to mirror the similar federal version that FDR had created. The Corps's purpose was to give youth training in various areas to help them find jobs and eventually learn trades. Thanks to the cooperation of Ignacio Piña, the then-director of the Camarillo CCC Center, an agreement was signed between the CCC and the SBTHP to provide a labor crew to help build the Chapel.

Remember: This was all being done outside the normal state-park process, but it was happening nevertheless. Thus, the CCC provided daily a crew of five to ten persons, young men and women, from different ethnic backgrounds. The crew was mostly Latino and Black but we even had a few Vietnamese workers, one of whom was later a first-class archaeology excavator. The first step was to make adobe bricks, and thanks to Richard Whitehead, a site at the Old Mission was secured in a field, formerly the location of the mission's Indian barracks. One might call that symbolic as the Chumash had been instrumental in building the original Presidio. Appropriate soil consisting of clay, sand, and silt was located on the same

The chapel foundations after years of volunteer and professional archaeological excavations. California Conservation Corps members at work just prior to commencement of reconstruction in 1982. *Courtesy SBTHP*

vacant lot that had provided the adobe for the padre's quarters. Pine needles or straw were added as a binder, and emulsified asphalt was added to strengthen the brick and to protect it against moisture. The latter was necessary because the bricks were sometimes left out on the site through a rainy season. General Telephone, owner of the property, gave permission to use and transport the soil by truck to the mission, a service provided gratis by Ozzie DaRos, owner of Santa Barbara Stone. As many as five thousand bricks were laid out at a time, eventually being stacked on pallets and then transported down to the Presidio by truck—Santa Barbara Stone, again, did this for the SBTHP gratis. Close to thirty thousand bricks were required for the thick walls.

Since Santa Barbara is a high-seismic region, a steel-and-concrete structure was required to support the building—thus, a concrete foundation and vertical and horizontal rebar were tied together with a concrete bond beam at the roof level. Norman Caldwell, a retired county public-works director and a civil engineer, served on the SBTHP restoration committee and decided we should also add a second bond beam at door height, which was indeed done.

The concrete foundations of the Presidio Chapel reconstruction. Padre's Quarters are to the left. Later SBTHP preserved the original foundations in situ for reconstruction projects. *Courtesy SBTHP*

Eventually the plans were approved at the state level and also by the City of Santa Barbara's Building and Safety Division. The first foundations were laid by April 21, 1982, as part of the celebration of the Presidio's two hundredth anniversary. In passing, I must mention a hiccup that arose after the foundations were laid. A historian pointed out that the original foundations of the Presidio were the reason that site had been placed on the National Register of Historic Places. By removing those foundations to pour concrete ones, one might argue that its designation should be decertified. The original foundation stones were reused to face the concrete foundations, but this issue needed to be addressed in future reconstructions at the site. The outcome of this intellectual argument will be discussed later.

Volunteers face the foundations with original foundations excavated during archaeology. *Author's Collection*

The chapel under construction. *Courtesy SBTHP*

California Conservation Corps crew on scaffolding in front of the nearly completed Chapel, with project supervisors Michael Pownall and Guy Wilson standing below next to Mike Acosta, descendant of a Santa Barbara Presidio soldier. *Author's Collection*

As commemorated on this plaque: The CCCs provided ninety-percent of the hard labor to rebuild the chapel. *Author's Collection*

Political Troubles for the Presidio Project

So far so good, one might say, but what about the chapter heading of the political maelstrom? That began to rear its head in 1981 and 1982, when the SBTHP sought funding to purchase the parking lot held in private ownership that had the foundations of the front gate of the Presidio beneath it. State Assemblyman Gary Hart said he would support that funding but asked us to hold a public meeting and to have the city endorse the funding. Until that time, the Presidio project had flown pretty much under the radar, but some local citizens and local businesses began to catch wind of the idea of closing down streets and removing buildings that were part of the full build-out of that project. Things didn't go well at the meeting for the SBTHP, and what eventually resulted was the SBTHP being required to prepare a plan for future park development.

The opposition to the Presidio project came from various people, but a community activist, a self-described local historian who lived in the neighborhood, and a Presidio-neighborhood restaurant owner were the three most vocal people who helped organize the opposition. Again, because I am giving my perspective of the series of events that transpired over the years, I am keeping these people anonymous. I have nothing personally against them except to say I thought the SBTHP's goal of rebuilding the Presidio a noble cause and that their views were grounded in what was then the here and now. A local political-advocacy organization also spoke against the project (the SBTHP had organizations on its side as well) and opponents formed into a group that called itself "Santa Barbarans for a Limited Presidio."

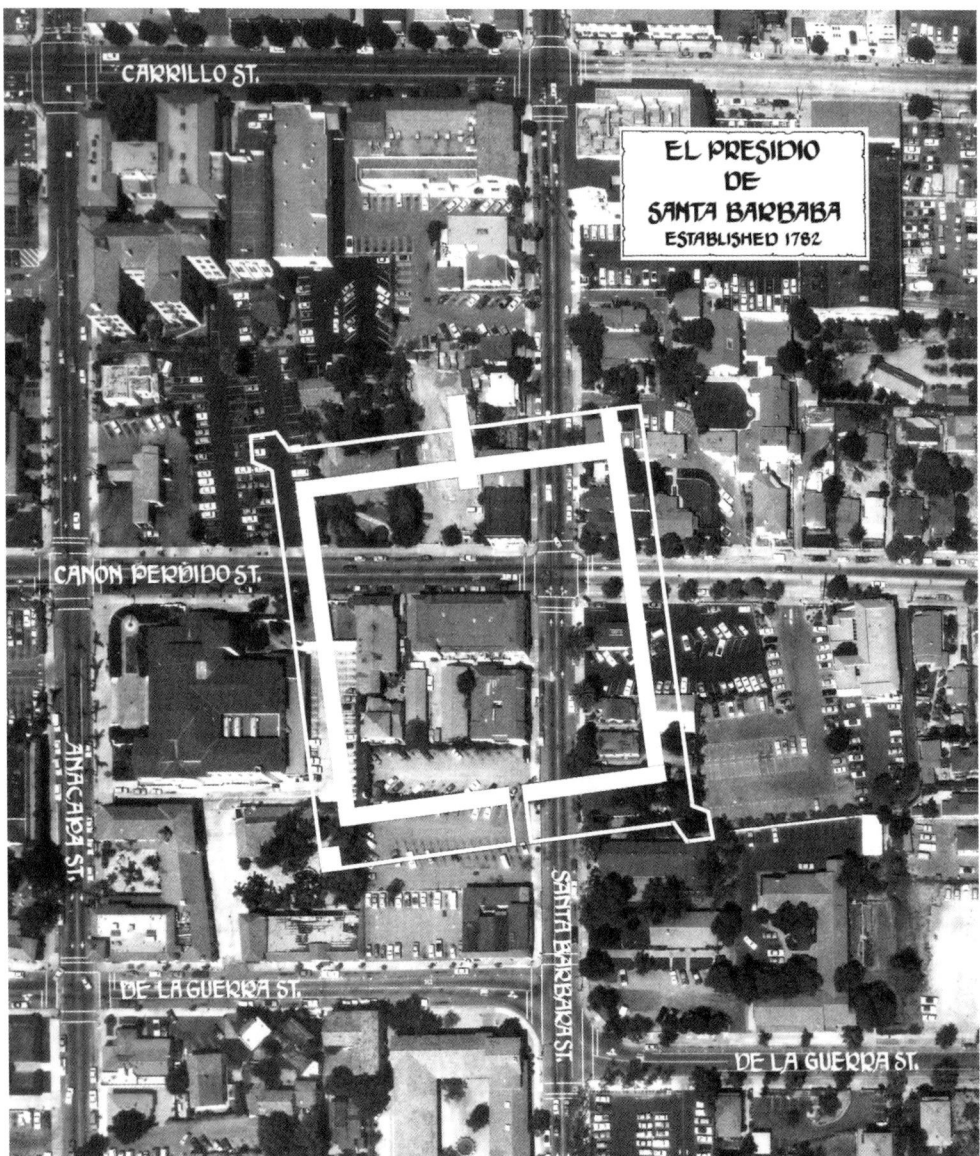

An original footprint overlay on modern city streets illustrates the challenges facing the Presidio project—requiring closing streets and removing buildings from later periods of history. *Courtesy SBTHP*

The challenge to the Presidio project was based on a series of attitudes as follows. First, there was other history on the site from later periods that had significance and was being removed and replaced with a history that was only part of the site's history. Second, the project would wipe out thriving businesses and some viable residences. Third, these businesses would be replaced by fake history, a Disneyland version. Fourth, the Presidio glorified the conquest of the local Indians. Fifth, the closure of the streets would cause a downtown-traffic nightmare. Also, for the most part, the local alternative newspaper under the name *News and Review*, later the *Santa Barbara Independent*, took the side of the opposition. One cover story ridiculed the project as trying to recreate "olde" Santa Barbara.

The SBTHP responded to this criticism in various ways, one of which was hiring an out-of-town architectural firm and another business firm to lay out the plan for development over five phases, but only the last phase would include closing the streets. The SBTHP went out and spoke to dozens of groups, most often yours truly as the spokesperson. The SBTHP tried to explain that there was a great deal of research and archaeology on which the project was based. We tried to establish the historical importance of the project as not only a local history site but also a state, national, and international historical monument, and as an opportunity to educate a generation and beyond of the interesting technology of adobe construction. The SBTHP also pointed out that the so-called Spanish soldiers came from diverse backgrounds; almost all were born in Mexico, but many of them had roots in Spain that traced to their Basque and Catalan heritage of diverse cultures and completely distinct languages. Father Serra's native language was Catalan, and Goicoechea was born in Mexico but traced his roots to Basque Spain. Lastly, the enlisted soldiers were ethnically diverse, with more than half being African American, Indians from Mexico, or of mixed Spanish and Indian blood.

Developing a General Plan for the Presidio

Dozens of meetings went back and forth and continued to drag on until around 1986, when the California State Parks Department decided it had to do a general plan for the Park and settle some of the many issues that were out there. They would do this through an official public process that would culminate with a plan that the State Park and Recreation Commission would review and approve. On the local level, the SBTHP, CSP, and the City of Santa Barbara entered into a memorandum of understanding that required each party to approve the plan before it went to the Commission. Finally, some order was being brought to a politically unpleasant, chaotic situation.

To backtrack and continue the happier activity of rebuilding the Chapel, that project continued until 1985. The CCC stayed with the project, and their labor substantially reduced the cost of the reconstruction. The Chapel project, and in fact all the Presidio reconstructions, we did on a time-and-materials basis—that is, they were not bid out. Under the SBTHP concession agreement, bids were not required. We had two full-time people who would supervise the construction, with Vince Pownall serving in a part-time consulting role. Adobe bricks brought down from the mission were laid by the CCC.

The labor and materials expenses for the Chapel ended up costing about $500,000. Thanks to the efforts of the fundraising committee led by Julia Forbes, we were able to keep the project on track without any stoppages. It was the first significant fundraising effort of the SBTHP, and it was fun to work on. Large donations came from the Santa Barbara Foundation, the local Jackson Family Foundation, and various oil companies drilling in the Santa Barbara Channel. Thanks to the contacts of board member and past-SBTHP president William Luton, Chevron, Exxon, and ARCO all gave grants to the project. Other foundations also contributed, with the remainder of the funding coming from individual donors, some in the low six figures, some much smaller. I remember a woman who sent in fifteen dollars per month for Chapel furnishings over the course of three years. Another favorite of mine was a woman named Josephine Harpham, who wrote checks on many different occasions. What I thought was interesting was the fact that while all the political controversy was swirling around the Presidio project, there were many who still supported our restoration efforts. This support was confirmed when the opposition decided to circulate a petition against the Presidio project and handed over to the city council fifteen hundred signatures mostly collected in a local restaurant. We, in turn, gave our volunteers a petition in support of the Presidio and asked them to circulate it. In less than two months, we gathered five thousand signatures.

El Paseo: Business Failure

Another problem reared its head for the SBTHP in the early 1980s. The SBTHP was trying very hard to solve what became the El Paseo restaurant failure. The consensus was that a new operator was needed for the main restaurant, so in early 1982 the longtime operator was given notice. Then the management committee and other board members began the quest for a replacement. It didn't go well and the SBTHP was losing rental income as a result. This was all a pretty heady brew for me, as board meetings were dominated by the tension of trying to solve the El Paseo conundrum. El Paseo dominated at least two thirds of the meetings until a replacement was found. The SBTHP had to sign for the new restaurateur's new equipment, a six-figure number. After the restoration, the opening followed in 1983, and the restaurant lasted less than a year before it went out of business. The SBTHP was stuck paying for the equipment as it searched for another operator. Not good! This continued until 1986, and these were not happy days at the SBTHP.

Sale of Old City College Site to State Parks and Its Aftermath

I think it has now become obvious that these were indeed challenging times for the SBTHP, and we were full-bore into the maelstrom. I stayed quietly in the dress circle avoiding the slings and arrows, but Executive Director Bob Cleveland had been at the center of all the misfires, and he was gone shortly after the restaurant closed. I asked myself after he left if I had been supportive enough of him, but I realized that really there was not much I could have done to prevent his demise. The best I can say from today's perspective is that he did work successfully with California State Parks to secure funding for the state's acquisition of the Old City College site. The SBTHP had purchased the site because it contained some of the original Presidio foundations—thanks in part to a donation for the down payment from board member Helen Pedotti. Looming was a very large balloon payment on the property that would have done further damage to the SBTHP's financial position, but all's well that ends well as Shakespeare tells us, and this one turned out just fine. Well, sort of: We now were to manage a property for the state that had potential rental income, although I think the SBTHP made a strategic mistake in re-renting it. The intention was noble to bring in artists to fill former studios and to rent the theater to a local theater company. The problem was these buildings were in ramshackle condition and many needed major renovation. Artists, however, do not tend to have a lot of money to pay market rent rates, nor the experience to undertake significant tenant improvements under what are called triple net leases. Thus, the rental rates were set at an affordable rate, and the buildings went unrestored. As the SBTHP tried to take over some of the spaces for Park uses and for tenants who could afford to improve the property, some of the artists turned on the SBTHP and showed up at meetings in opposition to the Presidio project. No good deed goes unpunished. There is much more to this story that would bring about a somewhat happy ending in the decades that followed.

What was I doing during all this? While I was not hiding under a shell, I tried very hard to present the SBTHP in as positive a light as possible by applying my historian training with UCSB graduate students in public history, researching and writing about the Presidio neighborhood, and putting on public events, many of which helped offset some of the negative images that had formed in the public mind about the Presidio. More on these later in summing up the decade of troubles that had the seeds of a positive next decade germinating.

Dealing with the State Bureaucracy—Persistence Pays Off

I have lost the exact time frame, but around the mid-1980s time of troubles for the Presidio project, I contacted our local legislators and Caltrans regarding getting a freeway sign directing the public to the Presidio from Highway 101. Our legislators

The Highway 101 Freeway sign at the Carrillo Street exit. *Author's Collection*

endorsed the idea, and I then began working with Caltrans. Nothing happens quickly with requests like this when working with the bureaucracy, but I was persistent and kept contacting various people at Caltrans. What was required was a justification of the importance of the site and that the Park would provide literature to other sites in the neighborhood. The justification was pretty easy: The Presidio is a state park, the site is a state historic landmark and on the National Register of Historic Places, and Highway 101 is a state highway. Eventually we won the day and large, prominent signs were installed on the northbound and southbound Carrillo Street exits alerting drivers that El Presidio de Santa Bárbara State Historic Park was accessible from these exit ramps. Until recently, there had been on ongoing problem with this signage, however, as the city had not provided adequate signs from the exits to the site, a route that requires several turns. We used to get occasional calls from people trying to find us after leaving the freeway. Today, surface-street signs have been upgraded. Those signs were to have a positive outcome later as they made the Presidio eligible to receive a federal highway grant. More to come on that fascinating outcome.

Una Pastorela: Saved by Archangels

One of the great cultural moments for the Presidio project was the completion of the Presidio Chapel and the arrival on the scene of Francisco Gonzalez. The year was 1985. Norman Neuerburg had finished his interior decoration with the help of volunteers. Speaking of volunteers: My father did all the electrical wiring in the Chapel, pro bono. The Presidio Chapel reconstruction was dedicated on the feast day of Our Lady of Guadalupe, December 12. The original Chapel had also been dedicated on that feast day in the year 1790. It was a grand ceremony, with a full house. Just before the celebration, Francisco showed up at my office and proposed doing as part of the opening of the Chapel a play called *Celebración de las Cuatro Apariciones de la Virgen del Tepeyac* (in English, *Celebration of the Four Apparitions of the Virgin of Tepeyac*). It is one of the most important Mexican events celebrating the conversion of Juan Diego to Christianity, a symbolic representation of the nation's conversion to Catholicism. Set to music by Francisco, this event was presented in three evening performances December 12, 13, and 14, 1985. It was one of the most moving events I experienced in all my years at the SBTHP, and it set the stage for the following years of reprieving the *pastorela* tradition in the Presidio Chapel. Having relocated to Santa Barbara from San Juan Capistrano, where he was musical director of the famous El Teatro Campesino, Francisco proposed that we stage a *pastorela* during the Christmas season in 1986 that was based on an original script copied down by Pablo de la Guerra and for which he would write the music and the bilingual text. It sounded very intriguing to me. I learned that he was one of the multitalented founders of the award-winning Chicano music group Los Lobos, and we moved ahead with a handshake.

The ancient story of the shepherd's journey to visit the baby Jesus has roots in Spain and Mexico and is, of course, biblical in origin. Francisco brought a Chicano perspective to the site; his wife Yolanda was teaching Chicano studies at UCSB, and he was sensitive to things being considered Spanish when in actuality they were more rooted in Mexico's heritage. I did not always agree with this perspective, but that was not a reason to balk at his desire to bring a historical play back to life. It definitely had a Santa Barbara connection and there is evidence that it was actually performed in the original Presidio Chapel. We know for certain that a version of it was performed in the presidio chapel in San Diego. There is a lithograph in Alfred Robinson's *Life in California* of the play being performed in that chapel.

It is possible that Pablo de la Guerra saw it performed in the Chapel in the Santa Barbara Presidio before his family relocated to the family adobe mansion that was completed in 1826 outside the fort's walls. What could be more perfect than having this play revived on the site where it was likely first performed in our community. Add to this the musical talent of Francisco and we were sure to have a winner. Francisco composed all the songs and music and with other musicians performed beautifully. The story, as mentioned, involves the shepherds on the quest to see the Christ Child—but the devil and the seven deadly sins are determined to block their way. Intimidated and terrified, the shepherds, with their unique personalities, are rescued by the archangels Saint Michael and Saint Gabriel, who trample the devils and deliver the shepherds to the manger. It is a real tearjerker, this happy ending—at least for me. Then after each performance, the audience and the cast met outside the Chapel, where a piñata was broken open and the children enjoyed the merriment of the Christmas season.

For the cast, Francisco brought in the local Mexican community, which was something new for the Presidio project. Truth be told, a lot of the members and supporters of the SBTHP and the Presidio project were not of Spanish, Indian, or

Una Pastorela was produced annually in the chapel into the 1990s. Here the devil, played by Luis Moreno, threatens the shepherds on their travels to Bethlehem. *Courtesy SBTHP*

The talented Francisco Gonzalez brought music and theater to the Presidio in the 1980s and 1990s. *Courtesy Francisco Gonzalez*

Mexican origin. That is not to forget that Russell Antonio Ruiz was among those early volunteers, and many of his fellow descendants were also of Mexican heritage. The Mexican cast in the play tended to be more recent immigrants and many of them were familiar with the *pastorela* tradition. The play is performed all over Mexico at Christmas and, besides California, in other US states such as New Mexico.

In Francisco's version, he insisted on costuming for the entire cast, the *pastores* in shepherds' clothing with their crooks; the devil and Lucifer dressed in black and red; and archangels outfitted in Roman dress, with their swords. The seven deadly sins in human form tempt the shepherds while they sleep, and the *pastores* wake up and begin fighting, while the lazy shepherd, Bartolo, continues to sleep as if nothing is happening. Of course, this is a story of good winning over evil, and it resonates at all levels, from children to adults. The play ran for two weeks, usually eighteen performances with matinees on the weekends. This allowed a large cross section of the community to attend as seating capacity was only 125 per performance. Audiences increased as Christmas approached and most of those later performances sold out. The play ran for ten years, into the nineties, and there was an extra production done in 1989 at Mission San Fernando Rey de España in cooperation with the UCLA Mexican art series; the entire cast made the trip and several performances re-created the Santa Barbara version of Francisco's *pastorela* for a Los Angeles audience.

During the early years of the *pastorela*, the SBTHP received much favorable press, which included front-page cover stories in the *Santa Barbara Independent* and in the weekend-scene section of the *Santa Barbara News-Press*. Believe me, this coverage was much appreciated as the Presidio project was under attack in the media at this time. It took place in the 1990s, but Professor Robert Potter of the drama department at UCSB wrote a play that slammed the Presidio reconstruction. I have conveniently forgotten the name of the play, which was performed at Center Stage Theater, but I do remember that I was a main character in the play called Colonel Bulldozer. The point was that I was destroying existing downtown history. I took it in the spirit of good humor. But really, some of the things being said about the Presidio and its supporters were over the top.

Violent Opposition to the Presidio Project

I remember a person coming into my office threatening me physically for being a Colonel Bulldozer in real life. I told him I appreciated his point of view and then asked him to leave. When he didn't, I picked up the phone to call the police. He grabbed the phone out of my hand, threw it down on the desk, and ran off. I never saw him again, thank God, although he wrote endless letters, one of which was appended to the final general plan and is available to read for anyone who wants to experience just how vicious a person can be in opposing rebuilding an adobe fort. That was a rare incident; most of the vitriol was spewed at public meetings and in letters to the editors of the papers—this was mudslinging of the nasty type. One of the worst attacks of the project came in the alternative newspaper then called the *Santa Barbara News and Review*. Just one example, and it's time to move on to more pleasant topics. In an article that appeared sometime around 1985, longtime volunteer Virginia Scott, then retired as a Santa Barbara High School history teacher, was ridiculed as "tiptoeing" through the foundations of the old Presidio. That may not be a direct quotation, but Scott, who for many years had brought her high-school students to work on the project, came into my office in tears. I have never forgotten that moment. This incident may help the reader understand my searching for positive experiences in the heat of the Presidio political wars. The *pastorela* provided that positive energy—a much needed spiritual boost.

Over the years, the *pastorela* never covered its costs because ticket prices were kept low and the cast and Francisco were being paid for their efforts. My staff was helpful in creating props and stages, but by 1995 it was getting more difficult to underwrite the play due to construction projects underway at the Presidio and Casa de la Guerra. As a result, we returned to a scaled-down version of the play, based totally on the Pablo de la Guerra script, no English, and sans the songs and music of Francisco. Elvira Tafoya of the local community has organized and directed this version (she produced one performance in 1984 in the Chapel while it was under construction) and it has been performed almost every year since the turn of the century; she does a first-rate job, and to her credit, she does it by and large at her own expense.

Before we move on to the tempestuous political events that closed out the 1980s, I must say some more about the Great One, Francisco Gonzalez. He also did for the Presidio state park a play called *If These Walls Could Speak*. It provided a cross section of individuals: a Chumash Indian, a Spanish African American soldier, and other historical personages from the nineteenth to the twentieth centuries. Also set to Francisco's music, it played for several performances. Added to this, he did an outdoor evening event called *"El Baile"* that re-created rancho life in early California—it included live horses, dancing, and much more. I was unfortunately out of town when the event took place, but I heard nothing but rave reviews about it. As if this were not enough, Francisco revived early-California songs with Presidio descendant and singer Elizabeth Hvolboll. With Francisco playing his harp, they performed numerous times in the Chapel. After Francisco relocated to Arizona with his wife, local musician Louis Moreno, who for years had been one of the leads in Francisco's *pastorela*, picked up for Francisco and played his guitar accompanying Elizabeth for a number of years. One of the disappointments was that our efforts to have the music and singing recorded never came to fruition.

In 2011, I nominated Francisco for the SBTHP's prestigious Pearl Chase Award for his many contributions that brought the Presidio to life in wonderful ways. This was, in my mind, living history at its finest. The award is given to a person who over the course of years has helped preserve and interpret Santa Barbara history. The SBTHP board voted him the award: Thus, the Chicano perspective has a permanent place at El Presidio de Santa Bárbara State Historic Park thanks to Francisco, who opened the Presidio's doors to the local Mexican community.

Gran Quivira Conferences: Seeing the Big Picture

I would be ungrateful if I didn't acknowledge the many opportunities the SBTHP provided to meet interesting people and learn about the Spanish history of Santa Barbara, California, and the borderlands of the Southwest. Regarding the latter, my introduction to it came through Gran Quivira conferences held every year—every third year at Salinas Pueblo Missions National Monument in New Mexico and the other two years at sites around the Southwest including California. The SBTHP hosted the conference twice during the 1980s. In the event, I was told by SBTHP insiders that I needed to attend these conferences and make presentations each year on the Santa Barbara Presidio. I pretty much did that from the 1980s into the 1990s.

The Southwestern Mission Research Center organized these annual events, but what was typical of these conferences was their informality. Just one example: The person giving the shortest timed talk was given a bottle of tequila. The key people were Charles Polzer S.J. and Dr. Bernard "Bunny" Fontana, both excellent scholars who eventually had a falling out and only Bunny stayed as the intellectual glue, so to speak. Attendees came from Texas, New Mexico, Arizona, California, and even Mexico. A couple of the conferences were held in Mexico. Among the conferees were historians, anthropologists, archaeologists, and some retired folks who were amateur researchers but who gave some of the most interesting talks. I learned a great deal about the big picture of Spanish colonial history—how our Santa Barbara Presidio was a piece of this Spanish empire that spread all across the Southwest. We *norteamericanos* tend to see the frontier as moving from east to west, but there was a Spanish version of the frontier that moved from south to north. There were similarities between these frontiers, but they would indeed collide, one might say, in the Southwest and to this day are shaping the world we are living in in the West.

One of the Gran Quivira conferences was held in Nuevo Laredo, Mexico, across the river from Laredo, Texas. I gave a talk on the Santa Barbara Presidio inside an original presidio room on the Rio Grande on the Mexican side.

Perhaps the most adventurous trip was a Gran Quivira conference in Sonora, Mexico, that proceeded in a caravan of about fifty cars and campers through various towns dating from the late seventeenth and early eighteenth centuries. Eventually we were to end up in Cananea, where we would spend time delivering our informal talks. Along the way we came across the adobe ruins of mission churches and visited the burial sites of Juan Bautista de Anza of California expedition fame and of Father Kino, the famous padre of Sonora. One glitch was leaving a town too late in the day and driving in the dark down a steep mountain. We were at the head of the caravan and watched the car lights as the vehicles negotiated the hairpin turns. When we arrived in the small town, Father Polzer, frustrated, said he "abdicated" and it was every man for himself. Fortunately, we had a VW camper and didn't have to worry. Others either slept in their cars or found a hostel to stay in. Quite an adventure.

Another Gran Quivira conference was held in 1997 in Loreto, Baja California, in celebration of the three hundredth anniversary of the first permanent Spanish settlement of the region in 1697. We did a little mission-hopping as well. Our Santa Barbara Comandante Goicoechea ended his career in Loreto as governor of Baja California, dying and buried there in 1814. His gravesite was washed away in a chubasco, a type of violent storm known to hit that region with some frequency. I should mention that the caravan on this trip came off without incident and the presentations of the Mexican scholars added something special to the conference.

But for me the most special moments were returning to the Salinas Pueblo Missions National Monument, which contains the remains of three Franciscan churches—Gran Quivira, Abó, and Quarai—all three of which predate the Puritans' settlement of New England. Without question, Gran Quivira conferences confirmed for me the international importance of the work we were undertaking in Santa Barbara. In addition, Michele, our daughter, Renée, and I, sometimes accompanied by a friend, took the time to visit just about every mission and Pueblo Indian site in New Mexico and Arizona, including the famous Chaco Canyon and Canyon de Chelly. Needless to say, we have also visited all twenty-one missions in Alta California. After the 1990s, the conference sort of faded away as many of its participants died or lost interest. But in their day, Gran Quivira conferences provided some of the most memorable encounters with people and history that I have had the privilege of experiencing.

CHAPTER FIVE

Presidio Reforger—and the El Paseo Solution

Around 1987, things didn't look too good for the SBTHP and the Presidio project. Pearl Chase had died in 1979 and so the SBTHP was without this force of nature. Then others of the SBTHP pantheon went to the other side: Bill Luton (1987), Richard Whitehead (1988), and Russell Antonio Ruiz (1988). How would the SBTHP fare with these losses? I took their loss as inspiration. They had given so much to the Presidio project that I said to myself that I must carry on their legacy. The bulk of Chase's estate came to the SBTHP for development of the Presidio. But the political opposition had gained support at the city council, where the issue of the future of the project would be decided. I did the Harry Truman thing to myself: "If you can't stand the heat, get out of the kitchen." My wife had worked on a military exercise called "Reforger" while employed by the US Army in Germany. This was a Cold War response to the possibility that the Soviet Union might someday try to attack the West through the Fulda Gap. It seemed to me an apt metaphor to describe how the SBTHP fortified itself to survive the political opposition. It had to give ground but not surrender. Call it a negotiation, but in the heat of it, it seemed more like a war. In my view, the SBTHP was fortunate to have the California State Parks Department to provide the bulwark against the Presidio naysayers. The Department kept the focus on the fact that the Presidio was a statewide, national, and even international project. The local flow of history was not to be ignored, but it should not prevail either. State support buoyed the SBTHP to stay the proverbial course.

At the same time, as became more apparent, El Paseo was barely able to stay afloat with the restaurant site still vacant and no new operator available. The

SBTHP really was struggling to survive, but one good thing was retiring the mortgage that the SBTHP had inherited when it accepted the donation in 1971. The board then broached a subject that seemed like a violation of its preservation mission: the sale of El Paseo. Two board members, who will remain anonymous in this account, were tasked with discussing the possible sale to Peter Kaufman, a trusted associate and friend of El Paseo donor Irene Suski Fendon. Any sale that might transpire she had to approve. But let us return to the Presidio political negotiations that were happening simultaneously with the El Paseo situation. I am not fond of the overused word "resilient," but this word does seem to capture the SBTHP at this moment in time. The board, many of our other supporters, and yours truly held firm in enduring the politics that were indeed intense. I have the highest regard for the board members who were serving as unremunerated volunteers. My role was becoming more significant as time went by. Having observed the SBTHP's struggles with El Paseo, I became a strong advocate for its sale. My thought process, I hope, will seem reasonable as the discussion of the sale proceeds.

I also remained a committed advocate for rebuilding the entire Presidio, but I also could be realistic. And the board had a realistic side as well: Compromise was the best, and really only, option. At least for the short term.

Before the sale idea came to the fore, work on the Presidio general plan was being coordinated in Sacramento. The person assigned to steer the general plan through the process for California State Parks was Art Camacho, an architect and planner in the Department. I liked his enthusiasm. But he was to have a rude awakening when he encountered some of the public backlash that felt like a whiplash. Some of the meetings mounted to a fever pitch: These included negotiations between some of the leaders of the opposition and the SBTHP board members and me. I can't remember how many meetings I attended from 1982 to 1988, some official meetings, some talks to organizations and interested parties representing Chicano and Chumash constituencies. I can remember missing only one meeting, when I was on vacation. It would become redundant to try to capture what transpired in each of those emotional encounters, as most of them were.

Finally in February 1984, some order was brought for going forward when California State Parks, the City of Santa Barbara, and the SBTHP signed a memorandum of understanding requiring that all three parties jointly review and approve a general plan that was to include freestanding phases of park development. The SBTHP as the operator of the park was to seek approval from both the state and the city before any reconstruction work commenced. If this sounds onerous, it was. As the person who shepherded the projects through state and local channels, I followed the memorandum of understanding to the tee, as well as the general plan that eventually was approved. The SBTHP's cooperative approach helped build confidence in the state and city that the SBTHP was a valuable partner, which to this day has pretty much remained the case.

Board-Member Chutzpah

By law, as I have previously emphasized, every state park has to have a general plan approved before any major development of the park can be undertaken. But that is not exactly how it works out. The California State Parks Department allowed the Chapel to be rebuilt without a completed general plan. Another example of park development taking place at the Presidio happened after the completion of the Chapel in 1985. It must have been around 1986 that one of the more intrepid board members of the SBTHP, Dr. Garvan Kuskey, said at a restoration-committee meeting that we should demolish the Shalhoob building on the corner of Canon Perdido and Santa Barbara streets, which was blocking the view of the Chapel as cars drove by Santa Barbara Street. I was wary of trying to do this, because we were in the heat of the Presidio war with a significant opposition. This was like flying in the face of our opponents and could be a political disaster. Garvan's response: What harm would it really do to ask? He took this idea to the SBTHP board, which endorsed it unanimously, and I was told to go make it happen.

I can't recall how this proceeded step by step, but I know we had conversations with Patrick Davis, one of the opponents of the Presidio project, and eventually this demolition idea ended up at a full-city council meeting. To my utter surprise, Davis stood up at the meeting and said he and others on his side did not have a problem with the demolition. I am not sure if anyone voiced an opinion against it but the council voted seven to zero to allow demolition of the building. I then talked to California State Parks and they also granted us permission.

The Shalhoob building was two stories, was made of unreinforced fired bricks, and consisted of a sandwich shop downstairs and two other commercial spaces. Upstairs were an office and two apartments as I remember. The first step was to give the tenants notice. Since all of them had signed rental agreements after the state purchased the building, they were not entitled to relocation benefits, but the Palm West Deli had been in the building for several years—as had several of the tenants. As a result, the SBTHP management committee found space at the Old City College site to relocate the deli, which stayed as a tenant for several more years before a new tenant renovated the site as a restaurant that today Zaytoon restaurant occupies. Regarding some of the other tenants, I don't recall exactly what was done for them, if anything.

What was required before demolition was a recordation of the building. While it dated from around 1910, it had not been designated a historic structure. To be honest, I don't believe the recordation went into the depth of photographing and drawing plans as is normally done today and are standards that the SBTHP followed after completion of the general plan. All told, several months passed before city permits were granted and the building was vacated. Eventually the SBTHP hired a local firm to do the demolition. I don't remember the type of equipment used, but it was all taken care of in about half a day. Santa Barbara and Canon Perdido streets were

The Shalhoob Building on the corner of Canon Perdido and Santa Barbara Streets, later demolished. *Courtesy SBTHP*

The same view today with the Shalhoob Building allowing an unobstructed view of the chapel. *Author's Collection*

Board member Garvan Kuskey, one of the Presidio project advocates who led the charge to have the Shalhoob Building removed, is shown here at a volunteer adobe day. *Courtesy SBTHP*

closed and the neighborhood came out to see the event. I remember waiters from the Sojourner Restaurant throwing debris on the site breaking windows. Demolition went off without a hitch, with one huge, dramatic moment as the walls facing the Chapel were collapsed inward away from the church, with the side wall facing Santa Barbara Street still standing. Suddenly the whole section of it was pulled down and fell with a loud thump as the wall collapsed on the street, leaving a dust cloud that hovered over the building. I was told later that you could hear the wall crashing two blocks away on State Street. A tractor next scooped up the bricks in the street into a dump truck.

Then there it was in all its glory: the Presidio Chapel for the world to see, with the debris of the collapsed building in front of it leaving the impression of a phoenix rising from the ashes. Without a doubt, this for me was the most dramatic moment for the Presidio project up to that point. The community could now see the Chapel that dominated the corner of that cross section of streets. It is difficult to say what impression this made on the community, positive or negative, in terms of resolving the Presidio project's planning process. For some, it was the first time that they could truly begin to understand what the whitewashed adobe fort actually looked like. It certainly blended into the Spanish-style architecture of the downtown Pueblo Viejo district. I know some people were won over as a result of this dramatic change in the architectural landscape of the so-called Presidio neighborhood. On the other hand, while I didn't talk to anyone directly about this, I am sure some saw the demolition and didn't like seeing the Shalhoob building disappear. If the measure of public dissent at the city hall in the months ahead was any measure, I would say that it didn't change much in either direction, positive or negative. Those for a limited Presidio girded their loins and fought hard to stop the full build-out. Some wanted not one more adobe brick of reconstruction to happen after the Chapel. One of our members came into my office to proclaim that she was no longer a supporter of our work. She, however, was in a minority of one, as far as I could tell, because the board was unanimous in pushing the project forward, as were members, who showed up in force at public meetings.

Around this time, another small building behind the Shalhoob also was demolished. It had been the home of Mimi Cruz for many years. The two demolitions would expose the foundations of the former commandant's quarters, and one of the major archaeological findings of the Presidio would be discovered. But that story takes place around 1988 and is best told after the Presidio's general plan is finally completed, a drama that more or less has a happy ending, for reasons I will explain.

Recently, my wife Michele found in my papers an attempt to write poetry around 1985, just as the Chapel had been completed. I spare the reader the full poem but it does contain a few predictions of things to come:

> *The besieged Telemachus, this worn out Don Quixote*
> *Hears the courthouse clock chime six,*
> *Lays a hand on the Cañedo's ancient adobe wall,*
> *Is drawn down the corridor to the padre's quarters;*
> *The Chapel looms above,*
> *The spirit pulls him to the street corner—*
> *Take courage, take away that building,*
> *So all the world can see your church, and*
> *Underneath you will find—hope says—*
> *Remains of the commander's office, where*
> *The Basque Goicoechea held forth:*
> *The eye glances across the street*
> *To memories of the students, a summer ago,*
> *Digging away with good humor but in vain,*
> *Looking for the foundations of*
> *The mythical two-story tower,*
> *When the glowing eyes of arche Benté appear:*
> *Eureka!*
> *An intact tile floor.*

That building was the Shalhoob building that was about to disappear, and yes, there was much to be found of the commander's residence foundations, and of the two-story tower foundations, and the tile floor. These were happy discoveries, but first let us finish with the not-so-pleasant, yet ultimately rewarding, weeks and months of political *Sturm und Drang* at the SBTHP that would not end until February 1989.

The Denouement of the Presidio's General Plan

When you are in the heat of the battle, things always feel more intense than they do in retrospect. Also, the pressure of not knowing how things are going to turn out has a lot to do with making one uneasy, to say the least. I really had no experience in being in the political arena, and it took me a while to learn that people will say just about anything about you and your project in a political situation. The truth suffers greatly in situations in which people strongly disagree. I had to learn to accept that people who didn't like or outright disdained the Presidio project had legitimate concerns. An ally told me when someone senses they are losing, they will double down on their attacks. The Presidio project being compared to Disneyland was a tough one for me to take. But then I thought maybe that's not so bad, as people love Disneyland, and when I was twelve years old, one of the greatest thrills of my life was when Disneyland opened and my friends and I tiptoed through Frontierland.

Later I discovered that Walt Disney and I shared a December 5 birthday, and that both of us years apart would be designated honorary state-park rangers by the California State Park Rangers Association. Few people today are aware that Disney ran a series of commercials in movie theaters supporting a state-park bond that was on the California ballot, and that was one reason he was named an honorary ranger. My honor came helping build our Santa Barbara Disneyland, called the Presidio. Would that we were able to attract all those Disneyland visitors to the site. Maybe someday it will.—if the vision of the Presidio project keeps moving forward in the years ahead.

As mentioned, California State Parks and the SBTHP presented the Presidio in freestanding phases, five in all. Only with phase five would the streets be closed. It was a pretty interesting approach because had it been presented as all or nothing, we probably would have ended up with close to nothing. Well, not exactly nothing as the Chapel was built and the corner building was gone, which meant the comandancia could be rebuilt. By proposing phases, if we couldn't get all of them, we could get at least some of them, which would keep the Park going and land acquisition continuing. This meant as long as the memorandum of understanding was in effect that the Presidio could be built out through a certain approved phase. And that was basically what happened. The SBTHP could go back later and ask for more. Times and attitudes change—who was to say what the community might think of a full build-out once the various phased reconstruction of the two-story tower, comandancia, and more was there to see. We are not all visionaries. Some have to see to believe.

Another concession California State Parks and the SBTHP agreed to from the outset was acknowledging the later history that took place on the site that wasn't related to the Spanish or Mexican periods. That meant interpreting in some fashion the presence of both Chinese and Japanese businesses and residences in the area. Fair enough, I thought, although no specific buildings were proposed to be interpreted to include that history. There were, however, structures in State ownership that were to be preserved, especially the Alhecama Theatre, which had been built in the 1920s. Its restoration would be the last project I worked on before exiting the SBTHP. The SBTHP also paid for traffic studies and another study that dealt with commercial cost benefits of the project. The phased plan made its way through the various committees of the City of Santa Barbara, and finally came to the city council. It started to look as if the project could achieve a Phase IV approval. But architectural historian Dr. David Gebhard made a comment at the landmarks commission that he was concerned that Phase IV approval would affect the operation of the post office, because Phase IV included building a section of the Presidio in the post office's parking lot. I don't believe he was opposed to the project per se being built there, but he wanted to make sure planning included finding alternative parking. Since it was in the docking area, the alternative-parking idea really wasn't feasible.

The city council would seize on that parking issue, and that was the end of Phase IV. Gebhard was a highly respected person on the landmarks committee, so much so that after he died, the meeting room of the commission was named after him.

So there we were at the city council, bruised but not bloodied. Phase III included building the front gate of the Presidio, a section of the soldiers' quarters, and a corral for the horses; on the other side of the street, this phase allowed for a section of the defense wall, plus the bastion. All good, because the state did not yet own these properties and that meant that it would seek ownership if Phase III was approved. Again, this is what happened. I will describe these acquisitions later as they have some rather fascinating details of interest.

Phase I contained the Chapel and comandancia; Phase II allowed rebuilding the northeast corner and the northwest corner of the Presidio. Those projects have in fact been completed with an important section of defense wall still to be rebuilt in Phase II. When it was all said and done, I started to realize that we had fared pretty well. The project had been on the books since the late 1950s when Pearl Chase had been talking to various people about rebuilding the birthplace of Santa Barbara and had the first study done. It was helpful to have Chase as the founding mother of the organization. She was the indomitable force that had helped plan Santa Barbara as a New Spain architectural landscape after the 1925 earthquake, not to mention that she also was involved with various social causes over the years. I also was very grateful to California State Parks for staying with the project with all the political controversy surrounding the Park. Parks Acting Director Les McCargo was there at the podium of the council meetings advocating for approval of all the phases. Staffer Art Camacho was a trouper, never shying away from defending the Presidio. The Presidio had an ironic quality that the fort was under attack, something that had happened only once before, in 1818 with the Bouchard raid. In both instances, one can say the Presidio people, military and civilian, had talked their way out of being captured by its enemies.

By the way, in fall 1987 I was elevated to the position of CEO, and that gave me even more responsibilities of overseeing all SBTHP activities, including the operation of El Paseo, although I had remained in the dress circle as negotiations commenced with Peter Kaufman about a potential sale of the property much earlier in the year. In spring 1987, while still projects administrator, my first duty was to help shepherd the Presidio's general plan through to completion. The key reviews of the plan took place in April and May 1987. First of all, the California State Park and Recreation Commission met in Santa Barbara in April and deferred action on the Presidio until the city gave its final review and approval of the draft plan.

The important interpretive elements of the Presidio were contained in this plan. Some examples are as follows:

> The essence of the Alta California presidio system is represented at Santa Barbara during this period [1784–1810], and the ultimate visitor experience should be centered around the complex as expressed at that time.

> Primary Theme: an Ethnic Brew: From [its beginning], the presidio and the mission were centers of many classes and races of people. The native Chumash and other inland groups were brought to this place to labor for the crown and church. Spaniards and Mexicans from Castilians to Indians were brought here to control, to protect and to build. The results of the mix were not always beneficial or peaceful. But the story is dynamic, and is a classic expression of the California experience.

Not mentioned in the above was the Spaniards themselves originated from an ethnic brew: Catalans and Basques were among the early settlers in Alta California.

Also in the plan were environmental-review documents, a parking study, and lots of maps with text that described each and every building and their uses, whether residential, educational, or commercial. Ample time was provided for the public to access and read the plan in advance of the final meeting, during which the city council was to make its final recommendations that would have to be accepted by the SBTHP and the California State Parks Department for it to be passed on for final approval to the California State Park and Recreation Commission.

The meeting took place in the evening of April 21, 1987. That happened to be the 205th anniversary of the founding of the Presidio on April 21, 1782. There was a packed house in the city-council chambers—both sides out in force, with the SBTHP having a strong representation of its board members, members, staff, and other supporting individuals and organizations. The meeting droned on for several hours, but finally the vote came—with a motion to endorse the state's general plan with acceptance of a modified version of Phase III, as described previously, and with the section on the post-office parking lot deleted. All the other elements of the plan, including the environmental impact report were accepted in the motion.

One by one they voted, and it was unanimous after Mayor Sheila Lodge cast her vote. Five-plus long years of public debate had finally been resolved.

It was time for celebration: The city had approved the plan through only Phase III but the relief of having it over was palpable among the twenty or so of us who left the meeting together. Afterward, we repaired to the Jimmy's Oriental Gardens bar (the SBTHP would later purchase the building), which is situated to this day inside the Presidio area. Among us was the current California State Parks Channel Coast District Superintendent Dan Preece, known by the nickname Can-Do Dan. Dan raised his glass and said emphatically: "Here is to Phase V." That brought a huge guffaw from all of us.

The endorsement of El Presidio de Santa Barbara Preliminary General Plan officially came in a letter from Mayor Lodge dated May 7, 1987. All the conditions required by the city were stated in the missive. Attachments included letters of support that very much outnumbered those opposed to the project, but the opposition letters were one last virulent blast at the Presidio as being fake and a monument to European imperialism.

There was one final step that was pro forma—the official endorsement of the California State Park and Recreation Commission—but it is worth relating as it is revealing about my personal feelings about the project and those of a board member who attended the commission meeting with me in Monterey in summer 1988. The final Presidio general plan had been presented to the commission previously for review and now at the hearing for its vote. A number of the members of the commission seemed surprised that the SBTHP was willing to accept endorsement of only three of the phases of development. They looked to us in the audience to comment. The board member, who will remain anonymous here, went to the podium and said that he and the board enthusiastically accepted the "limited Presidio." That was not really true. There were many on the board who felt disappointed with the outcome, and, like me, they accepted reality. This was the best that could be hoped for. At the moment, I thought we had somehow done less than we should have, but as time went by and the state continued its commitment to the Park, I felt that "all's well that ends well." The anonymous limited-Presidio board member would turn out to help advancement of the project in a number of ways, especially with regard to the eventual sale of El Paseo. That story is now front and center.

El Paseo: The White Elephant

What makes this story even more intense is the fact that the financial challenge of El Paseo was going on simultaneously as the Presidio was in the spotlight at City Hall. Only after the political maelstrom began to settle down in 1989 did I begin to appreciate what the organization had gone through. In the heat of the moment, we did what we could to keep the ship afloat. In the last section, I allowed the Presidio naysayers a last word regarding their attack on the general plan because it is a reminder that we were to get a double whammy from the public over our handling of El Paseo.

In the history of the ownership of El Paseo, there is very little indication that anybody made any money off the property, and that was reflected in the fact that there was a huge amount of deferred maintenance that had been passed on since its opening in 1922. Most of the SBTHP board members understood in accepting the gift of El Paseo their fiduciary responsibility was to preserve the property. But there were a few outspoken members who considered the gift a white elephant. Besides the mortgage, there was all this work that had to be done to bring the property up to snuff. That "snuff" was estimated to be at least one million dollars. Back in 1987, that seemed like a lot more money than it does today, but as it turned out it was hardly enough to cover what needed to be done. With the failure of the replacement restaurant operator and the inability to find another one, things were looking pretty bleak for the SBTHP.

After considerable debate over the course of several years, a stronger voice was heard from the board to consider selling the property. Among those supporting such an action were the Presidio advocates. They were interested in Spanish and Santa Barbara history, not operating a shopping center of more than fifty thousand square feet. To my surprise, the desire to sell became stronger and stronger, until two board members, one already mentioned regarding the state-park commission's general-plan approval and the other a banker, were authorized to begin discussions with local businessman Peter Kaufman as a possible buyer of the property.

Kaufman knew Irene Suski Fendon, who had made the donation of El Paseo to the SBTHP, and she looked on him favorably. This was important because the SBTHP could not sell the property without Fendon's approval as a result of restrictions in the gift. This was mostly taking place in early 1987 according to my memory, but the precise time period that will become most important is late 1987, just a few months after the city had approved the general plan. The city would have a lot to do with the outcome of our El Paseo financial challenge as well.

In fact, as things turned out, the gods of financial success seem to have been on the SBTHP's side beginning about this time. Machiavelli claimed that life is 50 percent virtue and 50 percent luck. I believe the SBTHP had both as the 1980s came to a close. I don't remember how much time went by before the two anonymous board members came back to the board with an offer from Peter Kaufman that provided cash and an exchange of properties. Again, according to my memory, the deal was contained on one page, and it went something like this: The SBTHP was to receive, after retiring its debt on the property, a multimillion-dollar amount; the SBTHP also would receive ownership of a parking lot in the exchange that contained the front gate of the Presidio. The problem with the latter was the SBTHP had to make the parking lot available to the present owner, Presidio Properties. That meant that the front gate could not be rebuilt until some alternative parking was found, but the SBTHP would receive income from the parking in the meantime. Not a perfect deal but not bad either. Also, there was a two-story office building that the SBTHP would receive in the exchange. In turn, the SBTHP would convey El Paseo to Kaufman and a partnership he would form. This included Casa de la Guerra, except for two rooms that would be retained by the SBTHP for interpreting the adobe. In addition, Kaufman agreed to spend a minimum of one million dollars to restore El Paseo.

I don't remember how much discussion and dissent there was on the board when the deal was presented to them. I do know that eventually the board came around and with only one dissension approved moving forward with disposing of the complex. Next was a notification of the potential sale to the membership. There was no big brouhaha at the board level over El Paseo, but there was a membership outcry. In fact, a rather significant piece of information in all this was that because El Paseo represented more than half of the SBTHP's assets, the membership would have to approve the transaction. Oops! That set the board back on its heels. Because of the membership backlash, our two anonymous board members returned to Kaufman and came up with a deal that was more palatable, at least to the membership. The deal change was that the SBTHP would keep all of Casa de la Guerra, and it would give up in the exchange the two-story office building. This was both satisfactory to the board and, as far as we could tell, satisfactory to the membership. All the other deal points stayed the same.

The next challenge was to take the deal to the membership for a vote. We had a sales job to do for sure. The board was behind the sale, but articles in the local newspapers did not make us look so great: "Preservation group to sell off historic property to make money to rebuild a fake presidio." Yes, the general-plan opposition spilled over to the El Paseo deal. One of the sadder sides of all this was a person I much respected and have come even more to respect in recent years opposing the sale. This was Jeremy Hass, whom I have earlier praised for obtaining the gift of El Paseo. He came to several board meetings in a highly emotional state trying to convince the board not to sell. I realize now how much he had invested in making that gift happen, and I regret that he didn't see the value of our cashing it out and then overseeing the complex's renovation.

But he was not the only one vociferous in opposition to the sale. The former manager of El Paseo came out strongly against it, and he had the support of one of the former board members of the SBTHP who was also a direct descendant of José de la Guerra. At the same time, the former manager organized voters against the sale, who then joined the SBTHP so they could vote in the election. Inside the SBTHP, we, in turn, began buying memberships for family and friends and other supporters. SBTHP membership nearly doubled to more than 750 members from about 400. I believe at this point we required an end date for people to join the SBTHP to be eligible to vote. At first, our members were coming in to register proxy votes against the sale; the other side was gathering votes by proxy as well. It was looking very bleak for passing this sale through the membership.

Enter my staff, whom I tasked with talking to our members about what we were doing to make sure they knew the details and the many long-range benefits to be derived from the transaction. Every staffer had some conversation or another with members, but the star among them was the director of the Santa Barbara Presidio Research Center, Cathy Rudolph. She single-handedly turned around more than several dozen votes. Votes that came by proxy against the sale were followed by other proxies canceling negative votes and voting instead for the sale. Those ballots are no longer around, I don't think, but I am sure the staff reversed a minimum of one hundred votes, and I include myself in talking it up and getting the support we needed.

What I thought would be the final showdown took place in November 1987 at a special meeting of the members at the Lobero Theatre. Less than half of the membership showed up for the vote. Kaufman spoke, Michael Arnold went over his appraisal of the property, and several people spoke for the SBTHP. I can't remember all the presentations, but I do remember the vote. The tally at the meeting put the naysayers in the lead. After the meeting was over, we returned to my office, where our CPA, Bill Nasif, was waiting to count the proxies that had been sent in. The staff and board members had been collecting them. The former property manager also brought in some proxies. After all the counting was completed, Nasif said support for the sale, which required a simple majority, had been attained. In fact, more than two-thirds of the votes counted were in support of the sale. Later, I did a count of the ballots of those who had been members before announcement of the sale and the rush of members after the announcement. The percentages of those for and against were almost exactly the same in both categories. In the event, a required milestone was reached, but it was far from over. Escrow had to be opened, and now the details of the one-pager had to be filled in.

Another step in the process was a review of the transaction by the state's Office of the Attorney General. This approval was required because we were disposing of a gift that had certain conditions; besides the cash, we were receiving something of importance—the Presidio's front-gate property, which was a huge step toward achieving our major goal of rebuilding the old Presidio. The attorney general's office responded favorably that the SBTHP could dispose of the property, but all proceeds from the sale must go toward restoring El Paseo, Casa de la Guerra, and the Presidio. That kept the SBTHP to its original vision of restoring the Presidio. I was totally on board with the attorney general's decision because the agreement contained protections of El Paseo, and it gave us money to advance the restoration of Casa de la Guerra and rebuild some of the Presidio. A true win-win. Moreover, it required Kaufman to restore the building to standards that we set in a historic preservation easement. I was actively involved with the creation of this easement. It gave us authority to oversee and approve all preservation projects at El Paseo—in perpetuity. An extra win for us.

Thanks to a major team effort, the sale looked like a done deal. Between the board and the staff and the members, it looked as if the SBTHP had turned a huge corner in its institutional history. But the struggle, as it turned out, was hardly over. As one of the local newspapers put it, the El Paseo sale and exchange was one of the largest and most complex real-estate transactions in Santa Barbara history. At this point, I became involved with the details of it. What previous real-estate experience did I have? Well, I had with Michele purchased a condo here in Santa Barbara, and we together acquired a small house in Ashland, Oregon, to be near the famed Oregon Shakespeare Festival. In short, I wasn't a real-estate whiz by any means.

What followed were a series of meetings, protracted affairs that went on for hours at a time, to hammer out the details. The individuals involved were Kaufman and his attorney and our attorney and me. I noticed that Kaufman was very intent to pull the deal as much in his favor as possible, and it was my responsibility to protect the SBTHP's interests as much as possible. There would have to be compromise, and sometimes we would get to details that could be deal-breakers. I remember two late-night meetings in which we had the parties meeting in my office and we called in SBTHP president Garvan Kuskey and some others on the executive committee. We would reach an impasse and both sides would repair to separate rooms in the Cañedo Adobe to decide how to proceed. Then we would come back and would finally reach agreement.

A lot of the disagreement was over details of the preservation easement and the requirement that the new owners would have to maintain the buildings in good repair. We had some very interesting times defining what was good repair and came up with some definitions. Another discussion point was the type of canopy that would be needed in the main restaurant. We brought in landmarks-committee chair Dr. David Gebhard to help us through this. He advised Kaufman to hire architect Henry Lenny to shepherd the restoration proposals through the landmarks committee, which Kaufman did.

There also were some disputes over the number of parking spaces to be allowed in the parking lot that the SBTHP was receiving in the exchange, how much to be charged per space, and allowances that had to be made regarding how many spaces had to be leased. These kinds of details were typical of the step-by-step development of the final agreement. For the average reader, they are pretty boring, but I paid careful attention because I knew the SBTHP's interests were in the attorney's and my hands. I thought we held our own pretty well, and on the whole we came out of these months of meetings with the primary agreement intact.

We should have guessed that the former property manager and board member who was descended from the de la Guerra family would not go away so easily. We received notice that they wanted to see our board minutes to look for any details that violated the deal. We went to a settlement meeting at the person's attorney's office. With me and our attorney was new board member Charles Storke of the well known local Storke family. He had spent twenty-five years in Mexico running his own advertising business and spoke fluent Spanish. He and the de la Guerra descendant rattled off in Spanish. It was a fascinating moment— Charles was a direct descendant of Comandante Ortega, so it was like history fast-forwarding across time to the present. Charming as this encounter was, it led to nothing, and so we ended up in court in front of Judge James Slater. I vividly remember that day in court at the historic Santa Barbara County Courthouse.

Slater came out and greeted the plaintiff and the defendant, us. He said he had reviewed the documents that both sides had submitted and was inclined to rule in favor of the plaintiff. At what appeared almost the last moment, our attorney arose and said he had a precedent case he would like His Honor to read. Judge Slater listened to our attorney explain why he thought the case pertinent and then said he would read it and return in a couple hours with his decision.

When we returned, he reopened the hearing and said that he found the case our attorney had given him compelling and he was ruling in favor of the defendant, the Santa Barbara Trust for Historic Preservation. With that, he gaveled the session ended. The plaintiff's attorney was stunned and rose to object. Judge Slater said the plaintiff's attorney was welcome to keep talking but he had made his decision, and then he left. This, for me, was one of the great legal moments for the Santa Barbara Trust for Historic Preservation, and I give full credit to our attorney. I have kept his name anonymous as well.

On the written page, it may appear that all the steps to the closure of the sale were proceeding rapidly, but that is deceiving because not all the details have been presented; I have placed more emphasis on the critical deal points that could have collapsed the sale. In fact, there were hurdles ahead as the opened escrow drifted beyond midyear 1988. I was worried about one aspect of the deal that I thought might get us in a big dispute and could be a deal-killer. I am referring to the carving out of Casa de la Guerra from the remainder of El Paseo. That required a lot split with a property line that ran through the interconnected roofs and shared walls of the adobe and several of the rooms of El Paseo. I was concerned that the city's environmental-review committee and the planning commission might nix this idea. The chair of the environmental-review committee was the wife of the former property manager who had been a thorn in the side of the SBTHP and its efforts to sell El Pasco. The day of the public meeting at city hall, the turnout was modest, but most importantly the aforementioned wife did not show, nor did her husband. It was perhaps a sign that they had pretty much conceded that their efforts had failed. The committees approved the lot split unanimously, which meant that any appeal to the city council was likely to have failed. We were inching closer.

One last problem reared its head. The lawyers determined that by the gift agreement, the SBTHP could not by itself dispose of the property. The lawyers came up with the solution, doing a twenty-four-hour turnaround deeding the property back to Irene Suski Fendon, and she would then convey the property to Kaufman. This legal legerdemain worked: Escrow finally closed February 22, 1989, almost sixteen months after we had opened it. I will never forget the escrow officer dropping off all the paperwork. We had a big celebration in the office.

State Passes Legislation Authorizing Long-Term Agreement at the Presidio

It is amazing to contemplate all that the SBTHP went through from 1982 to 1989 with the general plan for the Park and the El Paseo sale and exchange. From landpoor and being on politically shaky ground, the SBTHP now had no debt and several million dollars in the bank. We had our work cut out for us, but we were now in a position to make things happen at the Presidio. Not that they hadn't already—the Chapel would always remain one of the organization's top achievements. It was an honor to rebuild the first church of the community dating to 1785, but the relentless politics of the past seven years had for me been stressful.

SBTHP management of the Presidio was solidified in 1988 with the passage of a great piece of legislation carried by Assemblyman Jack O'Connell and State Senator Gary Hart, both Democrats. Introduced as Assembly Bill 2006 in March 1986, it finally became law and part of the state's Public Resources Code Section 5080.36 in 1988, signed by Republican Governor George Deukmejian. The basics of the amendment gave authority to the California State Parks Department to sign an agreement with a qualified nonprofit to operate and develop the Park. A key piece of the legislation required that all income generated in the Park must stay in the Park. Eventually this legislation became a model used by the state to help manage other parks, but the unions were not happy with the legislation because the unions would not control the employees of nonprofits, and they thus tried to limit the number of nonprofit agreements or at least tried to water the agreements down. I asked myself how it was that California State Parks had been willing to enter into this groundbreaking agreement in the first place. One thought that crossed my mind was when the California State Parks people came to Santa Barbara during the general-plan process, they experienced the intensity of feelings about the project on both sides and decided the SBTHP was best suited to deal with the Park on the local level— not to mention the SBTHP had already been managing the Park for twenty years.

In any event, with a growing amount of commercial rental income resulting from state acquisitions, the operating agreement was a major plus to providing basic revenue to operate and maintain the Park and to serve the public, as there were now a chapel and other rooms available for interpretation. Added to this was a multimillion-dollar quasi-endowment that could help advance both the restoration projects at the Presidio and Casa de la Guerra, and also to provide staff and board oversight of the renovation of El Paseo. I give full credit for the hard work of the board and the attorney who would eventually join the board. The attorney was remunerated for his services, but I note that there was no broker fee that had to be paid selling El Paseo, and, thus, that became a savings to pay the attorney. The sale couldn't have happened without him, as it was indeed a complex transaction that ended with a document more than a hundred pages long—the historic preservation easement alone was more than thirty pages. I certainly learned a lot about real estate by the seat of my pants, and in the years ahead it stood me in good stead as I became more involved in the real-estate world of the SBTHP, which was an important part of advancing the Park and other projects such as the Santa Inés Mission Mills acquisition. Timing is everything, as they say, and in the years ahead the SBTHP would benefit having money invested as the stock market boomed in the nineties. In turn, the SBTHP bought and sold real estate into the next millennium that it could invest in other purchases, which provided some income for the growing reconstruction and restoration program.

Starting with a lofty goal of creating a Williamsburg of the West may have been too lofty, as the public response cut the project down to size, one might say. But even then, we have seen that by 1989, the SBTHP had endured public opposition thanks to a strong board and a powerful group called the Presidio Volunteers. While the board, especially among its founders, contained the elites of the town selected by Pearl Chase, the Presidio Volunteers were a group who came from a cross section of the community and contained many who were actual descendants of the Presidio, led by Russell Antonio Ruiz. In the 1980s, the organization added me to an office staff and a bookkeeper—and as time passed, additional employees came on board: a curator, a director of the research center, some part-time help with fundraising, and some serving as museum attendants. By 1990, almost half the property that made up the Presidio footprint had been acquired—through what might be described as "friendly acquisition." And two buildings, the padre's quarters and the Chapel, had been built. Not bad at all, but much more was to come.

In retrospect, one of the most important remnants from the 1980s of the SBTHP as it went forward into the 1990s was a board rigorously committed to the Presidio project. This included Dr. Garvan Kuskey, whom Chase had recruited in the 1960s; one of "Pearl's girls," as Vivian Obern called herself; pharmacist Dr. James Mills, who became a driving force on the restoration committee; Michael Hardwick, who had started as one of the Presidio volunteers and was a key organizer of the volunteer Presidio Soldados reenactors; and Richard Lugo, a Presidio descendant who made replica animals for the site. Added to this group were new board members Charles Storke and his protégé Jack Theimer, whose exploits we will learn more about. On nonprofit boards there is always discussion of term limits, and the SBTHP didn't

Then State Senator Gary Hart (left) and Assemblyman Jack O'Connell present a Resolution to SBTHP board member Dr. James Mills circa 1990. Hart and O'Connell carried legislation that Governor Deukmejian signed authorizing a long-term operating agreement between SBTHP and California State Parks. *Courtesy SBTHP*

have any. With the aforementioned people leading the way, I was in no hurry to see term limits implemented. Two behind-the-scenes board members, former city-council member Alice Rypins and community activist Heather Bryden, who had both been staunch supporters, left the board, but I continued to consult with them and received their continued friendship and support.

There are multiple ways one can achieve a noble goal, two of which are to allow it to evolve while incorporating changes along the way or to strictly adhere to the goal unchanged. In the next ten years, both of these approaches would apply at the Presidio under certain circumstances. The risk of any organization is that it will go off in too many directions and lose its focus. The SBTHP, I would like to think, expanded its focus to include a complete restoration of Casa de la Guerra and development of a new state park for the people of California at the Santa Inés Mission Mills. The Presidio itself would continue its phoenix-like rise out of the adobe earth. The Presidio was indeed coming back to life.

CHAPTER SIX

Back to Adobe Mudslinging

AT ONE POINT, I titled an SBTHP fundraising pamphlet "On the Verge of Greatness." It felt that way to some of us even if it was maybe a little too hyperbolic. I remember a state-park historian stopped by who had been following the Presidio for a number of years. He said to me, looking around at the beehive of activity that included ongoing archaeology and adobe-making: "This used to be a sleepy little park." Not anymore. The question I posed to myself as we moved into the 1990s was how to explain these years of hyperactivity: They centered around people, events, projects, research, planning, and negotiating. Only those who have worked in construction in Santa Barbara understand the challenges of obtaining permitting in our town. In the case of the SBTHP, it was a double whammy, so to speak, because all its projects in the state park had to have both state and city approval per the memorandum of understanding the parties had signed. Truthfully, however, we generally had full support in Sacramento and Santa Barbara. Every project we took to the city's Historic Landmarks Commission received a unanimous positive decision, except in one case in which an architect didn't like the idea of the tile set on top of a defense wall. (He was wrong, by the way.)

In the foregoing I will continue to try to follow trust activities in a relatively chronological order, but in some instances I will follow something through to completion and then return to the chronology—something like the modernist novels that jump back and forth between time frames. I have learned well from Aldous Huxley's *Point Counter Point* and *Eyeless in Gaza*.

Major Archaeological Discoveries

When we left archaeology and reconstruction, board member Garvan Kuskey's chutzpah had prodded the SBTHP into requesting city and state permission to demolish the Shalhoob building. The importance of that became apparent the moment the building came down as the whole corner was now dominated by the Presidio Chapel. We immediately commenced archaeology to expose the site of the former Presidio comandancia, a series of interconnected rooms that included an office, an entry room called a "zaguan," and a living/dining room. Foundations of a bedroom lay under the modern city street. Archaeology began by late 1986 or early 1987, and I remember this because longtime volunteer Richard Whitehead, who had plotted the Presidio based on a Spanish-period ground plan over the modern city streets, was still alive when we made one of the major archaeological discoveries of the Presidio from 1987 until now. We hadn't expected to find much because we assumed that the foundations of the comandancia had probably been destroyed when the two-story building was constructed over it. But to our delight, archaeology exposed the lower courses of the foundations. Then as we lowered the backyard of the comandancia to historic grade, we came across a section of totally intact aqueduct! This was the earliest permanent construction of the Presidio, dating to 1783. Whitehead, an MIT-trained engineer, was ecstatic, as were we all. That the aqueduct came to the back of the comandancia led to all sorts of speculation that it continued under the building to somewhere in the plaza or that this section diverted directly to the comandancia. That speculation continues to this day. Restoration-committee member and civil engineer Norman Caldwell calculated how much water could have flowed through it and determined that there would have been more than ample water able to flow through the aqueduct to meet the needs of the Presidio. It would have flowed likely to a cistern, where overflow may have drained out the front gate from there. All of this was more speculation, but worth considering as a guide to future archaeological excavations. The water from the aqueduct also had solved the problem of water needed to make the more than three hundred thousand adobe bricks. At one point there was even an attempt to trace the aqueduct to Pedregoza Creek, which later was renamed Mission Creek. This idea was to follow the landform up to the source of the aqueduct. Nothing came of this.

Rebuilding the Comandancia

What did come of the excavations was a clear delineation of the remaining foundations of the comandancia. With the staff providing background research, the next step was to design the building. Three ground plans were consulted, the first two more or less as-builts of the Presidio, one signed in 1788 by Goicoechea and another of a slightly later date and with some added features and signed by Spanish Governor Pedro Fages. These ground plans are the most detailed of any found at presidios in North America and their accuracy has been confirmed through archaeology. The third map was called the "Vischer plan," drawn much later in 1820. This plan showed the comandancia had been converted into a storage facility after the 1812 earthquakes, and was not useful in this case as the period of reconstruction designated in the general plan was from 1790 to 1810 and the map dated from a later period. The two other ground plans clearly identified these rooms as the comandancia. Also, a painting from the 1850s of the Chapel showed that the comandancia had a porch overhang, which would end up in the final design for the reconstruction.

An interesting sidebar to the Vischer plan was that Richard had discovered it along with similar maps for three other Alta California presidios in the Bancroft Library at UC Berkeley. It showed some important details for later reconstructions, but one thing that bothered Whitehead was that the map indicated a bell tower attached to the Chapel whose existence Whitehead and some others had argued against for years. He told me he hesitated, but only hesitated, showing it to the committee. Eventually he published an article on the Vischer plans in the quarterly of the Historical Society of Southern California. The cat was out of the bag, but the SBTHP did not get around to building the bell tower until long after Richard's death in 1988.

Trying to keep costs down, I asked local architect Henry Lenny, born in Mexico and highly respected for his experience designing Spanish-style buildings, if he would design the building gratis. He agreed, but because he was busy with his normal practice, sometimes he would put our project on the back burner. I had to keep after him, but we finally got the plans from him, which were then approved by the city and the state. Norman Caldwell did the engineering pro bono.

Among the new approaches in this project was the problem of removing the original foundations. In contrast to the Chapel reconstruction, we decided this time to leave them in the ground to preserve them in situ and cover the foundations with concrete, then lay the bricks over the concrete foundation as we had with the Chapel. Lateral and horizontal rebar were used to the top course at the roof line, where a bond beam was thus formed to tie the building together as a protection against seismic events. Some purists go ballistic over this use of modern materials and see this as fake, but I have little patience with this attitude. Nothing of this modern building material is seen, and the visitor sees only what would have been seen by a person living in the eighteenth century. Another concession to protect the building from earthquake damage was using plywood above the caning to hold the roof tiles in place, which were then tied to the plywood sheets.

Another new feature of the reconstruction process was making the bricks on-site. Soil from the archaeological excavation blended with imported sifted soil provided the main material for making the bricks. Not that it made any difference to the purists, but I personally thought it was rather fascinating that the original melted soil of the comandancia bricks was being recast into bricks that went into the building. Having the adobe-making on-site was an added educational experience for the visiting public. Local adobe-maker and future board member Tim Aguilar was now more or less in charge of all adobe-making and would remain in such a capacity through my tenure at the SBTHP. We paid him only a moderate sum.

Vince Pownall, who had overseen some of the work on the padre's quarters and Chapel, was still involved as construction began on the comandancia. We used a lot of volunteer effort in raising the walls, and I spent many afternoons myself laying bricks. There is something really satisfying about picking up one of those fifty-five pound blocks and laying it in the wall. It gives you a real sense of the effort that goes into building an adobe fort. Things were moving a little slowly, so Aguilar said he knew someone we might hire who was in the construction business—Kenny Ruiz. I hired him and he was a big help in bringing the project to fruition. From that day forward, he was in charge of major on-site construction projects at the Presidio and Casa de la Guerra. He would build a team of mostly Mexican nationals who would stay with us into the turn of the millennium and beyond.

The foundations of the Comandancia uncovered after the Shalhoob demolition. *Courtesy SBTHP*

An original section of the Presidio Aqueduct, behind comandancia, one of the major archaeological discoveries at the site. *Courtesy SBTHP*

In 1992, the building was finally finished and partially furnished to a plan from art historian Norman Neuerburg, which would later be added to and somewhat modified. I worked with Norman acquiring a historic table for the office and other pieces. I had previously worked with the family of Don Dozier—a professor of Latin American history at UCSB and a former SBTHP board member—who donated several of his colonial paintings to the SBTHP, and we purchased a few others. These paintings ended up in the Chapel and the comandancia.

We decided on a dedication of the comandancia on Columbus Day, October 12, 1992, the five hundredth anniversary of the discovery of the New World by the Great Admiral of the Ocean Sea, as one historian called Columbus. Of course, these days one talks of Columbus's encounter with the New World, and even worse, he is being deconstructed as a monster who enslaved and destroyed Native peoples. There is no question that on his many stays in the New World he demonstrated a tendency to administrative ineptitude and some brutality, but a great brilliant sailor

The Comandancia under construction circa 1991. (Left to right): Kenny Ruiz, Tim Aguilar, and the author, with Moises Rodriguez standing below. *Courtesy SBTHP*

The Comandancia and Chapel today. *Courtesy SBTHP*

he was nevertheless. I will just leave it at that, allowing the most intolerant to categorize me as they see fit.

The dedication ceremony was very rewarding for me personally as I had commenced researching the life of the man who spent more years than anyone else in the quarters, Goicoechea. I emceed the event and had family from around the state who attended that day. Also, Michele and I attended a special event on the Spanish training ship *Elcano* in Los Angeles Harbor with board members and spouses George and Vivian Obern and Charles Storke and his wife, Elizabeth, and the evening of October 12 we spent at a celebratory dinner at the Beverly Hills Hotel. I remember sitting next to actor Timothy Dalton, who at that time was the designated James Bond in the movies. We were at these events as guests of Eduardo Garrigues,

The Comandanicia was dedicated on October 12, 1992, the same day as the five hundredth anniversary of Columbus's discovery of the New World. Attending the Columbus celebration on board *Elcano*, the Spanish training ship (left to right): Vie and George Obern; the author and his wife, Michele; Charles and Elizabeth Storke. *Author's Collection*

Spanish consul in Los Angeles, and his wife, Pilar. Earlier we were also invited to a special banquet at the Huntington Library whose guests included Governor Pete Wilson and his wife, Gayle, and the infanta of Spain at that time. I am not sure if it was Elena or Cristina. The event was a grand affair capped by the unveiling of a digitizing project of Spanish New World documents housed in the Archivo General de Indias. The documents were being beamed by satellite from Seville, Spain, to the Huntington. Spaniards were among the great bureaucrats and sent home millions of documents from the New World that were now housed in the Seville archive. I'm not sure how far along that project advanced, but it would take quite a few decades to complete if continued. In light of what is going on today as I write this—with Columbus, Lincoln, Washington, and Jefferson statues being torn down, it is hard not to look back to 1992 with a certain amount of nostalgia, although even by then Columbus was being vilified in some quarters.

I would like to think that the Columbus negativity was offset by a symposium the SBTHP sponsored with UCSB in 1991 called "The Spanish Beginnings in California." Scholars came from Spain and from California and around the Southwest to participate, and the guru of Spanish borderlands study, Dr. David Weber, gave the keynote address. I presented a paper that I later published on Goicoechea. In the chapters on Presidio history, I mentioned traveling to his birthplace in Cosalá in Sinaloa, Mexico, and found what was likely the comandancia where he was born; I photographed it and the church where he was likely baptized in 1747. I also made a trip to Los Alamos in Sonora, Mexico, where he grew up and lived for thirty years before coming to Santa Barbara. Later in the 1990s, I would do more research on him. I liked the idea that he was the man in charge of building the original Presidio and I was in charge of rebuilding it.

Brief Board Interlude: What to Do with El Paseo Sale Proceeds?

I am being a bit facetious talking in terms of board interludes, as if the board just came and went at my whim. In fact, it was in reasonable control of the organization on the whole and especially good with its conservative attitude toward finances. When you suddenly have millions of dollars dumped in your lap from the El Paseo transaction, it is tempting to think of all the ways to spend the money.

Around 1990, a new energy arrived in the board in the persons of Charles Storke and Jack Theimer. Storke was son of the powerful *Santa Barbara Press* publisher Thomas Storke, who was also a direct descendant of founding Presidio commandant Ortega. Charles, after a fight with his father while serving as executive editor of the *News Press*, left for Mexico City, where he created with a partner the largest advertising firm in Latin America. He had returned to spend his retirement years in Santa Barbara. Jack Theimer was in a way a protégé of Storke but also a developer on his own having done a much respected housing project in nearby Montecito. He also purchased some of the Storke property near the university, but never developed it and later sold it.

What Storke brought to the SBTHP eventually was a significant interest in, among other things, Casa de la Guerra, and he would adopt its restoration as his pet project. As he explained to me much later, he adopted that project because his father had built the *News Press* building on the opposite side of Plaza De La Guerra and Charles felt it was his duty to take care of the other side. That he did indeed; there are many who will contribute to that project, including me, but the project could never have happened without Charles. He and Patrick O'Dowd, the soon-to-be-hired manager of the Casa restoration, through the former's fundraising and the latter's skills as a historian, carried out the most thoroughly researched and accurate adobe restoration ever undertaken in California. More to come on this story.

Jack, originally from Oklahoma and a cousin of former president Bill Clinton, told me he had stayed in the White House on several occasions. He had the tendency to think big, which returns us to the multimillion dollars from the El Paseo sale. As I remember the discussions, Jack was the one who tossed out the idea that the SBTHP should use that money to build out the Presidio to the approved Phase III of the general plan. On the other side were those who had been on the board for a while, and they thought the money should form the basis for an endowment. There was never any big tension over this issue, and it was decided to invest the money and create what turned out to be a quasi-endowment. It wasn't a pure legal endowment because those require the corpus of the funds to be retained. The SBTHP could spend the endowment all in one fell swoop if it so desired. The virtue of having this fund available became obvious as it provided money to purchase other properties needed for the Presidio reconstruction and helped provide the basis for building a professional staff needed as the Park grew larger and public visitation increased. This would be the guiding budgetary direction of the SBTHP over time, a good fiscal conservatism, with only a few risks taken, one of which was the future purchase of Jimmy's Oriental Gardens, which I will talk about later.

Theimer, without question, added a liveliness to the board meetings and was one to recognize the importance of having a good public face. In 1990, a group that included longtime volunteer and then-board member Michael Hardwick formed *Los Soldados del Real Presidio de Santa Bárbara* (Soldiers of the Royal Presidio of Santa Barbara). Re-enactors really add something to historic sites, and Theimer took up their cause at board meetings. He donated money to the group and it paid off as they provided more than twenty years of presence at SBTHP events and at other sites, including in Washington, D.C. Their important contributions deserve to be more fully recognized.

Presidio Soldados fire their muskets at a celebration at the site. *Courtesy Mike Hardwick*

CHAPTER SEVEN

Making History Fun: Living History and Rewards of Research

Los Soldados del Real Presidio de Santa Barbara

Reenactors are a special breed. What makes them special in my opinion is that they burrow into history asking questions that help a site's interpretation. In many cases, they research and portray historical personages. For example, longtime volunteer Michael Hardwick decided to become Governor Felipe de Neve, who was at the founding of Santa Barbara in 1782. Michael outfitted himself in proper attire based on research and read up on Neve's life and career. He took his quest for accuracy to Spain, where he purchased an original medal of the Order of Charles III, similar to the one that Neve had been awarded by the king. Another key soldado was Jim Martinez, a Presidio descendant of Goicoechea who learned the manual of arms of the eighteenth century; he would lead the troupe onto the site and then bark his commands in Spanish and with some English. He would read appropriate documents to the audience depending on the occasion. This was usually followed by the firing of muskets and cannons.

The replica cannons needed special carriages made, and these came from longtime volunteer Bud Decker, a World War II veteran who is now deceased. He carefully researched the carriages and spent over a year working on them on his own, until he finally showed up with them and the cannons installed. He was in charge of firing the cannons for twenty years. Other loyal soldados included Marc Martinez and his significant other, Donna Egeberg. Russell Clay Ruiz, whose volunteerism dated back to the 1970s, also served as a soldier playing the trumpet and drums as needed. Later his wife, Diane, became a member as well. One did not have to be male to participate.

All of the above outfitted themselves in proper uniforms: Marc and Donna made their leather-jacket uniforms on their own. We had a professional seamstress in Ohio, who specialized in period dress, make the uniforms. The SBTHP paid for these; Jack Theimer's support helped fund the purchase of muskets and pistols and covered some travel costs. The number of soldados never grew to more than ten or so, but this small contingent was always impressive wherever they did their re-enactments. These took place not only at the Presidio, but they also became an active part of Old Spanish Days events held throughout the city during the month of August. One time at Fiesta Pequeña at the Old Mission, the soldados stood atop the mission between the towers and fired their muskets—more frequently they were at the church's front door during the introduction of Saint Barbara.

Their out-of-town events took them to the Tubac Presidio in Arizona, Mission La Purísima in Lompoc, founding day at the San Francisco Presidio, and as far away as Washington, D.C., where they participated in the second annual Hispanic Heroes parade. A major highlight for them was serving as the honor guard for the visit of Prince Felipe of Spain (now King Felipe VI) to the Presidio in 1995, one of the major events in the history of the Presidio project. The prince would make a return visit to Santa Barbara in 2012. The soldados to this day continue to play a role at the Presidio, but their numbers have diminished and their revival is the key to the future of interpretation that I will talk about in the last chapter of this history of the Presidio project.

It should be clear to the reader that I have much admired the volunteer soldados' contribution to El Presidio de Santa Bárbara State Historic Park to the point that I ordered my own uniform, became Comandante Goicoechea, and participated in a number of the events. There is even a photo of my firing my pistol on the cover of our newsletter, *La Campana*, taken by Paula Hardwick, the wife of Michael Hardwick. The soldados have done much more than just marching and firing weapons but became important parts of school visits to the sites. Staying in historical character, they explained what it meant to be a soldado on the frontier and described the daily life of a soldado and his family inside the Presidio. The encounters with young students in the fourth grade were very important because these students experienced living history, as it is called. One day I was listening in as a fourth grader asked a soldado: "Is that the kind of gun that was used to kill Indians?" Obviously the young boy had heard that part of the story of Indian-Spanish relations. It provided the opportunity for the soldado to explain his own origin as a person who was of mixed Spanish and Indian heritage. The unique relations between native Chumash and soldados is one of the stories of the Presidio, since in the early years of the Presidio there was no mission nearby and the soldiers had direct contact with the Indians in their villages.

In some ways, I think my grandson as we were talking about Indians and the Spanish asked a deeper, more difficult question: "Why didn't the Indians make some of the same things the Spanish had: guns, wagons, ships, and other things?" First of all, it is a pretty sophisticated question from a nine-year-old, but it did provide the opportunity to try to explain how the more complex society of the Europeans allowed them to create such things as cannons, a technology that the Spanish and other Europeans transferred to the New World. The docent can then talk about foundries and that there was even one in Lima, Peru. At the same time, one can respect the Indian side of the story, talking about their lifestyle that had sustained them over millennia.

In some respects, it is easier to answer the first question about violence between peoples as a reflection of human nature and the desire for power. Explaining why one society becomes more sophisticated and advanced technologically requires considerable thought and explanation. In the event, interactions between our soldados and visitors to the site are a key component in the interpretation of the site. It is a form of the dialectic—an active exchange of raising questions and responding to them. In addition, I think it is important to put the students in roles in which they act out being people living on the frontier. These learning methods are common around other sites in California and around the nation, and I witnessed firsthand how effective they were at the Presidio. On several occasions, we even invited professional re-enactors to perform in the Presidio Chapel: These included a Father Serra and a Richard Henry Dana of the famous book *Two Years before the Mast*.

A large part of the satisfaction I derived out of being director of the Presidio project and the other projects of the SBTHP was from the opportunity to learn about the business operations of the organization, but then find time to undertake and promote research and to contemplate the role of the historic site in education. The importance of archaeology in education was something I soon saw the value of; learning about adobe technology also was exciting and something that needed to be part of the learning experience at the Presidio. As I said at the outset, there is something very basic about mixing mud and making the basic building material of an adobe. People of all ages love playing in the mud.

SBTHP Research Program and Its Research Center

One would expect with a historian in charge of day-to-day operations of the SBTHP, research would become important to the organization. Such was certainly the case during my years as COO and CEO of the organization. Archaeology and research underpinned all that we did in terms of restoring and reconstructing buildings in the State Park.

I earlier introduced the story of the birth of the Research Center, but it bears further discussion as part of the 1990s heyday of the Presidio project. Richard Whitehead's efforts to collect and translate Spanish documents was something I tried to follow up on: although I did more collecting than translating. As I mentioned earlier, when Whitehead asked for a small room in the back of the Cañedo Adobe, I offered to convert a large double garage with a small apartment attached to it into our new Research Center. He was delighted, and fairly quickly in the 1980s he transferred his collection of books and other materials to the Center to form the basis of our library.

Admittedly there was a political component to my thinking in certain of the research we did. I was well aware of the public criticism of the SBTHP that we were only interested in the Spanish history and were ignoring much of the other neighborhood history of the Presidio site—the Chinese, the Japanese, and the art community in the Alhecama property. As a result, I discussed with the UCSB history department, which had a graduate public-history program, the possibility of one of its MA classes doing a project on the post-presidio history of the site. A half dozen students under the tutelage of Professor Carl Harris did indeed undertake such a project that we finally published in 1992 titled *Santa Barbara Presidio Area: 1840 to the Present*. Their research papers on the history of the Mexican period, the later Chinese and Japanese history of the area, and a study of the architectural landscape were included in the volume and would help define the interpretive element of the general plan for the Park. I admit my motivation for doing this was political to show our critics that we were not strictly interested in only the Spanish. That aside, the project really did have value in its own right, and I am glad we did it.

Cathy Rudolph, who we remember was so vital in the eventual sale of El Paseo, ably led the Research Center as its director through the 1990s. She started at the SBTHP while a reentry student at UCSB, eventually receiving her MA in history. While she did not have any previous library or archival training, she had the ability to learn these skills and head the center in a professional direction. She was the key staffer working with Professor Giorgio Perissinotto, now deceased, of the Spanish department in the project translating all of the fifty-two *memorias* (requisitions) and *facturas* (invoices) for the ships that landed in Santa Barbara during the Spanish period. The treasure trove of information contained in these documents, which I described in the Presidio-history section, was translated by students in the graduate program of the Spanish department of the university. As I remember, one student was from Barcelona, another from elsewhere in Spain, and some from Mexico. They convened for well over a year and we did pay them for their services. Under the guidance of Perissinotto, they toiled away translating each of the documents. Under the appropriate title *Documenting Everyday Life in Early Spanish California: The Santa Barbara Presidio* Memorias y Facturas, *1779-1810*, the SBTHP published in 1998 these translations in an excellent illustrated hardcover edition. Without question, this was the most important of the many publications of the SBTHP, a useful source for anyone interpreting a historical site of the same period in California, not to mention a useful tool to compare with archaeological findings at the Presidio and other Spanish colonial sites in the Southwest. One archaeologist told me that the book was the most important one ever published on the material culture of Spanish California.

One of the outcomes of this publication was a spinoff exhibition of some of the items found on the lists of requisitions and invoices, with the most prevalent the frequent shipment of chocolate in various iterations. The exhibition, housed in the rebuilt officer's quarters at the northeast corner of the Presidio, also reproduced an oversized complete version of one of the invoices in both Spanish and English. As of this writing, the exhibition is still installed and available for public viewing. Curator Patrick O'Dowd spearheaded this project—more on him later as the manager of the Casa de la Guerra restoration.

Another important publication of the SBTHP previously mentioned was printed in 1996: Richard Whitehead's *Citadel on the Channel: The Royal Presidio of Santa Barbara, Its Founding and Construction, 1782-1798*. One of Whitehead's main purposes in this work was to provide background of the history of construction of the Presidio to help guide those of us involved in the reconstruction. But it is also a freestanding scholarly effort that provides historical information on the Santa Barbara Presidio for the general reader. The SBTHP had well-known borderlands historian Dr. Donald Cutter edit and provide an afterword for the volume.

Also, the 1990s were the halcyon years for my own research on Goicoechea. I supplemented my previous short biography of him published in 1993 with more information on his genealogical origins from one of the most prominent families in Durango, Mexico—the Aragons. His mother, María Aragon, traced her lineage back to late-sixteenth-century Durango, and one of Goicoechea's uncles, Pedro de Aragon, was one of the leading ecclesiastics of the Durango diocese. I haven't been able to trace his father's lineage beyond Captain Juan de Goicoechea himself. He may have been born in Spain. This additional information, uncovered after the publication of his biography, has been printed in the SBTHP's *La Campana* and in *El Boletín*, the journal of the California Missions Foundation. A consolidation of my research on him into one publication is something I hope eventually to follow up on.

To stay with my own publication history for a moment, in the late 1980s, one of the *Santa Barbara News-Press* executives, Jeff Flanders, asked me if I were interested in possibly doing a book on Santa Barbara history that the paper would sponsor and promote. Why not? I thought, and it was a way to promote the SBTHP, which needed some favorable publicity with all the controversy swirling around its work at the Presidio. The book came out in 1988 under the title *Santa Barbara: Historical Themes and Images*. The paper heavily advertised it with full-page ads and sold three thousand copies by early 1989. In it, I gave plenty of coverage to the Presidio and the SBTHP's other projects. The director of the Center for the Study of Democratic

Institutions, then at UCSB, wrote me a note saying that it was the best book ever written on the history of the region. That made up for an error that was pointed out to me in another correspondence.

The 1990s were a very fruitful time for the Research Center, and viewed in the context of the 1990s, it was part of one of the most productive periods in the organization's history. Interestingly, there was much more to come for the Santa Barbara Presidio Research Center, as it became clear that the SBTHP's research program was outgrowing the current space. Plans began for relocating it to a new, larger facility across the street in a two-story 1920s building located next to the Alhecama Theatre in the Old City College site, which had been purchased by the state and incorporated into El Presidio de Santa Bárbara State Historic Park. This story belongs in the next decade.

Nihonmachi Revisited: From Idea to Brilliant Event

As we are learning, the Presidio project is more than a mud fort. Rather than following a straight line, the SBTHP zigs and zags through its own history. We know from the general-plan days that the public chastised the SBTHP for ignoring the Presidio neighborhood's Asian history. Thinking politically, I tried to address that issue with the aforementioned research project that eventuated in the publication *Santa Barbara Presidio Area: 1840 to the Present*. I suppose I was still somewhat thinking politically that something more should be done to interpret the Japanese community that existed along Canon Perdido and Anacapa streets beginning around 1910, thriving to World War II, and then more or less surviving in bits and pieces after the war into the 1970s.

I had a living reminder of this history in the person of Mas Shimoda, the gardener who took care of El Paseo and our Presidio properties. He had actually been part of the original neighborhood from early on, teaching Japanese in the Buddhist church and sharing his experience as an expert in the art of kendo, a traditional Japanese martial art that is descended from swordsmanship and uses bamboo swords and protective armor. Mas was an institution in himself, and was getting advanced in years. He would come to me and ask to retire and I cajoled him to please stay, which he did through the 1990s. At least once a year, he would barbecue for the staff. Mas, without saying a word, prompted me to think that we should do some kind of event at the Presidio honoring the Japanese heritage of the site.

That idea might have slipped away into my Don Quixote imagination, except a young lady named Valerie Yoshimura showed up in my office looking for part-time work. This was sometime around late 1990, probably early 1991. She was a student at UCSB studying French. She was looking to gain some experience in the museum world. How could I possibly know that this young genius was about to take the lead in putting on one of the greatest events ever to take place at El Presidio de Santa Bárbara State Historic Park? I shamelessly said to her that I did not have any paying

The introductory panel to the Nihonmachi Revisited Exhibition in 1991. *Courtesy Valerie Yoshimura*

Members of the Nihonmachi planning team with Valerie Yoshimura, far left *Courtesy Valerie Yoshimura*

positions, but if she cared to volunteer helping plan a Japanese American event at the site, I was game. As it turned out, she was game as well. What followed still amazes me to this day—some thirty-plus years later.

I am not quite sure of the exact time frame that ensued nor how many conversations we had before Valerie said she would do it. With her then-boyfriend and future husband, Bill Shay, a PhD candidate at UCSB, they began "planning" the event. She began on her own to do things such as go through microfilm of the *Santa Barbara News-Press* and print out any and all articles related to Japanese Americans in Santa Barbara from the 1920s on. She found and had done oral histories, and began to put together a proposed outline of the event. In addition, she gathered the names of locals who had connections to the local history of Santa Barbara's Japantown. She came up with a title: "Nihonmachi Revisited: A Celebration of Santa Barbara's Japanese American Heritage." She put together a large committee that began to meet once per week. I believe this was in February. I attended these meetings, as did several of my staffers. I am not sure how she put together a budget, that is, who she consulted regarding it, but fairly early on she determined they needed to raise about eleven thousand dollars for the event. Then she took the lead compiling a mailing list for soliciting donations from individuals and businesses. As the planning unfolded, the money came in. We helped mail out the requests and record the donations. I remember seeing fairly early that more than seven thousand dollars in donations had been recorded. Need I remind the reader that Valerie had not received one cent in remuneration for her efforts to that point, and it would not change? She remained a volunteer through this entire amazing moment in SBTHP history.

I know she would not like to take all the credit for the event, and for this reason I mention some of the key committee members by name who contributed. Some were descendants of Santa Barbara's Japantown and had been interned during the war: Kay Yamada Brown, Linda Yamada Weisman, Jan Inouye, Dave Inouye, and George Hirashima. They helped with the overall planning. Helping with the panels were Susan Kuromiya, Grace Murakami, Hideko Malis, and a woodworker named Ted Muneno, who crafted the beautiful panels that are still in the possession of the SBTHP. Various people helped create the eight photographic panels depicting the history of the Japanese American experience in the Santa Barbara area from early immigration and settlement on Canon Perdido Street, through evacuation and internment, to the present. Panels were complemented by historic artifacts and artwork and the personal histories of longtime Santa Barbara–area residents. All of this was installed in the Presidio Chapel, turning it back into, one might say, a Buddhist church. This was fitting as a Buddhist church had actually been built almost on the original Presidio Chapel site in the 1920s, later to be demolished by the city as the church was relocated to a site on the lower eastside of Santa Barbara.

The committee decided that the event would take place May 18 and 19, 1991, with a full slate of all-day activities—Japanese dancing, music on the Okoto, *taiko* drummers from Los Angeles plus a children *taiko*-drummers group, an Aikdo demonstration, a *konnichiwa* presentation by the Hollister Elementary School fourth-grade class, music from Bethany Congregational Church (formerly Japanese Congregational Church) singers, and a kendo demonstration from our very own Mas Shimoda. Japanese food and crafts also were for sale to help raise funds along with a raffle. At a special Friday-night opening, Kay Yamada Brown welcomed guests, and County Supervisor Tom Rogers thanked all for making the event possible. That evening, Roberta Fuji Cook did a special performance of classical Japanese dance. Mayor Lodge officially opened the outdoor activities on Saturday.

Then the crowds came—during each of those two days, more people visited the site than had visited in the entire month prior. Yes, several thousand people. The publicity that Valerie spearheaded was overwhelming. Full coverage in the *Santa Barbara News-Press* and the *Santa Barbara Independent*. We even were recognized in the "Angry Poodle" column of the *Santa Barbara Independent*, where we had so often been criticized. In the article in the *News-Press*, Valerie said that the event "was the idea of Jarrell Jackman, Executive Director of the Santa Barbara Trust for Historic Preservation." That statement was so typical of her—making sure everyone who contributed was recognized. I was happy to take credit for the idea but not for

The Presidio Chapel interior converted to a museum for exhibition of Nihonmachi Revisited. *Courtesy Valerie Yoshimura*

Mas Shimoda, longtime Presidio State Park gardener, member of Japanese community where he taught Japanese and Kendo, and later was interned during World War II. *Courtesy Valerie Yoshimura*

all the effort that Valerie and others put into this event. Volunteerism was again an essential part of the SBTHP's success story.

The upshot of the Nihonmachi event was, though not intending to, it made a profit. The funds were to help with a future display at El Presidio de Santa Bárbara State Historic Park on the history of Santa Barbara's Japantown. Instead, we used the funds to invite on February 16, 1992, the famous Fred Korematsu to speak in the Presidio Chapel. Korematsu had been convicted of violating Executive Order 9066 requiring all Californians on the west coast of Japanese descent to enter internment camps for the duration of World War II. He had resisted going to a camp. The US Supreme Court upheld his conviction on a 6-to-3 vote. In 1983, Korematsu filed a suit to have that conviction vacated, and it was. We filled the Presidio Chapel as Korematsu told us his story of years overcoming the conviction. The title of the event was "Reflections on Executive Order 9066: Japanese America, 50 Years Later." Besides having Korematsu deliver the keynote address, the event included a special symposium in commemoration of the fiftieth anniversary of Executive Order 9066. Guest panelists were Cressey Nakagawa, national president of the Japanese

American Citizens League; Karen Kai and Bob Rusky; Coram Nobis, attorney for Korematsu; and Frank Mori, local veteran of the United States Military Intelligence Service. It was an amazing capstone to the Nihonmachi event. To this day, I have the sincerest gratitude to Valerie, who earned her PhD in French from the University of Michigan; married Bill Shay, who also spent countless hours on the event; teaches at Laguna Blanca School; and has a son in college and a daughter off to Stanford University.

My own reflections on this event were that I had a whole different attitude toward the importance of preserving the Presidio area's Japanese history. The city block of East Canon Perdido was basically the home of the Japanese ethnic community. It supported both a Buddhist temple and Japanese Congregational Church, along with two grocery stores, a barber shop, a pool hall, a restaurant, and boarding houses. This history should find a permanent home, and I believe it would be great to rebuild the Asakura Hotel, which lies just outside the footprint of the Presidio, to house such a museum. But at the same time, this in no way changed my view of the importance of the Presidio project.

CHAPTER EIGHT

Creative Mudslinging in Full Swing

Presidio Northeast Corner Reconstruction

How does one transition from Nihonmachi back to the adobe world of the SBTHP? My answer: by focusing on volunteers. I remember a humorous moment as we were about to tear down a small wood-frame building that formerly housed La Playa Azul Mexican restaurant. The owners were longtime tenants of the SBTHP in the Park. A first step was to relocate the restaurant, which SBTHP Office Manager Phyllis Moore proceeded to do, to its present site where it is still located today, just up the street beyond the rebuilt Presidio defense wall. Playa Azul's new space had once been offices of Santa Barbara Adult Education and of Pearl Chase herself.

So here were George Obern and his wife, Vie, one of Pearl's girls, as the group of Chase protégés called themselves, on a Saturday afternoon wielding sledgehammers as volunteers began the demolition work of the building at 902 Santa Barbara Street. Underneath lay the foundations of the Presidio. Yes, volunteers do everything at the SBTHP. I remember board member and chair of the fundraising committee Julie Forbes making adobe bricks wheeling a barrel full of mud at the Old Mission. It is appropriate I mention her name at this point because after she died in 1988 and her husband, Wilson, died in 1992, their will bequeathed the SBTHP a handsome sum of money that helped pay for most of the archaeology of the northeast corner. A second source of funding for archaeology came from the joint powers agreement fund, whose primary purpose was to help pay for park acquisition. That fund lay fairly dormant and unused, and I talked to then-City Councilman Hal Conklin, who was the city representative overseeing that fund. The city had continued putting in ten thousand dollars annually; the county had backed out after passage of Proposition 13. I asked Hal if we could use that money for archaeology at the Presidio; he thought it was OK and the money was transferred to the SBTHP for that purpose. Over the course of my SBTHP decades, we did a lot of cobbling together of funding to reach our goals, and this was another example.

There also had been another building next door to the old Playa Azul restaurant, a small house. I remember an SBTHP member telling me that house once was the residence of a famous magician named Abel Maldonado, who went by the name Señor Maldo. He had a restaurant next door and she challenged me that weren't those buildings as important historically as the buildings we were going to replace them with—i.e., rebuilt adobes? I was taken aback by this then, but today I would respond that we should somehow acknowledge Maldo the Magician's presence on the site; however, what we have rebuilt was also the residence of José de la Guerra and his family for five years before he moved into his adobe mansion; in fact, it was also probably where the famous son, Pablo de la Guerra, was born. One has to make choices when interpreting history but also accommodate other periods of history. Perhaps a plaque someday mentioning Maldo and his studio and restaurant on this site?

With all due respect to the flow of history, it would have been really a lesser trade-off to keep those wood-frame buildings because underneath them was some of the best archaeology ever uncovered at the Presidio. I hired Michael Imwalle, who had arrived as a contract archaeologist, as our full-time archaeologist to proceed with the excavation of this site. Earlier, back in the 1980s, we had discovered a tile floor from the Spanish period, digging down between the two wood-frame buildings. We knew there was likely to be much more there. This is the major problem with the flow-of-history approach: it gives priority to the latest layer of history. What is underneath or behind it becomes second fiddle. This will be the major issue when we come to the Casa de la Guerra restoration.

The excavation took place over the course of a couple years. In the early 1980s, a UCSB public-archaeology class had done some initial work on the site. It was during that field school that the tile floor had been discovered. Mike Imwalle would lead a team of contract archaeologists to expose most of the foundations once the three wooden structures had been removed. As with all the archaeology at the Presidio, there was previous disturbance to the site with certain foundations of soldiers' rooms completely gone—in one case, one of the houses had a basement that resulted in complete destruction of the original eighteenth-century foundations.

Archaeologist Mike Imwalle had begun working at the Presidio in February 1987 on the comandancia excavation as a subcontractor of Woodward-Clyde, an architectural design firm. Vance Benté, who had done the final Chapel archaeology as a private contractor, had joined that company, and I thought it wise to keep Vance involved because of his previous experience with us and enthusiasm for the Presidio project. Continuing as a subcontractor with Woodward-Clyde, Imwalle then moved across the street and oversaw the excavations there from 1988 to 1991. After that, architect Milford Wayne Donaldson and his company were hired to begin to design the buildings. The archaeology had revealed sections of the foundations of ten rooms: an indoor kitchen, officer quarters, regular soldier quarters, a large section of defense wall, garden cross walls, and, most important, the foundations of a two-story tower. The tower foundations, almost double the thickness of the other room foundations, confirmed the existence of the two-story tower identified on the 1820s Vischer plan. Also, the previously opened small section of tile floor was completely uncovered and found to be fully intact inside one of the rooms. This was one of the common soldier and family rooms that normally would have only a packed adobe floor. It was reasonable to assume that after the 1812 earthquake that severely damaged the comandancia, the commandant and his family took up the common soldier rooms in this section of the Presidio. The room with the tile floor likely was the residence of José de la Guerra and his family from 1815 to 1826.

Aerial view of the northeast corner of the Presidio showing exposed foundations after archaeological excavations, circa 1988. *Courtesy SBTHP*

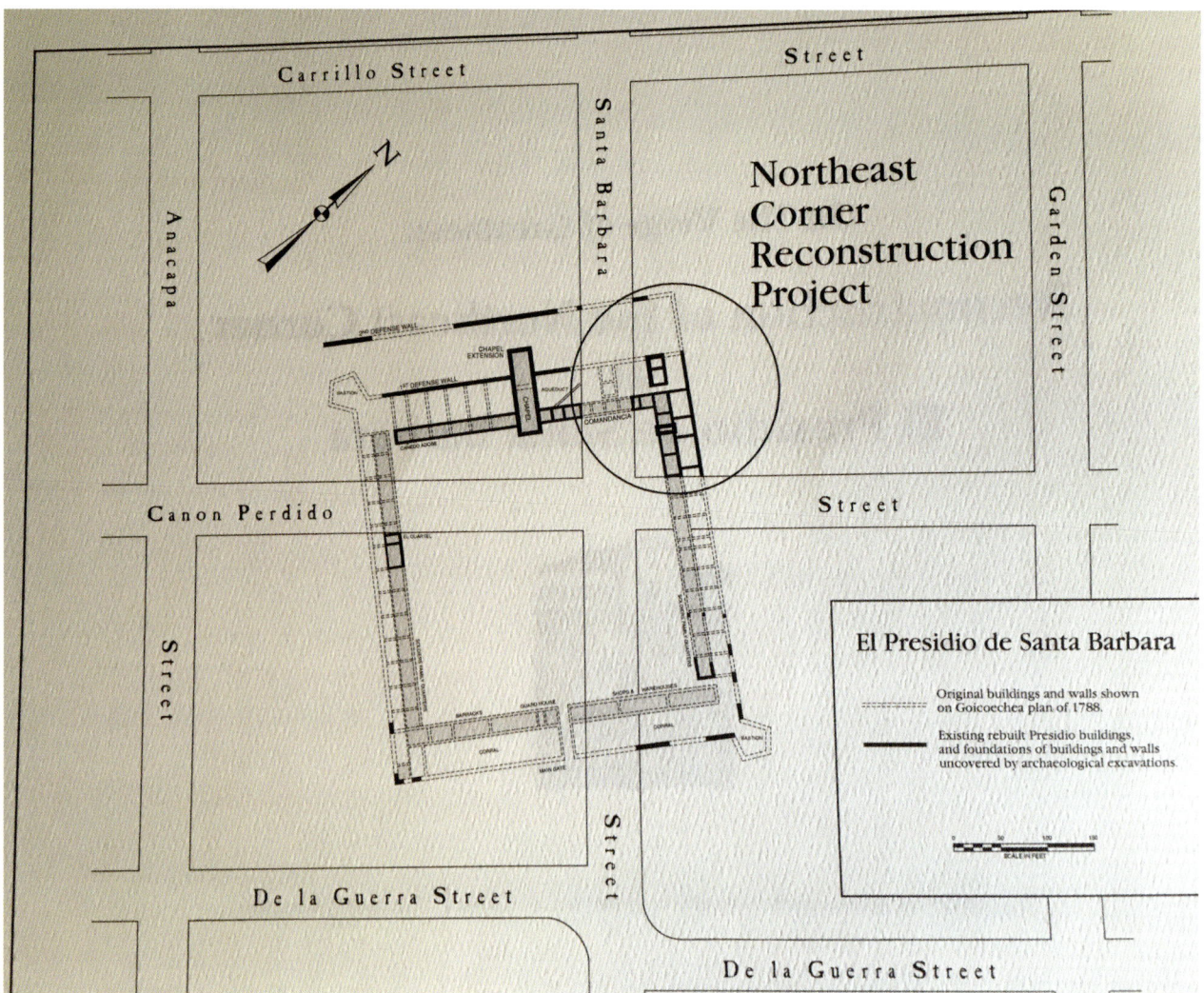

Overlay of the original surviving eighteenth-century ground plan of the Presidio on the modern city streets. This plan was used to fill in areas where original foundations had been destroyed. It is one of the most important documents for rebuilding the Presidio. A later 1820s plan confirmed the archeological discovery of a two-story on the site. *Courtesy SBTHP*

Evidence of the 1812 earthquake was found in one of the rooms where the roof had collapsed and there was a completely intact surviving roof tile, which confirmed the size of the tiles used on the building. It is possible that the building collapsed after the earthquake, but needless to say, the several thousand roof tiles made for the reconstruction of the northeast corner were based on the size of the discovered tile. All of our tile, beginning with the Chapel, came from local retired fireman George Davidson, who had a side-business in Tecate, Mexico, and with his Mexican crew fired roof and floor tiles there and then hauled them by truck to our site. He always produced high-quality tile during my years as director—and produced the tiles to the historical dimensions we requested.

As mentioned, there were sections of rooms that had been completely obliterated but also foundations completely intact that rose above the original historic grade. Among these rooms was the two-story tower. The question then became how to preserve as much of these original foundations as possible. Donaldson and his engineer Michael Krakower came up with a corner-pylon concept. That is: a pylon was sunk into the ground on the corners of all the buildings to a required depth. Then aboveground, a poured column for each corner was raised to the roofline. Horizontal steel rebar set at various courses tied the building together. This meant that 90 percent of the original foundations could be saved—a rather ingenious solution. Today when looking at the rebuilt two-story tower, one can see exposed some of the intact foundation on which the adobe bricks were laid. There were several rooms where the foundations were only partially remaining, and stonemasons built them to the proper height, making sure to identify what was original and what was replacement with a colored mortar. Where there were no foundations, we used the Goicoechea/Fages plans to design the floor plan. Remember, those plans had details telling us locations of doors and whether the rooms had planked or open-beamed ceilings.

Some questions were never answered and we had to use educated guesses. This included whether the defense walls had ramparts. Some on the restoration committee argued yes; others said there was evidence that muskets could have been fired from the rooftops of the buildings. We did put in a rampart but it turned out to be a bad idea because water pooled on it and damaged the building, and it had

The northwest corner under construction, with bricks in the foreground to be used to finish the adobe work at the site. *Courtesy SBTHP*

The northwest corner reconstruction crew celebrates the raising of the beams. Kenny Ruiz, the construction supervisor, is far left and the author is second from the right. *Courtesy SBTHP*

to be removed. Another interesting design issue was how to connect the northeast corner with the building across the street, namely the comandancia. The American street grid cut right through the section that was the commandant's bedroom. The solution was to project the officer's living room further out in the street, and have a glass window like the one across the street to look at both sides of the street at the respective buildings. We also would reset the stones in the street to where the original foundations had been. Since this required an encroachment permit with the city, we applied and received permission on condition that we would maintain the stonework. Now twenty-plus years later, it is getting close to needing repair.

Sources of Funding for the Northeast Corner Project

Around 1993, the SBTHP had finally a set of plans for the northeast-corner project to take to the city and the state, from whom we received approvals. Thus began the next phase of reconstruction. Builder Kenny Ruiz, who came on board with the comandancia project, put together a team of Mexican nationals, from whom we required documentation of their legal status. There were never more than five people working on the project. Plus, with Tim Aguilar and his team of two employees, we began filling the front yard of the Presidio with adobe bricks. The project was going to require twenty-five thousand to thirty thousand adobe bricks. All of this was going to require some fundraising and I began the cobbling-together process again. I wrote up copy for a brochure that I previously mentioned titled "On the Verge of Greatness" and solicited our members, foundations, and a few other sources. The Santa Barbara Foundation and the Jackson Family Foundation continued their ongoing support. Over the years, their grants totaled well over a half million dollars.

Two new sources of funding also came on board. The Redevelopment Agency of the City of Santa Barbara began funding our projects in an amount to well over a million dollars. The second source came in the person of Robert Erburu. Bob was one of the most distinguished businessmen of southern California, rising to be the CEO of the Times Mirror Company and becoming a leading philanthropist in southern California. He served as president of the board of the Huntington Library, the Getty Trust, and the National Gallery of Art in Washington, D.C. How did this distinguished gentleman become involved in our adobe-brick world? It turned out that Bob was a descendant of a Santa Barbara Presidio soldier and the cousin of one of our board members, also a descendant, Elizabeth Hvolboll. Bob made several visits to the Presidio with his wife, Lois, who continued supporting the SBTHP after Bob was struck down with Alzheimer's disease. The SBTHP began receiving grants from the Ahmanson Foundation (on whose board Bob served) for our projects, including for the northeast corner reconstruction, and we received grants from other boards that Bob served on, not to mention personal donations. Somehow the SBTHP always found a way to keep its projects going by its time-and-materials approach—the projects never shutting down due to lack of funding. By about 1995, the walls were halfway up on the northeast corner, and I remember walking Prince Felipe of Spain through the site during that time. More on the prince's visit to come.

Trees for Casa and Presidio Harvested in Local Mountains

Another example of taking advantage of a situation to the benefit of the reconstruction was the Marre Fire in the mountains above Santa Barbara in 1993. By this time, not only was the SBTHP rebuilding the northeast corner but also a full-on aboveground archaeology program was underway at Casa de la Guerra. In room one of Casa de la Guerra, we discovered that the round rafters were original from the 1820s. From a sample we sent out to a laboratory, we learned that the wood was white pine, such as grew in the mountains above Santa Barbara near Figueroa Mountain—yes, in the area where the Marre Fire had happened. We contacted the US Forest Service, which had helped us identify the wood of the Casa's rafters. In addition, during this time, the ever-busy Mike Imwalle had identified the rounded post-holes for the rafters of El Cuartel, one of the two surviving original eighteenth-century Presidio rooms. Thus we knew that similar construction was used at both the Presidio and the Casa—as pertained to the roof structure, at least.

Staff at the US Forest Service answered in the affirmative that we could cut down trees whose bark was fire-damaged and that would have to be cut down anyway. With our in-house construction team, we proceeded to cut down all the wood that was needed for both the Presidio northeast-corner project and the Casa restoration. So I count the US Forest Service as one of our great donors as that wood supply saved us thousands of dollars. The next step was to get the trees down to the Presidio and the Casa.

We rented large trucks and I can't remember who drove them. Maybe I don't want to remember as I might learn that the person did not have the proper licensing. But the driver was able to bring the trees down the mountain without incident and deposit them in front of the Presidio and Casa de la Guerra, where they were cut into beams, rafters, and possibly doors and floors, the latter for Casa de la Guerra. Also, the buildings at the Presidio needed Arundo reeds to lay over the rafters, and

Fire-damaged trees salvaged from Los Padres National Forest with permission of the US Forest Service. Many such loads provided lumber for the Presidio reconstruction and Casa de la Guerra restoration projects. *Courtesy SBTHP*

Unloading logs at the Presidio. *Courtesy SBTHP*

those grow along most creek beds in Santa Barbara County. It was easy to get permits to clip these out of the creeks as they are considered invasive and happened to be brought up to Alta California by the Spanish for the purpose we were using them for. The Spanish brought them over from the Old World, but in Michele's and my many travels in the Mediterranean, we encountered these reeds along creek beds in Spain, Italy, and Greece. Native to the Middle East, Arundo reeds are a caning material that looks like bamboo. One of the nastiest jobs is tying the reeds down on the rafters with straps made from cowhides. The stench of the straps while soaking and then being sliced into strips is very unpleasant—probably the most unpleasant of all the work. The lack of iron and forges on the frontier led to hides becoming a substitute for nails. For the first couple projects, including the Chapel, board member Bill Luton, who contributed in so many ways to the SBTHP, brought down some hides from his ranch. After his death, we had to go to Los Angeles to purchase them.

Some of the rebuilt rooms had tile floors put in (such as in the officer's quarters; in the common soldiers' quarters, we retained the adobe-packed floors). In some instances, human urine was used as a hardening substance for the dirt floors. Life could be pretty primitive on the frontier.

There are other details that went into the northeast-corner project that included things like disguised plugs in the floor for lighting at night events. The locks as well were of a modern variety but hidden inside the door so that the visitor would not see them. Also, the doors were planked rather than paneled as had been done on the padre's quarters—this the result of more recent, better research on the subject. Every time I think back to those accusing the SBTHP of creating a fake fort, I am reminded just how much effort went into trying to make the reconstruction feel as authentic as possible.

The construction phase of the northeast corner was over by 1998. That was followed by installing exhibits, one of which—the Memorias and Facturas exhibition—I mentioned earlier in the discussion of the publication of *Documenting Everyday Life in Early Spanish California*. Also, we hired the guru of early-California kitchens, Edna Kimbro, who designed the *cocina* in the rebuilt northeast corner. With an *horno* (oven), *comales*, and other appurtenances, the *cocina* serves to this day as one of the leading living-history rooms during our special public interpretive days. The tile-floor room has been left empty but open for viewing. One unanticipated wonderful thing that resulted from this project was thanks to the green thumb of Mike Imwalle, who comes from a family that operates a wholesale-vegetable business. He introduced early-California fruits and vegetables to the backyards of the soldiers' quarters, including original vines from Mission San Gabriel. The wine produced from them—not so good. While I end on a sour note—admittedly a bad pun—I think my enthusiasm for the reconstruction peaked as we moved into future reconstruction projects that would have their progress impeded by major political and economic events at the turn of the millennium.

Casa de la Guerra: Restoration Versus Preservation

During the 1990s, our adobe world was front and center. As we were doing the northeast corner of the Presidio, we had another major project underway at Casa de la Guerra with its thirteen rooms and large porch (or *corredor*, as it is called in Spanish) that doubled its square footage. With so much going on at the same time, I eventually supported hiring my longtime friend from graduate school in the history department at UCSB, Patrick O'Dowd. He would be mostly in charge of the Casa restoration.

Before Patrick moved from the board to the staff, the SBTHP had begun to look at the building and think about where we wanted to end up with this historic site. Escrow had closed in 1989 and El Paseo was sold, and Casa de la Guerra was ours mortgage free and, as a museum property, tax exempt. By 1990, with most of the rooms still rented as stores, we decided to take one room back of the thirteen and began peeling back the walls. That particular room had been Don José de la Guerra's office with a stairway that led to the two-story tower behind it. That tower had been demolished by the time El Paseo was built, but we had a good photographic record of it. Interestingly, it was about the same size as the tower at the Presidio, and it is likely that Don José copied it for his very own tower. That is, if the Presidio tower still existed when he lived in the Presidio. That fact is not certain. So today if you look at the two-story tower at the Presidio, it looks very much like the one that was at Casa de la Guerra to the end of the nineteenth century.

The office itself still had most of the original beaded ceiling beams and we peeled off plaster from the walls. There was an outside door to the veranda, and archaeologists soon figured out that this door had originally been a window. When we got to restoring this room later, we closed off the door, leaving a window with the reveal. This archaeological discovery became very typical of what was to be uncovered at the Casa as we ventured deeper into the adobe walls, floors, and ceilings in the other rooms and veranda. We initially hired two preservation professionals to come up with a plan for restoring the building. They were typical in their notions of treating a historic building and came up with a flow-of-history proposal. I went along with it at first, and at the same time we decided to move ahead with a seismic retrofit for which we received a state preservation grant. The retrofit used the typical method of tying the building together with a bond beam that wrapped around the top course of each room's adobe walls. That retrofit would be reversed later when we changed our approach from preservation to restoration.

The acting director of the State Historic Preservation Office (SHPO) in Sacramento came down to the site to discuss the professional preservationists' proposal to capture various phases of the building's history, which ran into four different restorations over the course of the building's 170-year history. The SHPO said that proposal was not acceptable because it included rebuilding and thus adding different periods of history to capture the flow of history of the adobe. Secretary of Interior standards encouraged preserving the flow of history, but not re-creating it. The SHPO had some control over us because he could require our returning funding for the seismic retrofit that his office had provided a grant for. We were at a bit of a standstill. Never a dull moment at the SBTHP—we were also back into the political maelstrom.

Meanwhile, the ever-present Mike Imwalle, who was still working in 1990 with Woodward-Clyde, moved from room eight in the Casa to the east wing and began a major uncovering of all the rooms in this section. Mike and his helpers removed

Archaeologist Mike Imwalle at Casa de la Guerra. Archaeology started slowly in one room of the house, circa 1989. *Courtesy SBTHP*

The interior of the east Wing of Casa de la Guerra after archaeology. Eventually SBTHP decided to do a total restoration of the Casa de la Guerra inside and out. *Courtesy SBTHP*

all the wood floors in these rooms. One of the first discoveries was there had been a change in the configuration of the rooms. There were two walls that were made of wood and plasterboard, but on the ground between where the walls had been were the remains of the foundation of an adobe wall. As we approached committing to a restoration of the early period of the adobe, one of the results was to rebuild the adobe wall on its original foundations and not the later walls. Thus the adobe shrunk by one room to twelve rooms. Doors and windows were also reconfigured, and ceiling beams had to be replaced. Also, it was determined that there was an attic above the ceilings in these rooms that may have served as play or sleeping areas for the children of the large de la Guerra family. A model of the house that is today in the museum shows this attic.

I will be presenting some of the highlights in what follows, but eventually a separate publication on all the discoveries made through archaeology should be condensed from Mike's final Casa de la Guerra archaeological report completed in 2003. These discoveries were astounding and served to guide the restoration. I would say that at least 90 percent of areas restored were based on the physical evidence archaeology provided.

Among the phenomenal finds were those uncovered on the porch or veranda or, as the Spanish sometimes call it, *el corredor*. In the history of the adobe, there were four different versions of the porch or *corredor*. The original Spanish one came down in the Fort Tejon earthquake of 1857 and was replaced by a wood-post porch. Yet another appeared after 1900, and the El Paseo version happened around 1923. It was assumed based on some local history lore that the tile floor on the porch was original. We weren't so sure that was the case and began looking underneath certain areas. I am not certain of the precise time this work commenced, but it turned out to be one of the major revelations. No, the tile floor was not original to the early adobe, we learned. Under the tiles, we found the cement bases of the original adobe columns for the porch-roof structure. This meant the tile had been laid over the foundations sometime after the Fort Tejon earthquake and thus was there at the earliest sometime after 1857. If you don't look, you don't find. It turned out that that first flooring of the porch was packed earth mixed with some lime. This flooring too was re-created in the final adobe restoration.

The next revelation came when the chicken-wire plaster was removed from the wall of the porch area. One of the great conservation measures of the Casa de la Guerra restoration was the removal of this chicken-wire plaster, which in the long run does damage to the original adobe walls—pulling away from the walls in time and damaging the bricks, and then allowing moisture to be wicked up and do more damage to the unamended adobe blocks. Tons of this plaster was removed all around the adobe and replaced with a natural adobe plaster and then re-whitewashed. This requires that every so often, the walls be patched and re-whitewashed. A perfect job for volunteers—sometimes done by students as a school project.

Behind the wall underneath the roof of the porch, the archeologists noted that there were post holes in the walls. These turned out to be the original holes for the rafters of the 1820s porch—another exciting discovery. So we now knew from the bases of the original columns their size and shape. The archaeologists then measured the angles of the holes, and the architects for the projects then determined the height of the original roof over the porch. Square columns at Mission Santa Barbara were used as examples for the former adobe columns. There was no way the replacement columns would survive earthquakes and therefore they had to be made of concrete with rebar, but faced with adobe material to look as they would have originally. A similar issue of a structure surviving an earthquake was encountered when the SBTHP built the Presidio Chapel bell tower. More on that to come.

Casa Corredor during restoration. All lumber came from harvested trees in Los Padres National Forest. *Courtesy SBTHP*

Completed Casa de la Guerra Corredor, circa 2005. *Courtesy SBTHP*

Casa de la Guerra fully restored. *Courtesy SBTHP*

There you have it—thanks to archaeology, the SBTHP was able to reconstruct the Casa's porch to the appearance of the 1820s to the 1840s. By now, the SBTHP was totally committed to one of the most intriguing restoration projects ever undertaken on any building in California.

How to Pay for This Expensive Project

Perhaps it is best to take a break from this detailed look at the Casa de la Guerra restoration and ask the question of how we paid for it. Enter Charles Storke, whom we have already met in this epic story of the SBTHP. As noted, Storke took a great interest in the project by the very fact that it faced Plaza De La Guerra across the way from the *News-Press* building, where he had spent his early career. Interestingly, while still at the paper quite a few years before he left for Mexico, he was spending December 7, 1941, at the celebration of the completion of the restoration and reconstruction of Mission La Purísima in Lompoc when he received a phone call from his publisher father to get back down to Santa Barbara—Pearl Harbor had been bombed. He liked to tell that story, and it seemed fitting to retell it in connection to another restoration that he gave so much of his time to—the home of the most prominent person of nineteenth-century Santa Barbara, José de la Guerra.

Charles decided to take on the task of raising the money needed for the Casa restoration—and one couldn't have had a more committed, appropriate person to do it. His father, by most accounts, was considered the most prominent and powerful man of twentieth-century Santa Barbara, and it seemed fitting the son would be involved with preservation of the adobe mansion of the most prominent man of nineteenth-century Santa Barbara. It was splendid to be with him and watch him in action. I had at least a half dozen lunches with him, several at the Casa de Sevilla restaurant, where he would broach the subject with the person he was hosting of donating to the SBTHP. It was really hard to say no to him, and usually after the lunch, a check would come in the mail. Many checks arrived also from people I never met and only a few dared say they couldn't contribute, writing letters of apology. Many of these checks had several zeroes after the numbers, and the amount quickly rose to well over several hundred thousand dollars. Storke also had his friends working to raise money for the project, including banker Roy Gaskin, who was also on the SBTHP board and a president during this time. One day, Roy brought in a check from a local insurance company for a cool twenty thousand dollars.

Probably the individual donation that pleased Charles the most came from local philanthropists Pierre and Ailene Claeyssens. Charles invited them to see the restoration and we gave them the tour. Two days later, a check for one hundred thousand dollars arrived, and I called Charles, who drove down to see it. We named the dining room in the Casa after the Claeyssens, and the plaque is above the front door of the *comedor* to this day. The staff, including myself, helped put together solicitation pieces that were mailed to SBTHP members and other prospects. Patrick O'Dowd also became a player in the fundraising, helping open the door to the city's Redevelopment Agency, which provided significant funds.

It was wonderful to be part of this successful effort, albeit as time went by, Charles came in one day and asked how much more we needed to finish the project as he was getting a little burned out from all the time he was putting in. Estimating the cost of a restoration project that was being carried out by the typical SBTHP approach of time and materials was a little tricky. I consulted with Patrick and we decided that the number was about five hundred thousand dollars. Charles then sold some stock that went up the day he sold it another twenty-five thousand dollars or so, and we received a check for five hundred thousand and change within a week.

Not to my surprise, we turned out to need more funds to complete the project, and the Redevelopment Agency came to our assistance. All told, the project cost well over two million dollars and would have never happened without Charles. That is why there is a plaque honoring him on the east wall of Casa de la Guerra facing the plaza. As if this were not enough, he set up a charitable remainder trust through his children, one of which came to us after the untimely death of his son Paul; a room in Casa de la Guerra has been named after Paul.

Charles Storke, major donor and fundraiser for the Casa de la Guerra restoration. *Courtesy SBTHP*

One other room in the Casa, the sala, was named after the E. L. Wiegand Foundation, which had made a large grant to the project. Patrick had been responsible for that donation, making an interesting connection with José de la Guerra being a devout Catholic, as was E. L. Wiegand, who had made his fortune as an inventor. Again, as I explained before, the SBTHP had an uncanny way of piecing together funding for its projects.

Which brings me to one last example of this at the Casa: The area on the west side of the house is an alleyway between the Casa and the Westen Building, which faces State Street on the corner of De La Guerra Street. That area for years was an eyesore collecting trash and homeless flotsam. After a conversation with Derek Westen, who was in the process of restoring his building, we approached the Redevelopment Agency with a joint plan: He would create an upgraded enclosed trash area behind his building and we would restore a historic drainage area that archaeology had identified. The Redevelopment Agency of Santa Barbara funded our portion of the project, and the problem was solved to the benefit of both parties and the surrounding neighbors. For his efforts, Derek was given the George and Vivian Obern Preservation Stewardship Award in 2007 by the SBTHP for restoration of his building. (There is an even more fascinating story to come at the Alhecama Theatre with Derek in the pages ahead.) To say the least, Charles Storke, who had died by the time we did this alleyway project, would have been pleased with this outcome.

CREATIVE MUDSLINGING IN FULL SWING 129

Final Phase of the Casa de la Guerra Restoration

Looking back at all we did in the 1990s, I think I was too busy to be overwhelmed by it. Plus, it was really exciting to be part of something that was making a significant impact on Santa Barbara and on the whole state, for that matter.

The revelations kept coming in one by one as the archaeologists continued their aboveground excavation at the Casa. Room five at the northwest corner was one of the early places we had begun to examine use of the various rooms. Once the tenant had vacated the room, around the time we closed escrow, we noted an adobe counter that wrapped around the back of the room. We asked historian Norman Neuerburg to take a look, and his first surmise was that this could be the Casa's kitchen. That would have been unusual, as most early kitchens were built in separate, freestanding buildings. The danger of fire obviously was an issue. As we got further into the project in the 1990s, we soon learned that this was the *bodega*, or wine cellar/room. This made sense as de la Guerra's personal wealth had spread to the Simi Valley south of Santa Barbara, where he was growing vineyards. Through research, we learned that some of the wine produced from these vineyards won prizes at the 1776 Centennial in Philadelphia. This room was right next to the dining room with a *zaguán*, or entranceway, between the two rooms, where wine and supplies could be delivered. In the *zaguán*, we discovered a loft (at least the post holes were there from it) where supplies were probably lifted to the attic above.

Eventually it was determined that a lean-to outside the back of the house was the area for the kitchen, and the SBTHP was in possession of a painting of the back side of the Casa that showed this lean-to. By the way, the doorway into the *bodega* turned out to be originally a window, and that was reconverted to that configuration.

One of the major concessions of the new owners of El Paseo was giving up the large opening that had been cut through room six into El Paseo. This happened after the major rehabilitation work at El Paseo had been completed, and local developer Bill Levy, then managing the El Paseo partnership, agreed to our closing this opening in exchange for reopening the historic *zaguán* previously mentioned. This was a real coup for the restoration and it enabled us to have the whole dining room intact.

But what a story that turned out to be, as tons of concrete had to be removed and power tools had to be used carefully to protect the adobe walls, which lacked the strength of reinforced concrete. Too much vibration might have cracked and seriously damaged the adobe. Then the roof structure above had to be braced while the adobe walls in the front and rear of the rooms were rebuilt. By the way, the adobe bricks used in Casa de la Guerra were measured and found to be slightly larger than the blocks we had found intact at the Presidio, so the adobe size was adjusted to align with those at the Casa. Details, details. Today a visitor who sees the dining room has no realization that there was once a gaping hole in this room, or that with the passageway the room was reduced in size by about a quarter. I should mention also at this point that Kenny Ruiz was in charge of the construction team that he brought over from the Presidio. One can't say enough about these workers—the best thing one can do for them is keep them employed, which we did without stop using our time-tested time-and-materials approach.

As work on the west wing commenced, the Casa de la Guerra committee made restoration decisions based on evidence archeologist Mike Imwalle presented to them. One of the doors between the *sala* (living room) and José de la Guerra's office was determined to be original, and duplicates for other rooms were made. One of the myths of the house having tile floors was put to rest, so to speak, when evidence of sleepers and markings left on the walls set the height of wood floors, and all the floors were rebuilt using random planking. Not to be forgotten were the logs brought down from the national forest not just for the Presidio but also for Casa de la Guerra, which provided the lumber needed for ceiling-beam replacement, door frames, and doors.

A disguised lighting system was put in all the rooms in the north wing, which was to be restored to the prime interpretive period of the 1820s to the 1840s. The east wing, which was to accommodate changing exhibits, was fitted with a special museum-lighting system.

The archaeology of the west wing of the Casa had more than its share of exciting discoveries. One of the more important ones came to light in room one facing De La Guerra Street, which I alluded to in my discussion of the northeast corner of the Presidio. This room had, as mentioned, the original rafters. Crossbeams supporting a ceiling were removed and that meant, as in the original room, it was now open to the roof structure with the rafters visible. The same situation abounded in the *bodega*, an open ceiling to the roof structure. The problem was, with the cross-ceiling structures removed, the retrofit had to be rethought. The architect of the project, Milford Wayne Donaldson, came up with the solution: This was to tie the roof together higher up crisscrossing the room. The only way to do this so that a visitor would not see this modern construction was to lower the beam and caned ceiling, which hid the modern construction. Today when one enters room one and room five, one looks up and sees the historic method of construction, thinking one is looking all the way to the rooftop. Not so, as we now know.

In the west wing, SBTHP research indicated the rooms were used primarily for storage with a store selling goods and supplies in room one, which the SBTHP has furnished. The other rooms were put to practical museum purposes—a small kitchen, a restroom, one room for possible future interpretation of a bedroom since the east wing today is primarily used for changing exhibits. Lastly came the *bodega*, which has been furnished with wine barrels. For a while, the SBTHP had a winery serving in there, but that has been an on-again, off-again situation.

Casa de la Guerra: The Finest Restoration?

Having a reasonable knowledge of the surviving early-California adobes that are primarily from the Mexican period and earlier, I feel I can make the claim that the Casa de la Guerra restoration was one of the best ever undertaken. Patrick O'Dowd and I made road trips to see these adobes: I also saw many of them on my own. Monterey, San Diego, Santa Barbara, Los Angeles, Sonoma. At Sonoma Barracks, Patrick and I answered one of the open restoration questions at Casa de la Guerra: Behind each window, we found large holes in the reveals. We assumed they were from some sort of hinged mechanism connected to the windows. Norman Neuerburg thought it might be some type of wrought-iron fixture. At the Barracks, we noticed these exact holes in the wall, and they turned out to be post holes for logs that secured the shutter windows. Question answered; problem solved.

Besides picking up other hints along the way, we observed how almost all the early adobes were covered inside and out by later periods of history, and what we saw was not what had been there originally. I prefer not to name names, but we saw also some poor restorations, beams that were badly adzed or not adzed at all and in some cases looking more like telephone poles. Many adobes have cement plastered walls, which bodes badly for the future conservation of the original walls; some buildings have machine-made tiles of improper sizes. One example of a good restoration is the Petaluma Adobe, now a state park near the town of Petaluma. It is a large two-story structure dating from the 1830s—it was supposed to be enclosed but was never finished, and was the property of Mariano Guadalupe Vallejo. The California State Parks Department has been responsible for preserving and carefully restoring some sections of the building.

This is in contrast to Casa de la Guerra, which was a total return of a building to its earliest period that had been covered over with multiple layers of history, some of which were damaging to the building. An example of the damage was the outside west wall that had significant moisture erosion. That has been repaired, by the way. I believe I have given a good sampling of the work undertaken. But there is much more found in the final archaeological report that Mike Imwalle prepared and completed in 2003 on this fascinating ten-plus-year restoration project. I have urged Mike to extract some of the key details from that report and publish them for the knowledge of the docents, the public at large, and anyone interested in how to undertake a detailed restoration project. I do not believe that every adobe in California should have all its layers of history stripped away. That is up to the people who will have to decide when they are faced with repair and maintenance of these fragile buildings. But you will never get an argument from me if one decides to strip away chicken-wire plaster. That is guaranteed to damage the building severely if left in that condition.

Regarding the flow of history, the SBTHP had its own way of letting people know about the various phases of the adobe's history: One was preservation of the layers of paint on the chair railings in the *sala*; another was to rebuild one of the wooden porch columns from after the 1850s and display it in the museum.

It is really important to acknowledge the key people who made this project happen: Charles Storke, the primary funder and the project's inspiration; Patrick O'Dowd, who guided the project through the city's landmark commission and received unanimous votes all along the way; Mike Imwalle, whom I call the Jesuit Genius (he is a graduate of a Jesuit high school) and who with his fellow workers and archaeologists gave us the physical facts we needed to restore the building; and Kenny Ruiz, who with his team did the bulk of the physical labor. The architectural firm of Milford Wayne Donaldson helped us make the right decisions, as did the Casa de la Guerra committee, especially one of its members— art historian Norman Neuerburg.

Yes, I thank them all for the finest restoration of an adobe so far achieved in California.

The Casa at the End of the Millennium

The Casa since its restoration completion in 2001 has been home to important activities and events to this day, and I will touch on some of them as we move into the next millennium. But there were two that bear discussion and elucidation as part of the decade of the 1990s—and were the particular brainchild of Patrick O'Dowd.

First of all, in December 1995, a horrible thing happened during the holidays as Patrick O'Dowd and his wife, Anne, had gone to her family home near Marseille, France, to celebrate Christmas. They have a chalet in the Alps, which they visited, but on the way home with Anne driving, a truck crossed over the road and smashed their car and many others, nearly head on, with such impact that the seat belt actually severed one of Patrick's lungs. Both were seriously injured, but Patrick's injuries were the more severe. He was flown by helicopter to the hospital and received excellent medical attention, in part thanks to his brother-in-law's wife, who was a physician in Marseille. There he remained in critical care for more than a month, after a surgery that involved using a metal-bar method to assist the healing of his lung. It was about two months before he could return to the United States.

After returning to Santa Barbara, he had to ease himself back to work. Fortunately, thanks to Charles Storke, who said forcefully to the board that Patrick needed to be supported in this emergency, he was kept on salary during his time of recovery. I was concerned, as he was in severe pain as the bars that had been installed began to push against his rib cage as he healed. Eventually he found a surgeon here who could remove the bars and he then was able to head toward a real recovery. Full recovery? I can only say yes, from my perspective, because he eventually was able to assume his full duties at the SBTHP and achieve important successes, one of which has been described in his contributions to the Casa de la Guerra restoration. Three other activities had to do with exhibits and a symposium that he organized. I have already described the permanent installation he oversaw in the northeast-corner rooms of the Presidio on the subject of the *memorias* and *facturas*.

Patrick also curated a special exhibition on Bouchard at Casa de la Guerra in its completed east wing in 1998. Patrick's interest in all things French triggered his interest in the Frenchman Bouchard, who is known in California history for his raid on the California coast in 1818, stirring up insurrection with his ships and several hundred sailors and men. His story I told in the section on the original Presidio's history, but Patrick added new information based on his research in French documents.

Besides learning that Bouchard had sailed with Napoleon to Egypt, museumgoers and attendees at his talks became aware that Bouchard was more than a pirate, as he is often portrayed in California history. Bouchard and his crew are seen instead as insurgents in the spirit of Napoleon. In this perspective, he was fomenting revolution in sailing around the Pacific to the Spanish colony of the Philippines and the west coast of North, Central, and South America. In fact, he is a hero of the Argentine independence movement against Spain, and there is a central square in Buenos Aires named after him, as I mentioned in an earlier chapter.

The Bouchard exhibit included borrowing the Van Cina twentieth-century mural that normally hangs at the Santa Barbara County Courthouse and portrays Bouchard's landing in California. The SBTHP also borrowed materials from Argentine museums with the cooperation of the Consulate General of Argentina in Los Angeles. Among the objects borrowed was a bust of Bouchard. All told, the exhibit played off an opening-night event that had as special guest the Argentine consul from Los Angeles, and a local superior court judge who hilariously vacated the charge of piracy against Bouchard and installed him as a local hero and freedom fighter. I also remember an artwork that Patrick had painted of a likeness of an Indian auxiliary soldier who fought alongside his fellow Spanish soldiers. The exhibit and event were fun and educational at the same time.

Plus, the reader sees that a better understanding is derived from seeking the international perspective. Bouchard was more than a pirate. His story is international—French, Argentine, and Spanish. In this, Patrick and I share a way of looking at the world—at history.

Ode to O'Dowd

Patrick and I share something else—the same mentor, Dr. Harold Kirker. We met in fall 1970 at UCSB. From there, both of us began to find Europe as a place to explore and think about. In the 1970s, Patrick left UCSB to teach in Marseille, France. I had already left for Germany with my family in 1974. One might say we both became Europhiles—he more of a Francophile, I more or less a Germanophile. He lives at present with wife Anne in Marseille; I spent all total almost six years in Europe—mostly in Germany and Austria. In 1963, I spent a summer studying German in Salzburg, Austria; in 1966, I spent six months in Europe traveling about;

from 1974 to 1978, Michele, our daughter, Renée, and I were in Germany, where I was on fellowship and taught; then I took seven monthlong trips, some longer, to Europe between 1993 and 2011. Whenever I study something, I like to trace it to its origins and oftentimes that leads back to Europe. Once when I was on the board of a nonprofit, a board member accused me of being Eurocentric, that epithet used these days for those of us seeking a broader perspective in studying the past. I am unrepentant regarding this alleged Eurocentrism. I believe Patrick shares this attitude as well. It is why I much respect his contributions to the SBTHP. José de la Guerra was Spanish born and spent his youth in Mexico City; thus, it is very appropriate that he and his Santa Barbara world be thought about in broader terms than local history.

When we fast-forward to 1999, we close in on completion of the Casa de la Guerra restoration—there is a whole plaza the house is facing and it also happens to be named after José de la Guerra. Patrick, in partnership with the SBTHP, the city of Santa Barbara and its Redevelopment Agency, and UCSB organized an exhibition, symposium, and publication titled "Plaza de la Guerra Reconsidered." The timing of the subject was tied to the fact the city was taking under consideration upgrades to the plaza. So, Patrick jumped into the political cauldron.

Curated by Patrick, a team of others helped him design the exhibition. Among his chief collaborators were Edward Cella, who was a student of architectural history, served on the city's landmark commission, and was a local businessman at the time; and Kurt Helfrich, an architectural historian who was curator of the architecture and design collection of the University Art Museum at UCSB. They put together the exhibition in the east wing of Casa de la Guerra—organized around the history of the four sides of the plaza, and including some of the proposals for the plaza from the 1920s to the present. Unfortunately, to this day the plaza remains a parking lot with a grassy area in the middle. Living in the age of the car, one can imagine the resistance to change among many, including a nonprofit that called itself Cars Are Basic. The exhibition ran from May to the middle of August 1999.

Midway through the scheduled exhibition, a symposium was convened in the chambers of Santa Barbara's city hall under the same title, "Plaza De La Guerra Reconsidered." Patrick brought in scholars and professionals in the fields of historic preservation and urban planning to participate—some who spoke extempore and others who had prepared papers. Among this group were architectural historian Dr. Robert Winter; city Community Development Director Dave Davis; historian Dora Crouch; Milford Wayne Donaldson, FAIA; and Professor Carroll William Westfall, chair of the School of Architecture at the University of Notre Dame. This was an all-star team if there ever was one to hold forth on plazas, past and present. In fact, much time was spent on the past history of plazas as public spaces, from the Greek Agora to the Roman Vitruvius, from the Spanish Plan for the Reformation of the Indies to our very present. A sour note seemed to be struck by Donaldson when he opined why *gringo* plazas don't work. In fact, it was the intrusion of the automobile that was the hallmark of the modern plaza. He contrasted these with earlier examples of plazas that had been more pedestrian and people friendly. In fact, his statement proved prescient, as discussions in the community after the symposium centered around removal of the parking; resistance to that removal prevailed and to this day nothing has changed at Plaza De La Guerra some twenty years later.

But actually, times, they are changing. In the midst of the Covid-19 pandemic, there seems to be a different attitude growing. I have heard that millennials are not as car friendly; in fact, I can remember a few employees of mine who did not even have cars, and that was in the 2010s. In addition, the famous downtown Santa Barbara Pueblo Viejo district, re-created in the Spanish colonial and Mediterranean style of architecture after the 1925 earthquake, has suddenly found itself languishing economically. A lot of this has had to do with the new Amazon economy, and the transition from retail to the service industry of restaurants and bars. Whatever the cause, the main roadway through town, State Street, has been closed and discussions are again underway about what to do with Plaza De La Guerra. There seems to be a much stronger desire not to let the automobile dominate the discussion, and this attitude may spill over to the plaza.

Another area of disagreement previously was the large swath of lawn in the plaza. Most proposals have involved reducing the amount of lawn, if the idea is to make it more of a public gathering space. During Old Spanish Days in August, thousands crowd the plaza for the food service provided by nonprofits and the concerts. By the end of the week, the grass is trashed, and the grassy area has to be fenced off for a month to bring it back to life. There are those who shudder at the thought of the removal of the grass, and those on the other side who prefer more hardscape, which is more event friendly and costs less to maintain. Some sort of compromise will likely result in the long run.

That has brought back to the fore the 2002 publication the SBTHP prepared with funds from the city's Redevelopment Agency: *Plaza De La Guerra Reconsidered: Exhibition and Symposium*. This handsome volume contains a condensed version of the exhibition and essays by the aforementioned authors; it presents for discussion various alternatives for upgrading the plaza. It is possible that the time has come, and all the important research efforts that were put into this symposium and exhibition will bear fruit and have the public impact they deserve. After this time, Patrick O'Dowd left the SBTHP, eventually moving to Monterey, where he became involved with the early Spanish history of that town, and today he is sharing his knowledge of American history, especially of historical personages Thomas Jefferson and John Quincy, through talks at and involvement with the US Consulate General in Marseille. Such is a great way for a historian to spend his retirement.

The Importance and Joy of Archaeology

By now, the importance of archaeology should be apparent in the way it enabled the SBTHP to achieve its goals. Without it, both the Presidio reconstruction and Casa restoration would have been a joke. I feel it is important to single out the personalities and good times that archaeology brought to the SBTHP—from the early days to my later time as CEO. Since 1981, California State Parks staff has been actively involved with approving and reviewing all archaeological work at the site—with reports as required prepared by Mike Imwalle. We have been thorough and had fun at the same time.

I remember my first encounter with archaeology in Alexandria, Virginia, in 1979. This was the town closest to Washington's Mount Vernon and where our

Trust volunteers (clockwise, starting at top): Richard Whitehead, Russell Ruiz, Lynn Spear, and Mary Spear at the excavation on the southwest corner of the Presidio in the 1970s. *Author's Collection*

CREATIVE MUDSLINGING IN FULL SWING   137

Students in Dr. Robert Hoover's Field Sch[ool] working at the back defense wall of the P[re]sidio in recent years. *Courtesy SBTHP*

first president frequented the famous Gadsby's Tavern. There was a historical-archaeology program in place and the person in charge was Pamela Cressey, a PhD in archaeology. I think she hired me part-time primarily because we grew up in the same town—Glendale, California—and attended high school there, I at Glendale High School and she at the crosstown school of Herbert Hoover High School.

Emerging in the 1960s as a new field in anthropology, historical archaeology, unlike prehistoric archaeology, has a written, documentary record to compare with what is found in the ground or aboveground when dealing with extant structures. Prehistoric archaeology has to re-create the past in most instances based solely on what is found in an excavation. Another fellow historian who was working with me at the Alexandria Archaeology Research Center housed in the old World War I torpedo factory along the Potomac used to be a kindred spirit, so to speak. He shared my resistance to some of the assertions of the archaeologists who seemed to me a little too quick to speculate on the meaning of the physical evidence they had uncovered. I was trained in documentary research and hadn't thought much about other ways to go about writing history. I used to go back and forth with a PhD archaeologist from Brown University and I remember when it appeared I might be getting the upper hand in the argument—he would say to me, "That sounds like a California idea." I did notice a decidedly anti-California attitude in some of my intellectual encounters on the East Coast. One of the graduate-student interns whispered to me one day that I sure seemed to get people riled up. That said, I did come to appreciate the information derived from excavating the privies of Alexandria, which contained some fascinating trash remains. Even the remains of a baby had been found in one of the privies. That experience in Alexandria was very brief—about six months—but it foreshadowed a world that was going to become vitally important to my day-to-day work at the SBTHP.

I have recounted earlier how we left Washington, D.C., to return to California in 1980 and I soon was hired to work at the SBTHP. My first assignment put me right back into archaeology as I went to a National Trust conference in San Francisco to meet with a contract archaeologist named Vance Benté. One last phase of archaeology was needed to expose the Chapel foundations before reconstruction, then remove them and finally replace them with concrete foundations faced with the original excavated foundation stones. I immediately hit it off with Vance, and the Presidio reconstruction committee voted to accept his proposal.

I liked Vance's no-nonsense, high-energy approach that included some use of California Conservation Corps workers. Once we completed the Chapel excavation, we contracted with him for more site excavations that eventually led to the tile-floor discovery on the northeast corner. When Vance went to work with the firm Woodward-Clyde, we stayed with him and hired Mike Imwalle as a subcontractor with that firm. Around 1990, both of them also began the archaeology at Casa de la Guerra.

I need not repeat all the wonderful discoveries made over the years that have already been related. And again I refer the reader to Imwalle's report from 2010 on Presidio acquisition and development for details on the vital importance of archaeology in increasing our general knowledge of presidio history and of building practices at the time.

There were some practical sides to the archaeology that at first seemed less exciting but turned out to be extremely interesting. One of these discoveries began from a near disaster in an El Niño rain year in the 1980s. After a night of heavy rain, I came to the office in the morning to find the floors of seven rooms of the Cañedo Adobe covered with two inches of mud. To the rescue came the CCC members, who spent a couple weeks removing the water-saturated debris. To the day I left the SBTHP, I could still see the mud line at the bottom of the walls, a reminder of that unpleasant incident. What had happened was over the years of archaeology undertaken under archaeologist Julia Costello, the ground surface of the padre's quarters foundations had been lowered, but not the accreted soil behind it. On that rainy night, there was nothing to hold back the mud as it flowed under the back door of the rebuilt padre's quarters.

The first thing we did was make sure to sandbag that area to prevent a future mud event. Next, over a period of several years in a two-phased excavation, Mike lowered the grade behind the padre's quarters to the first defense wall. Some corrective measures were also implemented that helped the flow of the water in a pipe that ran underneath the padre's quarters to the street. Much later in 1992, Mike Imwalle lowered a section of the surface between the first and second defense walls down to the historic Spanish grade. This also improved the drainage situation. The Redevelopment Agency of Santa Barbara funded this phase.

As usual when you dig on a historical site, something turns up unexpected. In this case, we came across a burial that was excavated and sent to UCSB for study. It was determined that the remains were of European origin. What started out as a simple, practical attempt to fix a drainage problem surfaced a site that turned out to be a cemetery of the Presidio. This was fascinating enough, but SBTHP board member Paul Mills, who had been instrumental in bringing a bronze statue of King Charles III to Santa Barbara cast from an original eighteenth-century mold in Spain, suggested to me that we relocate the statue to the Presidio from an area next to Plaza De La Guerra. I thought it was a capital idea.

The statue was then with approval of the SBTHP restoration committee (name changed from "reconstruction committee") moved to the site where the Presidio burials had been found—outdoors next to the Chapel. This was indeed a fitting place to have the great Spanish king resting over his California colonists and soldiers. That statue, as of this writing, is still in the same location.

There was more archaeology that took place in the 1990s but I am deferring that to the turn of the millennium and the northwest-corner project. I had started out as a big skeptic of archaeology in Virginia, only to be converted to a true believer in the incredible value of it interpreting our site and many other sites, for that matter—Casa de la Guerra perhaps being the best example. Moreover, I grew to love having the archaeologists around. It's a bad pun to say they were down to earth, but they shared personality qualities of construction people who provide valuable physical skills; when the day was done, they were fun to spend some time with. I used to get a kick out of the archaeological team having their safety meetings in the bar of Jimmy's Oriental Gardens across the street. I joined them on many occasions. I felt right at home with them. I will mention only one name: Bob Sheets, who is no longer with us, but was a favorite. "I slit the sheets and sheets slit me" was harder to say after a beer or two.

I can't help with my Shakespeare obsession but think of the Bard's *Henry IV, Part 1* and Prince Hal's jovial moments with Falstaff and others at the Boar's-Head Tavern. But like Prince Hal, I had to come to the awareness that my fate was to move beyond the jolly to the more serious business: that is, property acquisition, which I came to realize was a critical part of the future of the Presidio project. To this story I will turn after discussing the SBTHP's learning process in its conservation practices at El Cuartel, a surviving original adobe from the eighteenth century.

Saving El Cuartel

While Mike and his team enjoyed revelry, they could equally get down to serious business. El Cuartel is a case in point. I'm not exactly sure why, but El Cuartel is considered the oldest surviving adobe at the Presidio—built in 1788 with the oldest status in the city. I mention this because the Cañedo Adobe across the street is probably a few months older, as the original fort was built in sections and the Cañedo was in a section that was built before El Cuartel. Part of the issue with the Cañedo may have to do with the significant alterations that took place on it in the 1940s, leaving doubt about just how much of the remaining adobe could be considered original. Elmer Whittaker and his wife had restored and built their residence around the original structure. The same probably could be said of El Cuartel, however; when Canon Perdido Street was cut through the Presidio site, half of one of the rooms of El Cuartel had to be lopped off and then a wall rebuilt. In addition, the roof on El Cuartel is not original, and its roof tiles are smaller than the originals and are machine-made .

The SBTHP also made some other non-historic changes to El Cuartel when the SBTHP acquired it in 1963. Pearl Chase had installed a heated concrete-slab floor; in addition, a cement plaster was used that traps moisture in the adobe walls. The concrete floor also moved moisture toward the walls. Water is the enemy of unamended adobe. One last inherent problem was a high wall constructed by the post office on its property that shielded the back of the building from sunlight and thus also led to moisture deterioration of the bricks.

Adobe repair at El Cuartel in 1980s. Note the concrete, which later is removed. *Author's Collection*

When I arrived at the SBTHP in 1981, I hired two professional preservationists to repair that back wall. Adobe blocks had to be replaced, but we made the mistake of using blocks that had been stabilized with emulsified asphalt. In follow-up studies, we became aware of the rule of thumb to use like materials when repairing a historic building. We should have used unamended adobe. One of the reasons is in an earthquake, the building may be prone to more damage if stronger materials push against and damage weaker materials.

Mike Imwalle learned from these mistakes of others and in the 2000s worked with his team to stabilize the adobe—this included basal-erosion repair (with unamended materials), some roof repair, and, most important, removing the concrete slab. We also had an agreement with the post office to remove the wall behind the adobe to permit sunlight to help keep the adobe wall dry. Unfortunately, with the attack September 11, 2001, security overrode this agreement, and the agreement has never been implemented. Nor has a seismic retrofit of the building been done. I am sure Imwalle will keep the SBTHP board and the California State Parks Department apprised of the need to lower that wall and do the retrofit, which includes reengineering the building to hold the larger, historical-size roof tiles. Meanwhile, I still think it is worth having a discussion about whether the Cañedo Adobe at least deserves to be considered a coequal as the oldest building in the California State Parks system, oldest in the city, and second-oldest in the state of California.

Chapter Nine

Some Amazing Presidio Real-Estate Stories

From my experience at the SBTHP, I know that I do not have the temperament to do real estate for a living. The selling part is pretty easy if you believe in your product, but the details of real-estate transactions require patience and concentration and, most of all, the ability to endure the worry of closing escrow. No doubt, my involvement with the El Paseo sale and exchange would have tried anyone's patience, especially considering the escrow remained unclosed for over a year. Real estate is definitely one of those professions in which you never count your chickens before they hatch.

Yet in retrospect, I find almost all the property negotiations were in some fashion unique, and worth the trouble. Nothing could match the El Paseo deal—but I learned a lot about people and human nature in general when one enters real-estate deals. Plus, I made some significant contributions that had long-term, positive economic impacts and advanced the Presidio project. Those contributions came to fruition mostly after the turn of the millennium but sprang from actions and events that took place in the 1990s. Perhaps the most significant of these actions surrounded a parking lot owned by Lino Castagnola that straddled the southeast corner of Santa Barbara and Canon Perdido streets.

To keep somewhat to chronological order, let me first describe several acquisitions that preceded the interesting development around the Castagnola property. One of the no-brainers was the purchase of the store at 137 East De La Guerra Street—within a year of the SBTHP purchase, the state came in to acquire it from us. That was the last parcel that secured the row of stores the SBTHP had acquired in the El Paseo exchange. Per the general plan, those stores were to be demolished sometime in the future.

Then in 1996, Mrs. Leontine Phelan died at age 100. She occupied the historic Rochin Adobe on Santa Barbara Street, which contained the largest section of Presidio foundations still in private ownership. Through the efforts of longtime volunteer Jeremy Hass, the SBTHP had obtained a right of first refusal in case the property were put up for sale. I can't remember the exact details, but at first the family had declined selling the property to the SBTHP, but there was a legal misstep on their part that allowed the SBTHP to force their hand. In essence, the SBTHP threatened to sue the family but at the same time offered to pay the appraised value of the property. To avoid the lawsuit, the family accepted the SBTHP's offer, so in 1996 the SBTHP assumed ownership of the property, which included, besides the adobe, two 1910 wood-frame houses that had been relocated to the site after the 1925 earthquake.

The adobe itself, built in 1856 from the bricks of collapsing Presidio buildings, had significant historical significance and was to be preserved according to the Presidio general plan. The buildings were in dilapidated condition and over time the SBTHP would improve these properties—including putting on a new wood-shingle roof to replace the historic one. That needed a waiver from the city as wood shingles had been banned by city ordinance. Other improvements to the property were made by Anacapa School, which used the adobe for office space. There was a metal garage at the back of the property of close to two thousand square feet. Perhaps someday the SBTHP and the state will use that shed for indoor archaeology as some of the Presidio's foundations lie underneath it.

I mention the state because the California State Parks Department will eventually buy these properties from the SBTHP, but that story is tied to the creation of a new research center, which I will go into in more detail in the twenty-first-century world of the SBTHP.

The SBTHP Purchases the Santa Inés Mission Mills Property

The other big acquisition in the 1990s took the SBTHP northward to Mission Santa Inés near Solvang. Longtime SBTHP supporters Harry and Ellen Knill had acquired the parcel next to the mission that contained two historic mills dating from the mission period, built around 1820. The land amounts to about thirty-five acres. While the owners, the Knills, did archaeology at the site and partially restored the buildings and the reservoirs, reconstructing the walls to their historic height and rebuilding the roofs with handmade tiles. The mills included both a grist and a fulling mill, the latter used for processing wool.

I much admire the Knills to this day for their incredible commitment to interpreting and preserving early-California history. One of the classic examples of this commitment was purchasing land next to the Monterey Presidio chapel in the hope that someday a section of that important Spanish fort, which was the capital of

Harry and Ellen Knill, who sold Santa Mission Mills to SBTHP. *Author Collection*

Alta California for fifty years, could possibly be rebuilt. Unfortunately, the Catholic diocese decided to build a large dining and reception center in the middle of the Presidio parade ground. Seeing the futility of there ever being a revival of the adobe fortress, Harry and Ellen sold their holdings and moved on.

Santa Inés Mission Mills. *Courtesy SBTHP*

Their purchase of the mills was another admirable act of historic preservation. The Knills had offered the restored mills property to the SBTHP to purchase at the amount they had paid for it. The timing didn't seem right in the early 1990s, but the stock market was booming, and by 1995 the SBTHP was, I felt, in a position to acquire the mills. I brought the idea to the SBTHP board: There was some resistance but there was a strong majority who were willing to take the leap. The problem was that most of the SBTHP's assets were restricted to the Presidio and Casa de la Guerra. There was just enough in some unrestricted funds, which included money from Pearl Chase's bequest, to allow the SBTHP to move forward. At the back of the board's and my minds was eventually California State Parks would acquire the property from us and create a new Santa Inés Mission Mills state historic park.

The SBTHP made the great leap from its downtown Santa Barbara and adobe world to Santa Inés Mission Mills entering escrow on the property in 1995. All seemed to be going well, except there was a significant lien on the property—I'm not sure how he worked his magic, but Jeremy Hass got the lien removed. It looked like we were about to close when there arose a glitch, details of which are best left undescribed. Here we were again, stuck in an escrow, and I thought back to the El

Paseo deal and realized that escrow can mean limbo. But it all worked out in the end. There is plenty more to this Santa Inés Mission Mills story that will come out in the next chapter.

God Bless Lino

The 1990s were truly an amazing time at the SBTHP. El Paseo was sold and restored, Casa de la Guerra completely restored, the commandant's quarters and nine rooms of the northeast corner rebuilt—and the Rochin Adobe and the historic mills acquired.

The icing on the cake came in developing an agreement with Lino Castagnola, a member of the famous local Castagnola family, who previously owned the liquor store that his parking lot surrounded and which the SBTHP and the state had previously acquired. The SBTHP had earlier purchased a right of refusal on his parking lot, and unfortunately, after the right of refusal expired, Lino gave no indication of a desire to sell.

A board member came up with the idea of our entering into a lease agreement on his lot, which would keep us actively in contact with Lino and his wife, Helga. There was at least one other developer interested in the property and that made it more imperative that the SBTHP try to protect its interests. At the time, this lot contained the last significant section of Presidio foundations still in private ownership—these included portions of two rooms and a large section of the defense wall. I can't remember now the duration of the lease, but I think it was a long one—I believe twenty years. One of the SBTHP's board members was adamantly opposed to the deal—twenty years, and having to pay Castagnola an agreed-upon rate that was tied to annual cost-of-living adjustments (COLA). It could be a big loser. But the pro-lease board member prevailed and we entered the lease. The outcome was beneficial for the SBTHP. Within a couple years, the value of downtown parking far exceeded the COLA, and the SBTHP actually began turning a significant profit on the lot.

In the meantime, I stayed in contact with Lino, who, with Helga, retired to Ashland, Oregon. In one of those strange coincidental situations, Michele and I own a house in Ashland and we were making two trips per year to attend the Oregon Shakespeare Festival. We made a point to visit Lino, but by the time we did this, his wife, who was twenty years younger than he, took ill and died, so we never met her. On these visits, I just reiterated our desire to acquire his property, and explained its importance in containing a significant part of the original footprint of the Presidio.

Lino hit it off with Michele because of their mutual Italian background, and it turned out that Lino for a couple years had lived in the Italian neighborhood near Griffith Park in Los Angeles, where Michele had been raised. When we met with Lino, there usually was a woman present who was more or less Lino's guardian. Then on one of our visits, there was another person present he had invited—his CPA.

A painted footprint marks the location of the original defense wall on the Castagnola property. *Courtesy SBTHP*

Lino Castagnola, major benefactor to SBTH. *Author's Collection*

He then announced to Michele and me that he was putting the SBTHP and his local Lutheran church in his will, each to receive from his estate half the proceeds from the sale of the property, which would be sold to the SBTHP from his estate at an appraised market value. It meant we would have to pay half its market value. Of course I was blown away by this, and we thanked him for this incredible news. There are some interesting twists and turns to this story that will be unfolded in the chapters ahead—but just let me say at this point: It does have a happy ending.

Managing the Growing Presidio Real-Estate Empire

When El Paseo was finally sold, the SBTHP relieved itself of managing a shopping center with stores, offices, apartments, and, at the time, three restaurants. Conversely, as more and more properties were acquired in the Presidio area, property management was on the rise at the State Park. By the end of the 1990s, the state- and SBTHP-owned properties under SBTHP management were two restaurants, a print shop that turned into a sandwich shop, a private school, one apartment, three residential units, many parking lots, a theater, and artist studios from the 1920s at the Old City College site. The studios were occupied by artists. Many of the rentals, especially the artist studios, were to be temporary income-producing properties while the adobe fort was built out. The parking lots were great income-producers and relatively easy to maintain; the artist studios that I described previously were in poor condition but the artists were paying barely market prices.

The SBTHP still had a management committee, and from 1985 into the 1990s, Office Manager Phyllis Moore took care of renting the properties. Property management has its challenges and one of the biggest was artists in the studios who came to see themselves as permanent fixtures. That would cause some conflict over time, but gradually the SBTHP took back much of that space and put it to other uses, which will be described in the next chapter. Also, the Ensemble Theatre Company (ETC) occupied the Alhecama Theatre but had trouble making a go of it because of the small seating capacity of around 140 seats. Because ETC had a significant following in the community, we felt obliged to work with them and tried hard even though there were times when they missed rent payments. Their situation would finally be remedied near the end of my years at the SBTHP. Both parties came out of the rental situation quite satisfied with the outcome. I am saving the icing on the cake for later in this SBTHP history.

After a while, Phyllis wanted relief from the day-to-day management responsibilities, so I took them on for about two years. I increased the rents and re-rented some of the spaces, but it takes just one or two tenants to ruin your day. Eventually, I welcomed board members' suggestion that we hire a property-management company. The district superintendent of the California State Parks Department agreed to the suggestion and we hired a company. Since the end of the 1990s, professional management has taken care of both the state-owned and SBTHP-owned rental properties. Here I mention again that important business sense of the SBTHP board. I valued the experience of learning something about property management, but the board saw this was not a good use of my time. Handing off property management allowed me to concentrate on our restoration projects and research, museum, and education programs.

Planning: Pluses and Minuses

The staff was growing during these years and now we had around twelve full-time and part-time employees (not counting the construction team that was on payroll because of our time-and-materials approach to our restoration projects). During the 1980s and 1990s, the SBTHP had done a series of board- and staff-planning sessions that called out three- to five-year goals, with the Presidio reconstruction remaining the main focus. With the help of a curator, furnishings were installed in the padre's quarters and comandancia. Now that there were multiple rooms available at the Presidio and the grounds were gradually being returned to the historic dirt hardscape look, elementary school classes started visiting in increasing numbers. Volunteer Cathy Chalfant, a retired elementary-school teacher, handled the dozens of fourth-grade classes that came to the site. We also had a docent team that did other tours. But by the end of the 1990s, the board, led by one board member in particular, felt we needed to have an official education department and a director of it. It did happen, although outside of the planning process and in the middle of a fiscal year. That wasn't a problem financially at the time, as the stock market was growing almost out of control. That wouldn't turn out so well at the end of the 1990s when the NASDAQ went into a spin and salaries had to be cut.

One can argue that this might have been avoided with a better planning process, but in the life of a nonprofit and any business, for that matter, there are moments of irrationality that are seen only retrospectively. This may have been one of those moments, but all's well that ends well. In fact, I remember a couple board members who said they literally hated strategic plans, because when completed they were put in the drawer and forgotten. There is a lot of truth to that, but in the case of the SBTHP, I also remember looking at one of the plans from years earlier that had dozens of objectives and goals and we had completed every one of them. One thing we didn't do was establish long-term financial goals. We talked about increasing the endowment and eventually hired a person to help develop an official endowment program. All said, the SBTHP, because of its financial conservatism, kept deficits to a minimum, and that conservatism seemed more important than having specific financial goals. Also, a healthy relationship with the state ensured that we would remain operators of the Park, whose income continued to grow with each state property acquisition. The operating agreement between the SBTHP and the Parks Department, at first resisted by state unions because it existed outside their influence, became the model for working with other nonprofits around the state when hard times hit the state government and trickled down to the park system. Those hard times tended not to affect the Presidio's operation because our agreement, locked in state law, required that any funds generated in the Park stayed in the Park.

CHAPTER TEN

POMP AND CIRCUMSTANCE: ROYALTY COMES TO THE PRESIDIO

WE COME TO THE CLOSE of the 1990s focusing on one of the great events in SBTHP history. Actually, I am turning back the clock to 1995. My emphasis at the Presidio and at our other sites—including Casa de la Guerra and Santa Inés Mission Mills—has been on the international importance of these historic places. In 1993, we hosted the British consul general at an event celebrating the two hundredth anniversary of the visit of Captain George Vancouver to Santa Barbara; another time, the ambassador of the Philippines came to visit the site where the first Filipino known to be buried in California is located—in the floor of the Presidio Chapel. I previously mentioned the Argentine consul's participation in our Bouchard events at Casa de la Guerra, and just a few years ago the Mexican consul came to the Casa to celebrate Mexico's Independence Day. On more than a dozen occasions, the Spanish consul has come from Los Angeles to participate in SBTHP events at the Presidio.

Towering above all these was the visit of Felipe, the prince of Asturias, heir to the Spanish throne. Spanish dictator Francisco Franco selected Juan Carlos to assume power as Bourbon King of Spain upon his demise, which took place November 20, 1975. After a rocky start that included an attempted military coup in 1981, Juan Carlos stood with the parliament, and democracy was secured for Spain. First in line to the throne after Juan Carlos was his son, Felipe, who came to Washington, D.C., where he completed in 1995 a two-year master of science degree in foreign service at Georgetown University. Before returning to Spain, he did a tour of the United States that included a visit to Santa Barbara.

Fortunately, we had strong relations with the Consulate General of Spain in Los Angeles, which I encouraged, and we were asked by then-Consul General Víctor Ibáñez-Martín Mellado to help coordinate a prince visit to Santa Barbara June 8, 1995. SBTHP past president Vivian Obern, who had close contacts with the Consulate General of Spain in Los Angeles, was going to be out of town during his visit and asked me to take over planning. I was thrilled to help but inexperienced regarding protocols and details such a visit entailed. Enter Carmen Farreras y Duran, vice president of the Casal dels Catalans organization of Southern California and a resident of Santa Barbara and loyal member of the SBTHP. Originally from Barcelona, she put on a major exhibition of artwork in the east wing of the partially restored Casa de la Guerra on the sardana, an ancient folkloric and traditional dance of Catalunya. She even brought a group to dance at the opening of the show. The dancers formed a circle and followed one another in various steps. Carmen, who had become a dedicated volunteer at the SBTHP, was the perfect person to help me with the prince event. By the way, after this event, Carmen traveled to Atlanta to dance with a troupe at the 1996 Summer Olympics—in 1992, Barcelona had hosted the Olympics.

Farreras took the bull by the horns (which I know is a bad Spanish pun) and made sure that the prince spent most of his day with us. I in turn arranged a lunch banquet with the local Wine Cask restaurant; the Northern Trust bank donated the money for it, and Firestone Vineyard donated the wine. In attendance at the lunch in the Presidio Chapel was State Assemblyman Brooks Firestone. (An interesting side story was the buzz that Firestone created among the Spaniards; I found out later that Firestone Tires, pronounced *fee-ray-stoh-nay* in Spanish, had more than 50 percent of the market share in Spain.) Following the opening ceremony with a musket salute and a cannon firing, and after the lunch in the Presidio Chapel, we repaired to a tour outdoors to see the statue of the prince's ancestor King Charles III, where the prince laid a wreath and heard from SBTHP board member Paul Mills, who explained that Prince Felipe's father and mother had donated the statue to Santa Barbara in advance of their planned future visit to our city—a visit that never happened because of the political goings-on in Spain I described above. The prince also greeted around a dozen Santa Barbarans who were direct descendants of the Spanish Presidio.

Farreras, the miracle worker, had arranged that after lunch I would take the prince on a tour of the Presidio's northeast corner (then under reconstruction) and after that walk with him over to Casa de la Guerra. On the way, I showed the prince the plaque and then the wall in the Street in Spain at El Paseo, where the plaque was to be installed commemorating his historic visit to Santa Barbara. Inside the Casa, I talked to him about José de la Guerra and his family, and I asked if José's Noriega name was of Basque origin; the prince responded, "No, Noriega is a Galician name."

As the prince of Asturias, which is a principality on the coast of northern Spain between the Basque country to the east and Galicia to the west, he demonstrated knowledge that helped explain the history of José de la Guerra, who was born in the state of Cantabria, which adjoins Asturias to its west.

The prince also demonstrated his knowledge of history when I showed him a ground plan of the Presidio drawn by California Governor Pedro Fages in 1788. He said that was the same year his ancestor King Charles III had died in Spain. I know if I had asked him about the background of Fages, he would have known he was a Catalan. In fact, many years later in 2007, I visited the town where Fages was born, about thirty miles outside of Barcelona.

SBTHP board member Paul Mills explains that Felipe's parents, King Juan Carlos and Queen Sofia, donated the Charles III statue to honor Santa Barbara's 200th anniversary of the founding of the Presidio. *Courtesy SBTHP*

The author with the prince and Carmen Farreras, who made many of the arrangements for the Prince's visit. *Courtesy SBTHP*

We had the prince for over three hours and enjoyed every minute of it. He is a delightful person and speaks fluent English. At the opening ceremony, the *sargento* of our Presidio *soldados*, Jim Martinez, said to the prince: "Your Highness, it has been 173 years since we turned our facility over to the occupation. We have a faithful garrison now and are ready to restore this Presidio to its rightful allegiance. We request that you be our honorary comandante." To which the prince responded: "I accept, as long as it is honorary." This moment of levity was typical of this wonderful visit that none of us present would ever forget. Jim, by the way, is a direct descendant of Santa Barbara Presidio Comandante Goicoechea.

After leaving the Presidio, Carmen accompanied the prince to Mission Santa Barbara for a tour of the church and mission archive library, which houses the most comprehensive collection of original mission documents and other research materials. This was followed by a reception at UCSB. I heard later from Carmen that after all the hoopla, the prince asked to go for a walk back into town. He, Carmen, and some of his entourage later that evening strolled down State Street, and the handsome 6-foot-5 prince went into a few shops and a bookstore unrecognized. The prince would make a return visit to Santa Barbara in 2013 for a special meeting of

A special issue of SBTHP commemorating the prince's visit. *Courtesy SBTHP*

US and Spanish businessmen held at the Bacara Resort. The SBTHP held a special reception for him at the Biltmore hotel in Montecito, where he greeted a host of SBTHP members and special guests. At that event in November, we showed him the medallion of the Order of Charles III presented to the city in the 1950s—Santa Barbara is the only city in the United States to ever receive that decoration. We also had on display another plaque commemorating the visit of him and his wife, Letizia. Just a few months later, his father, Juan Carlos, abdicated and the prince, now King Felipe VI, ascended to the throne with his wife, now Queen Letizia. More on the Prince's second visit will be mentioned in chapter twenty.

The Santa Barbara Presidio, thanks to the prince's visit, became a popular place for Spanish officials to come visit (such as Mariano Rajoy, who at the time was minister of education and later was prime minister of Spain from 2011 to 2018). Even members of the famous Barcelona soccer team paid the Presidio a visit. Of course, Carmen Farreras had a lot to do with all this. And what better way to end this happy moment in SBTHP history than thanking her for all she did to make the prince's visit memorable. I would be remiss, however, if I didn't thank the staff and volunteers, especially our Presidio soldados, for their participation in the royal visit. We heard later that Santa Barbara had been splashed all over Spanish TV reporting the event, and Carmen's mother was all excited to see her daughter in faraway America. Clearly, a day to remember.

Later that year, the SBTHP published a special edition of *La Campana* on the prince's visit covering all the activities of that day, detailing even the meal served at the lunch banquet. Local businessman Richard Berti underwrote the cost of this special publication and also, I should mention, underwrote a series of photographic competitions that brought Brooks Institute students in David Litschel's class at the local school to photograph SBTHP sites, including the Presidio, Casa de la Guerra, and Mission Santa Inés. These photos have been used over the years in many SBTHP publications.

CHAPTER ELEVEN

My First Twenty Years

AS THE TWENTIETH CENTURY came to a close, I might sum up its last decade at the SBTHP as the "busy nineties." One time I came out of the office when there were people coming and going, meetings, and a spin of activities that seemed to be out of control. I said: "Things are really crazy around here." Jean Liston, our longtime office receptionist, said in response: "Jerry, this is a craziness of your making." *Agreed*, I said to myself.

Both the 1980s and the 1990s had been decades of great progress at the Presidio—restorations and reconstructions, publications, great public events. Comparing the two decades, I would say the main difference was anxiety versus pressure. In the eighties, there were times when one could not know for sure how the politics of the Presidio were going to end up, and one felt left hanging as the El Paseo sale and exchange might collapse during the escrow; in the nineties, there was plenty to worry about with all the balls we had in the air, but that was pressure and the feeling I had was that we would get all our goals done and get them done right, which we did. At the same time, we had museums now open to the public at two sites, and we added more events that kept us even more busy.

I remember several board members complaining that we had too many events going on. In fact, they probably had a point. During Cathy Rudolph's tenure as director of research and of the Research Center, she kept a chronicle of events for a number of years, and the chronicle captured the day-to-day activities of the SBTHP, which included a weekly Elderhostel program that brought on average forty to fifty visitors to the site and required docent-led tours. Elderhostel did, however, donate on average about ten dollars per person and that funding went into general operations. Glancing through the 1995 chronicle, I have to admit I had forgotten many daily activities that kept us more than busy—almost-daily tours, exhibit openings, volunteer adobe-brickmaking days, lectures, concerts, internships, wedding rentals (new at this time), and the regularly scheduled annual park celebrations. And donations were flowing in regularly. No, El Presidio de Santa Bárbara State Historic Park was no longer a sleepy little park, as a state-park historian once described us.

I have mentioned that every year we did a founding-day ceremony April 21. I like to point out that April 21 also is the date of the mythical founding of ancient Rome. Because the Presidio was the first military site of Santa Barbara, I thought we should consider doing a Veterans Day event. The soldiers, most of whom were veterans, thought this was a capital idea. Thus every November from the 1990s on, we had such an event at the Presidio. One year we had military vehicles and equipment on the street and on the site—and the soldier re-enactors from Fort Tejon State Historic Park came to fire their cannon—a loud howitzer. Another year I arranged to have an F-18 fly over. After his speech, the commander of Point Mugu gave the signal to his officer to send the message to the pilot circling the city and it then happened—the plane dipped just above the Presidio. Oops, it rattled windows and the boom apparently scared a lot of the neighbors. I received a call after the event from the mayor telling me never to let that happen again.

That reminds me that during Old Spanish Days in August, we always had an entry in the Friday parade, including some great floats, many designed by Presidio descendants Jim Martinez and Richard Lugo. One year we had not only our contingent but also Mission La Purísima docents in the parade—one of the soldiers in that group had his musket and fired it along the parade route. This very much pleased the crowd—but was not such a great idea for the equestrian entries. Nothing bad happened, fortunately, but word came back to me—no more musket firings during the parade. In the nineties we also started a cantina during Fiesta, but Charles Storke did not like the loud music and raucous behavior and we discontinued it, only to revive it later.

Research in Spain

On a personal level, during this decade, my wife Michele and I did a lot of travel, starting in 1993 with a two-month leave that I took from the SBTHP—one month was spent in Greece and the second in Spain on a research grant that I received from the Spanish Ministry of Culture through a program administered by the University of Minnesota, Twin Cities. Michele was with me for the first two weeks as we went to archives in Madrid and Segovia following research leads on Goicoechea. At one of the military archives in Madrid, there was a giant mural of Franco dressed as a knight errant with his followers surrounding him. I wanted to take a photo of it, but Michele was adamantly opposed to it. I later saw a photo of that interior and the mural had been removed.

After Michele left, I traveled by train to Valladolid to do research in the *Archivo General de Simancas*, an archive containing many military records. On the way, I was as usual sitting in the nonsmoking compartment of the train. Two large well-built passengers came in, sat down, and lit cigarettes. That really annoyed me, so when the conductor passed by, I pointed this out, and he made them get up and leave the car. They made a fuss, then turned to me, gave me dirty looks, and left. A few minutes later, a young man leaned over from his seat and said to me in Spanish that it was very brave of me to assert myself against those bullies. We struck up a conversation and he was interested to know I was going to the archive, which he knew about. He insisted once we exited the train that his brother, who was there to pick him up, take me directly to the archive by car, saving me a bus ride there—a kindly act in return for my brave behavior on the train. Once at the archive, I had before me a castle with a moat and a bridge across it. The castle dates from the fifteenth century and was chosen to house documents as a place easy to protect and defend. I had a letter signed by Professor Giorgio Perissinotto of UCSB testifying to the legitimacy of my research. I was then signed in and given a brief introduction on how to use the archival materials. I found service records of Goicoechea and other Santa Barbara Presidio soldiers and made copies for the Presidio Research Center.

That adventure under my belt, I bought a ticket for the bullet train from Madrid's Atocha Station to Seville and the *Archivo General de Indias*. I intended to spend a week there but ran into a few holidays and was able to use the archive for only three days. While there, I came across Dr. Joseph Sánchez, a national parks historian in New Mexico and then-head of the Spanish Colonial Research Center. He helped me figure out the collections with their millions of pages of documents. I requested *legajos*, which are bundles of documents that are not necessarily in chronological order nor bundled by subject. Nevertheless, they have been reasonably cataloged and there is much to be found in these documents related to Santa Barbara's Spanish history. The staff is very good about copying materials and sending them to your home address. A lot of the documents in the archive have been microfilmed and are available at the Bancroft Library at UC Berkeley—but by no means all. During the evenings, Joe took me to tapas bars, as he had been doing research in Seville since the Franco era and knew the city inside and out. I walked some of the city and went to the cathedral with its famous Giralda bell tower, the Alcázar with its famous Mudéjar architecture, and the Plaza de España.

On the weekend when the archive was closed, I took a train to Huelva, then a bus ride across to the Monasterio de Santa María de la Rábida. Why to this monastery? This was in 1993, a year after the Columbian Quincentenary, and I wanted to see the place where Columbus had spent the last night before his first voyage to the New World. When the bus arrived at the monastery, the site was closed but reopening three hours later. I decided to walk to a town to the north to find some place to have lunch. It was at least a mile away and it started to rain, but I was determined to keep going, found a restaurant, and had an excellent fish entrée. As I walked out of the restaurant, I remember seeing a statue on a high pedestal of one of the Pinzón brothers in the plaza—these were the captains of the other two ships on Columbus's first voyage. I did get to see the monastery and the room where Columbus spent his last night. As should be apparent by now, I am not the politically correct type—Columbus was a great man, albeit with flaws. Ye who have not sinned cast the first stone.

Continuing my political incorrectness, I had another day of the archive being closed due to a saint's day, so I took a train to Cádiz, the port city where Father Serra spent his last night before leaving for the New World, never to return. I walked around the coastal walkway of the city and then treated myself to another fish dinner. Between the archives and these visits to historic sites and towns, I came away with my Europhilia intact. What comes to mind when I think back and relate the anecdotes of my experiences is Don Quixote and his adventures—Cervantes's great novel is in some ways a series of encounters told through anecdotes. My *Muses Flee Hitler* coeditor Carla Borden once told me that her mentor at the Smithsonian wanted to write a book titled *Anecdotal Anthropology*. Not a bad idea, I thought—maybe someone someday will write a book titled *Santa Barbara's Anecdotal Spanish History*.

Several other trips Michele and I took in the 1990s were to Germany and Greece, which are not pertinent to the subject at hand. Plus, I have already touched on the research Michele and I did in the archives at New Mexico State University in Las Cruces on the ancestry of Goicoechea. We spent two separate vacations focused on him in Las Cruces—it had become somewhat of an obsession.

Staying True to the Founder's Vision

In some respect, that may also be a good way to end the first forty years of this success story of the SBTHP, twenty of which I spent as the "hired gun" of the organization. That was the appellation one board member pinned on me. I liked it. The SBTHP was an organization able to maintain its focus on the Presidio during these years yet expand to be able to restore Casa de la Guerra and start a whole new park at Mission Santa Inés. At the helm was the hired gun, who had grown to appreciate what had come before him and was a soldier riding shotgun into the future. Practically, one can point to good business practices, solid relations with city and state government agencies, and a unique approach to fundraising as the keys to its success—but in my opinion, it was the continued focus on the founder's vision that kept the SBTHP on track. That vision will continue into the twenty-first century.

CHAPTER TWELVE

"We Are the Mud People"

A NEW MILLENNIUM seemed to frighten some, manifested in the fear that all computers might go haywire in a phenomenon known as Y2K. While it all turned out to be nothing, the first decade of the twenty-first century presented some hugely challenging moments—that is, the infamous attack September 11, 2001, and the Great Recession starting in 2008. The SBTHP had to adapt to the economic challenges of these events and in some ways was positioned to survive them as well as any nonprofit could expect to. The reason for the organization's survival had to do with the balance of its financial resources in rental income and stock-market investments. In fact, as I remember, the SBTHP did not lose a dollar in rental income after 9/11 and the same was the case after 2008 as the Great Recession hit, with one exception—the case of Jimmy's Oriental Gardens, which I will talk about later. The SBTHP's investment portfolios did take hits in these recessionary events, but it meant only about 30 percent of our revenue was affected. This meant that cuts had to be made and these were done primarily with reductions in staff salaries. But we did not have to furlough or lay off any employees.

Thus, up to 2013 and the SBTHP's fiftieth anniversary, we sailed along with less trauma than some organizations faced during the economic meltdowns of this time period. We, "the mud people," as one board member called us, could continue our adobe world unabated. I like the term "mud people" as a way to describe the SBTHP. We definitely did other things and our restoration projects during this decade were not solely mud related, but we began as mud people. I like the notion that mud was an essential part of the meaning of the organization, which connects to a wider world of earthen architecture and should remain central to the SBTHP's work well into the future. Let me explain the connection.

International Earthen Architecture Conference

We live in an age trying to become greener, and one of the better ways to do that is to become browner—building with earthen materials. Mud—a wet version of the earth—is a unifier. This came home to me when I attended the International Conference on the Conservation of Earthen Architecture in Las Cruces, New Mexico, in October 1990. People came from all over the world to participate in this event. The conference is held about every five years in various places around the world. The other conference I attended was the eighth one that took place in Torquay, Devon, England, in May 2000—at the beginning of the decade of the new millennium. Why in England? In fact, there is an interesting earthen-architecture tradition primarily in Devon known as cob construction. Cob is earth mixed with sand and straw—very much like adobe, indeed. Instead of being cast in blocks, it is laid out in layers about 20 inches in depth and allowed to dry, and then the next layer is laid down until you eventually reach the roof level. In years past, a thatched roof was constructed over the cob walls. Today, the thatching comes from Turkey and is no longer available in England. This cob tradition was used in many thousands of houses and farm buildings dating from the fourteenth to the nineteenth centuries. Many of the houses we saw on our tours of the countryside had been gentrified and were being restored and used as country homes for city dwellers.

Mud, one finds out at these conferences, is much more extensively used in construction around the world than is generally recognized. People from all over the world attend the conferences—from South America, East Asia, the Middle East, and, of course, the United States. I felt right at home among these people. One learns that there were many earthen homes built along the Hudson River in New York in the nineteenth century, that modern unamended rammed earth is being used in construction in modern Germany, and that after World War II thousands of structures were made out of adobe throughout the Fatherland. China has an earthen-building tradition with something like 10 percent of the population of that country living in adobe structures. Then there are the whole towns made of adobe in Morocco that date to the twelfth century.

The Torquay conference provided sessions on the latest conservation methods, the latest uses of adobe in modern buildings, and the value of promoting earthen architecture as a key to long-term environmental sustainability. Hosted by the University of Plymouth, the series of events provided time to meet many fellow conferees—among them was an architect from India who said he hoped to help shift his region away from concrete to earthen structures; another was a gentleman from Saudi Arabia who told me his country was seeking to develop adobe technology as a major building method. I was amazed to see a woman from Peru seven months pregnant attend most of the sessions and go on most of the field tours.

The tours were to sites where we saw cob buildings being restored. There was an overnight bus tour that took us to underground earthen sites that predated

Stonehenge. California architect Gil Sanchez was on these tours with his wife, Daryl Allen. SBTHP people will remember that Gil was the architect of our Presidio Chapel. With Gil's infectious laugh, we had a great time on the bus tour and ended up walking on the ancient path that led to Stonehenge itself, which was opened specially for us by archaeologists from the National Trust for Historic Preservation. It was an unforgettable moment to be among those giant boulders. Before returning to London, I walked around the seaside town of Torquay. I came across a large building that had a sign on it: "Spanish Barn." When I went in, a plaque explained that its name came from the fact that this was the place where prisoners from the defeated Spanish armada were brought in 1588. I wondered what happened to those prisoners.

Back in London, I took a few days to visit the British Museum (my hotel was a block away from it) and the famous Victoria and Albert Museum. That evening, I went to the new Globe to see a production of the Bard's *The Tempest*. All seats were sold out, so I had to do standing room, which is in an area in front of the stage. I arrived early enough that I was in the first row, leaning against the stage. The lead part of Prospero was performed by Vanessa Redgrave, and I had to duck when Caliban threw a sardine into the audience. Hard to top that Shakespeare experience.

From London, I took the train under the Channel to France to a week's vacation of research work in Germany on Thomas Mann, which included several days in Lübeck, Mann's hometown and the setting of his famous novel *Buddenbrooks*. That evening, I noticed that Nobel Prize author Günter Grass was giving a talk in the former Lübeck Cathedral, now a lecture hall. I showed up to find a long line waiting to get in to see the famous novelist. When I came to the front of the line, the woman said that she was sorry that the hall was now full and she couldn't let me in. I pleaded with her that I had come all the way from America, and she relented and let me in. After Grass's talk, I purchased a copy of his most famous book, *Die Blechtrommel* (in English, *The Tin Drum*), and waited for the right moment when no one was talking to him to ask him to sign his book to my wife and me. I told him on our first date we had been to see the movie *Who's Afraid of Virginia Woolf?* and we both saw on the bookshelf in one of the scenes his novel *The Tin Drum*. It turned out that Michele and I were both reading it at the same time, except I in German. I said to Grass we had been married thirty-plus years. He really liked that and said his book had brought us thirty years of happy marriage—and signed the book to both of us. That was one of those once-in-a-lifetime experiences.

When I returned from Europe at the end of May, I brought with me *Terra 2000 Postprints*, which contained copies of all the papers delivered at the conference—it has been archived in the Santa Barbara Presidio Research Center. Santa Barbara staffers also attended other adobe workshops and events in Arizona and New Mexico during these years. With retirements and employee changes, there is really only one person (Mike Imwalle) left on staff today with knowledge of adobe technology. I will discuss in a later chapter how this skill might be revived and used to place the

SBTHP in the position of being a site promoting sustainability while at the same time rebuilding sections of the Presidio approved in the city- and state-approved general plan.

Its Time Has Finally Come: Reconstruction of the Presidio Chapel Bell Tower

To return to the world of Presidio reconstruction: Probably nothing caused more consternation at the SBTHP than the idea of rebuilding the Presidio bell tower. A few voices against, more or less, kept the rebuilding of it in a state of limbo. From the time I began at the SBTHP in 1981, there had been discussions ongoing about the bell tower. While sections of the foundation apparently had been located, some, such as Richard Whitehead, remained skeptical. Then the 1820 Vischer plan surfaced due to the research of the leading skeptic, Whitehead himself, that clearly indicated a bell tower attached to the Chapel in the area where the foundations of the tower were located. There was still resistance by certain members even after Richard died in 1988. Finally, by the end of 1998, restoration committee chairman James Mills decided it was time to bite the bullet, and Mike Imwalle and Bob Sheets did a final excavation of the bell-tower foundations, establishing the width and length of the tower. Then came the time to design it. With no images of the bell tower known to exist or at least still not found, various ideas based on examples of other mission towers were put forth. We knew one thing—the tower had to hold two bells, as those bells still existed and the SBTHP had reacquired them. One of the bells had ended up at the Milton Academy in Massachusetts and was returned to the SBTHP in exchange for a bell that we had cast for them; the second bell was located at the Jesuit retreat center in Los Gatos, California, and it was purchased from the Order.

One of the board members came in with an idea of a tower that soared about five feet above the church. That was soon nixed and finally one that everyone could agree to brought the bell platform to the lower ridge of the roof, with the rest of the tower rising only slightly above the top of the ridge of the roof. Its proportions, to my mind, seemed just right. Norman Caldwell, longtime volunteer engineer on the committee, engineered a version that the city public-works department rejected for reasons I am not sure of to this day. We then turned to another engineer, who designed a tower that because of its height and its narrowness could not be made entirely of adobe. The engineering plan that was finally accepted was a tower built of reinforced concrete blocks that was to be faced with adobe blocks several inches thick. By the time all the approvals had come through, the year was 2000, and then the money was raised, which turned out to be a fairly easy task. The tower was built and was dedicated April 21, 2001, the Presidio's 219th birthday. There was quite a turnout for the dedication, one of the largest crowds I can remember at Founding

The bell Tower under construction. *Courtesy SBTHP*

Day—including many of the major donors, who participated in the ceremony by ringing the bells. The director of California State Parks at the time, Rusty Areias, also was in attendance.

To me, this is a classic example of SBTHP persistence, especially of James Mills and Garvan Kuskey, both longtime Presidio-reconstruction zealots. You will remember Garvan was the person who had, years before, prodded us into demolishing the building blocking the view of the Chapel. They just would not be denied.

It has made a big difference ringing the bells in the tower at weddings and other events, just as would have been done in historical times. Is it an accurate reconstruction? Based on what was found in the ground and other examples, it is what one can say "might well have been." Should we come across a rendering or painting of the original Chapel and its tower and it is different from what has been created—well, I would say tear it down and rebuild it as history tells us it was.

The Presidio Northwest Corner

After the nine rooms of the northeast corner had been completed in 1998, the SBTHP moved headlong into its next reconstruction project—the northwest corner of the Presidio. Again the mud people would have their work cut out for them, eventually having to make another twenty thousand-plus bricks. First was the archaeology, then the design, raising the money, and the actual construction—a by now familiar pattern. Except there were to be quite a few different ways of doing this project, different, that is, from the northeast-corner project. In part that had to do with the archaeological remains left in the ground—or lack thereof. I can't remember the context, but someone told me about a photo showing the foundations of this section of the Presidio supposedly taken by a state-parks person before the area was lowered to put in a parking lot. No one has ever located such a photo, and what remained were mostly the bottom courses of certain rooms and a feint area of the defense wall.

When I first started at the SBTHP, the area of the northwest corner was rented out to a local businessman of some ill repute and he had some business failures, and the SBTHP received the lot back. Next to the lot was a driveway that led back to the garage that had been turned into the Presidio Research Center. Eventually we would connect the driveway with the parking lot for staff parking and keep the area in the front of the lot for future archaeology. That all happened in the mid-1980s.

In a summary history of the acquisition and development of the Santa Barbara Presidio, Mike Imwalle reported the first archaeology he knew of in the northwest corner began with an uncovering of a small section of the outer defense wall by Presidio volunteers in 1971. The site also had structures on it dating from the period of Japanese occupation. Apparently, this occupation, combined with the leveling of the lot, caused significant disturbance to the original Presidio foundations. Much fewer intact foundations were found during the excavations in the lot than in the northeast corner. Up the slope of the driveway toward the Cañedo Adobe, excellent foundations were uncovered connecting this former room with the Cañedo Adobe. Also, we found the foundations of another room that was not on the original ground plans of Goicoechea or Fages. It was decided not to rebuild this section but to preserve the foundations—that could change in the future as more museum space may be needed, and this room could help meet that need. Also, the excavation of the defense wall gave no evidence of the bastion that is shown on the original ground plans. It has been surmised that the bastion may have existed originally, but when the back wall of the Presidio was extended and a second wall created, the bastion may have no longer been thought to be necessary. One thing that was ascertained was that the second defense wall's foundation had been built and extended in the same direction toward a section coming from the opposite direction east to west. A mysterious gap exists between the two foundations that to this day remains unexplained. Also, a small 15-foot section of the foundation lies underneath a neighbor's parking lot and is thus not part of the Park. I tried very hard to get the owners of that small piece to sell it to the SBTHP, but the job was left unfinished when I retired in 2016. It is one of the most important acquisitions still needed, albeit adding up to only about five hundred square feet of land.

All the above archaeology of the northwest corner was going on between the years 1998 and 2002. Mike Imwalle supervised most of this work with Bob Sheets, and Dr. Bob Hoover, retired professor and member of the SBTHP board, oversaw a number of California Polytechnic State University San Luis Obispo field schools at the site. The SBTHP retained architect Milford Wayne Donaldson again to come up with the plans. Wayne had been the architect of record for the northeast corner and the Casa de la Guerra restoration. After the SBTHP restoration committee reviewed the plans, they went to the city's landmarks commission and then to California State Parks for approval. The plans included four rooms, backyard cross walls, and a huge section of the defense wall that extended more than 275 feet—all adobe, but using the pylon system that had been developed for the northeast-corner project. We also were going to try to extend the stonework out in Canon Perdido Street to connect the reconstruction with El Cuartel, one of the two original adobes (with the Cañedo) from the eighteenth century. In trying to do this, we were hoping to duplicate what we had done in the northeast corner, setting stones in the road marking the original room that had been the bedroom of the comandante and connecting the room with the comandancia on the other side of the street. For whatever reason I don't remember today, it was decided not to submit the plans with the encroachment onto the street. As mentioned earlier, this project was undertaken in a different way from our earlier reconstructions because of the funding sources. The project was broken down into three phases based on the complete set of plans. By this time, around 2005, Wayne was about to leave his firm and turn it over to the other architects, who included Stuart Sawasaki, and they renamed the firm Heritage Architecture and Planning.

As a quick aside: Later, in 2008, I would nominate Wayne for the Pearl Chase Historic Preservation and Conservation Award, which recognizes someone for an outstanding career in historic preservation. He had been the architect of three SBTHP projects and his firm also did the restoration of the Santa Barbara Railroad Station. Added to this, he was named state historic preservation officer by Governor Schwarzenegger in 2005, and later went even higher up, being named President Obama's chairman of the Advisory Council on Historic Preservation, a position he held into the Trump presidency. Without question, he deserved the award. The SBTHP voted unanimously to present him with this award.

Phase I: Northwest-Corner Reconstruction

For this project, I had one of my bright ideas. I'm not sure how it came to me, but I remembered that I had worked for two hard years to get a freeway sign for the Presidio on Highway 101—these signs we asked for from both north and south at the Carrillo Street exits. Working through our local state legislators, we finally were able to get Caltrans to commit to installing the signs. A great victory in itself. I next connected the signs to the Intermodal Surface Transportation Efficiency Act (ISTEA) grants given out by the federal government. It seemed like these grants were about transportation and roads, but when I attended a National Trust for Historic Preservation conference in Louisville, Kentucky, I learned that there was a historic-preservation component in the Act. Sure enough, when I got back and looked it up, I came across the section supporting historic preservation. The wheels

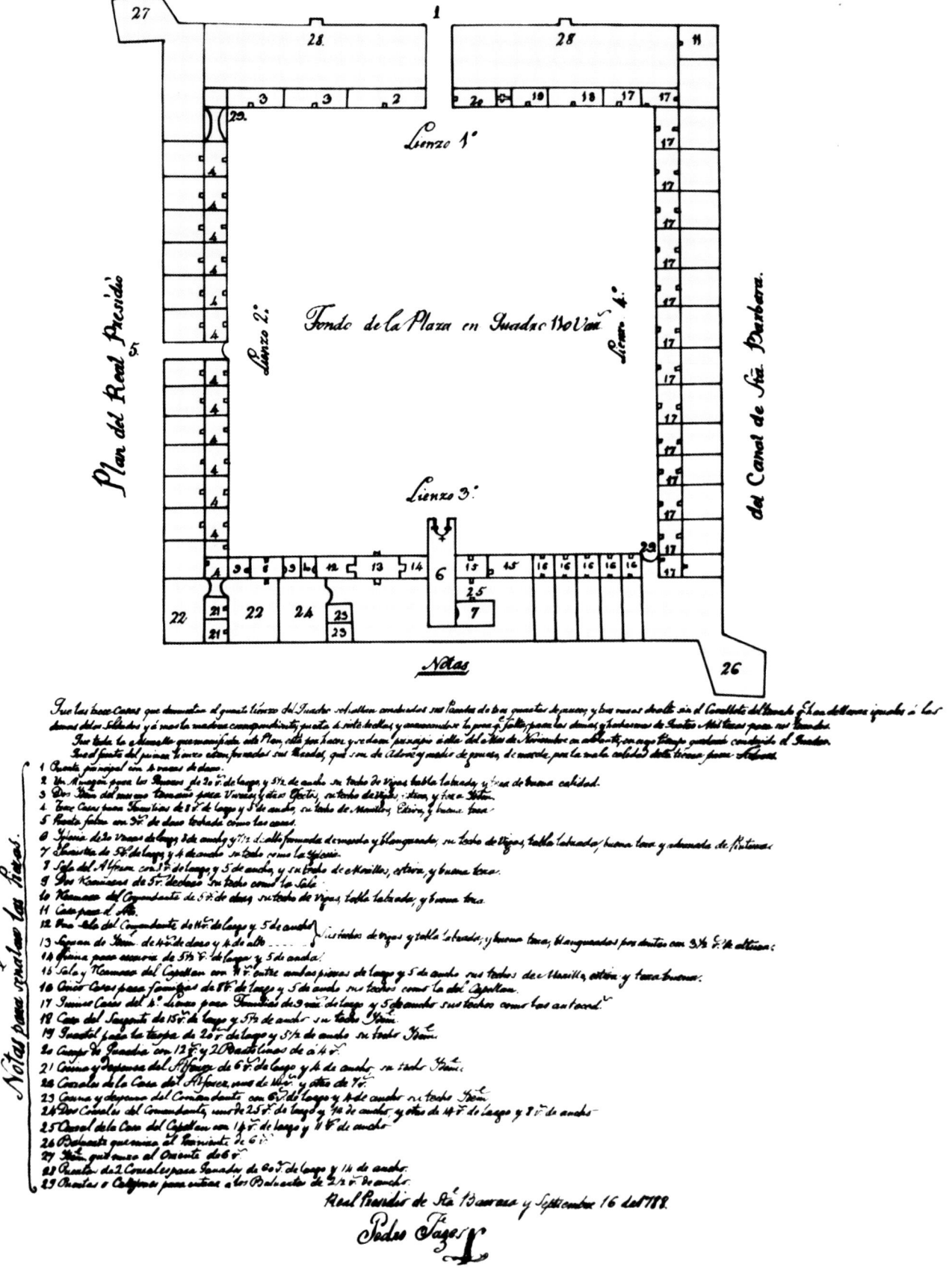

The Fages Plan of the Santa Barbara Presidio. The design of the northwest corner depended more on this plan because much less original foundation was found than at the northeast corner. *Courtesy Newberry Library*

Detail of ceiling work in the northwest corner—lumber was harvested from the local forest, caning from a local creek, and leather straps from hide obtained by Channel Coast Construction. *Courtesy SBTHP*

started turning. Then I learned that the ISTEA funds locally were controlled by the Santa Barbara County Association of Governments (SBCAG) with members from all the cities in the county plus the supervisors. One of my wife's former business partners, Susan Rose, was on the board of supervisors and I felt she would support a grant for the Presidio. Also, Susan asked me to serve on the county's Historic Landmarks Advisory Commission, which I will discuss later.

I'm not sure why I asked for the amount of five hundred thousand dollars—probably because I thought a lower amount was more likely to be approved, but if I had to do it again, I would ask for more. I talked to the then-SBTHP board president and dragged him around to meet city officials in Lompoc, Buellton, Solvang, and, I believe, Santa Maria and Carpinteria. The president was extremely skeptical about our getting the money, but we did pitch it, and by the time it got to the SBCAG, I felt pretty confident, and yes, it did happen. The problem was it was not enough to do the entire northwest-corner project and required bidding.

We broke the project into phases and bid out the first two rooms, which included the future visitor center. Only two companies expressed interest in the project and only one bid on it: Channel Coast Corporation (CCC). We accepted their bid and they did an outstanding, high-quality job—which included creating an excellent new ADA entrance, packed adobe floors, and the traditional leather-tied reeds on the rounded roof beams. I don't remember that there were any change orders, but if there were, they were minor. From that time until the time I left, most of our restoration work was done by CCC. That included Phases II and III of the northwest-corner reconstruction. I should mention also that while CCC did the construction, SBTHP board member Tim Aguilar was still in charge of making all the adobe bricks—around twenty thousand, as I mentioned previously. These were being made on-site and left to dry in the front- and backyards of the site, and then stacked on pallets and moved near the location of the buildings. Prior to us beginning construction on this phase, California State Parks funded new restrooms on the northwest-corner site in 2005. One glitch for the restrooms was the city requiring a 2-inch versus a 1-inch drainpipe—at an expense of thirty thousand dollars. City council member Roger Horton, a former SBTHP board member, helped get the fee waived. By the time we obtained the permit for the two rooms, construction did not begin until 2006 and was completed in 2007.

The lessons of this Phase I story were twofold: First, going to conferences has some paybacks I could compile a list of all the knowledge I acquired at conferences, but my attending the Louisville National Trust conference ended up with a five-hundred-thousand-dollar return on investment. In addition, that favorite word "persistence" made some difference again—making contact with SBCAG members was important lobbying that paid off.

Phase II: Northwest-Corner Reconstruction

Our first bid project had worked out just fine. For the next phase, we asked CCC to do a bid on the next two rooms. That in hand, we went about raising the money. There had been more money needed to be raised beyond the ISTEA grant for Phase I—thus , we were still receiving individual donations, and the Ahmanson Foundation, among others, helped fund this phase. Yes, there were smaller donations of one hundred to one thousand dollars coming in, but we couldn't start Phase II, the final two rooms, until we secured more funds.

Somehow we always find a way. We had hired on short term Debbie Arneson, one of the better contract fundraisers in Santa Barbara, in my opinion. We had her for only a short time in 2006 and 2007, but she delivered. We were bringing in individual donations of smaller amounts, and then larger grants from the Santa Barbara Foundation, the Jackson Family Foundation, and the Ahmanson Foundation, the latter thanks to one of their board members, Robert Erburu, who had retired as CEO of the Times Mirror Company in 1996 and was, as previously mentioned and most importantly for the SBTHP, a descendant of a Santa Barbara Presidio soldier. But we were still coming up short in 2006, and Debbie kept working away and, to be honest, putting the pressure on me to contact potential supporters of our project.

A couple named Jon and Lillian Lovelace helped raise and contributed funds for the making of a video on the life of SBTHP founder Pearl Chase, and Debbie kept reminding me to call Lillian to give the Lovelaces a tour of the Presidio site and of the Ranchero room upstairs at the El Paseo complex, which contained murals by some of the best Western artists of the early- to mid-twentieth century—such artists as Edward Borein, Carl Oscar Borg, Joe De Yong, Will James, Frank Tenney Johnson, Eunice MacLennan, and Channing Peake. When we sold El Paseo, the SBTHP maintained a historic easement to preserve the artwork in the room, which was the first meeting place of the renowned men's riding group Los Rancheros Visitadores. The room is open only for special tours. When I finally called the Lovelaces, they expressed interest in the tour, and we set a date. The day came and we showed them the northwest corner, under construction, and then walked to El Paseo to view the Ranchero room. They were impressed, especially Lillian, with her deep interest in art. She was at one time president of the Santa Barbara Arts Council.

After the tour, we repaired to the Wine Cask restaurant downstairs for lunch, where the stars started to align. By pure chance, Supervisor Susan Rose was at the table next to us. She and Lillian were good friends—Susan had been the executive director of the Santa Barbara Arts Council during the time Lillian was president of the organization. The organization's office had been on the Old City College site in a building that had subsequently been removed to make way for the Presidio's northeast corner. Susan also had been a business partner of my wife in the Forte Group—the company's business being consulting and training. We had a lot to talk about on various topics, all positive. After lunch, the Lovelaces thanked us for a good time.

Within two days, a check from their foundation arrived that covered Phase II of the northwest-corner project. Thus, the project proceeded and, according to Mike Imwalle's report from 2011, it was completed by 2008.

CCC hired some of the crew who had worked previously on the northeast-corner project. The foundation work, adobe laying, and construction of the roofs were all first rate. Adobes came from Tim Aguilar again, and the roof tiles were made by George Davidson in Tecate, Mexico. There was a kicker, however: Because we had not pulled the complete permit for the project—we had to slightly reengineer the plans because the seismic code had been stiffened—more steel and concrete were used, but the buildings were still 90 percent made of adobe. The roof structure used beams left from the Marre Fire; the leather for the strapping tying the reeds to the beams came from a source in the Los Angeles area. Those hides had to be soaked and then cut into slices. As I have reported in earlier adobe projects, it is one of the most unpleasant jobs as the leather has a bad stench to it after being soaked. But the rest of the project smelled like a rose and came out as I said: just perfect. On to Phase III.

Phase III: Rebuilding the Northwest-Corner Defense Wall

Michele and I have said to ourselves that something happened to our sense of time when the year 2000 arrived—the new millennium. Both of us seem to remember dates and fit events into them up to 1999. Since then, we seem to have trouble keeping things in chronological order. And that is important as we move into Phase III of the northwest-corner project. The SBTHP was finishing the two rooms of Phase II just as the Great Recession hit us like a Category 5 hurricane in 2009. Also, the SBTHP made some economic moves in real estate that I will discuss later, and we faced a stock-market collapse that put us in a tenuous financial situation.

Still, the SBTHP tried to move ahead with the northwest-corner project and had hired a full-time development person, Kendra Rhodes. In her research, she found the Hind Foundation, which was located in San Luis Obispo and, most importantly, was one of those rare foundations that provided most of its grants to historic-preservation projects. Perfect for us.

Looking at the 990s of the Hind Foundation we determined the amount we might ask for in a grant and then matched it with a bid from CCC to do the foundations of the northwest defense wall—all 275 feet of it. The bid was about $150,000, and we applied to Hind and received from them that exact amount. The project included construction of the stone foundations, the original of which had been mostly erased when the parking lot was put in before the SBTHP and the state acquired the site. In addition, the wall, which was more than 10 feet high and 4 feet thick, required the pylon system burrowing more than 6 feet into the ground and concrete columns rising to the top height of the wall. All of this was to be completed, only to leave unfinished the adobe work on the defense wall and the cross walls connecting to the

A section of the rebuilt defense wall of the northwest corner. It represents less than 10 percent of the original defense wall built in the 1780s. *Courtesy SBTHP*

rooms. I shouldn't use bad metaphors, but from this point forward, the SBTHP ran into a stone wall in terms of fundraising—the first time that we had experienced this during my years working on the Presidio reconstruction. What happened?

For one thing, the recession deepened and many of our donations began to shrink, even though we put together some promotional literature to help find potential donors. Also, Bob Erburu, later to be diagnosed with Alzheimer's disease, stepped down from the Ahmanson Foundation, and that source of funding was substantially reduced. Bob's wife, Lois, during his incapacitation had the foundation at least send us a grant every year of ten thousand dollars, but it was not nearly as much as we previously received. In addition, the Santa Barbara Foundation, which had for years been a major source of support for cultural institutions and provided more than five hundred thousand dollars in grants to the SBTHP over the years, changed direction to support more of the social-service nonprofits and programs.

Thus Phase III came to a standstill. To be honest, it was embarrassing to have those ugly concrete columns left visible as we shut down the project. The SBTHP had already cut salaries and funding, thus finishing the wall out of SBTHP operating funds just wasn't feasible with all the financial challenges the organization was facing. Literally several years went by until the SBTHP board, in 2013, said the wall had to be finished and authorized using funds from its cash reserve. Added to this were grants from the Outhwaite Foundation and other outside sources that made completion of the wall a reality by the time of Prince Felipe's visit in late 2013. Today, when I see that magnificent adobe wall—all 275 feet of it—I realize that, all things considered, we got it done in the face of very difficult economic times. This wall is one of the great legacies of the mud people.

CHAPTER THIRTEEN

SOME OUTSIDE ACTIVITIES: DID THESE BENEFIT THE PRESIDIO PROJECT?

Santa Barbara Historic Landmarks Advisory Commission: Some Nasty Mudslinging

Intertwined with all the other goings-on, I became involved with county preservation politics when Supervisor Susan Rose in 2000 asked me to serve on the county's Historic Landmarks Advisory Commission. It turned out not to be the most pleasant experience. Chalk it up to a learning experience. The commission over the years dealt with designating sites as structures of merit or historic landmarks. Really, hardly any controversy was involved as designations usually came with owner approval. Those were the "old days." During the time I served on the commission, some big issues came to the fore, and there was considerable contention that arose between the commission, the public, the county staff, and the board of supervisors. Shades of yesteryear and the controversial Presidio project.

During the first meeting I attended at the commission, the issue of setting term limits for commissioners came up. The matter was fairly advanced in discussion from previous meetings, I surmised, and I sat quietly listening. It may have been in about the third meeting when I spoke up. I got the feeling that this measure was being put forth to get rid of "dead wood" on the commission. There were a couple members who had been on the commission for well over a decade. My comment was that I wasn't sure I supported term limits because I felt that the appointments were the responsibility of the supervisors and it should be up to them to determine how long someone served. Others on the commission also spoke out in support of my point of view. There were eleven members on the commission, two per district and one at large.

There were two commissioners who were pushing term limits. Eventually the matter died for lack of support. I don't remember there even being a vote. Both of the members supporting term limits were livid and resigned. One of them, an anthropologist at the Vandenberg Air Force Base (now the Vandenberg Space Force Base), wrote a hate letter against me saying basically I was an idiot and the only skill I had was fundraising. He sent the letter on Air Force letterhead to all the supervisors. The other term-limits person had his wife, who was a city employee, write a letter to the SBTHP president saying that I was incompetent and an embarrassment to the SBTHP. I did contact the commander of the Air Force base, asking him if it was appropriate for this person to be writing a letter like this—I received an apology from the commander and shared the letter with the board of supervisors. I wondered if I would have been better off if I had kept my mouth shut.

As I mentioned, quite a few bigger matters came up at the commission that resulted in large public turnouts for the meetings. We had to move to a larger meeting room. Among these matters was a proposal from the Botanic Garden to add some buildings for their education programs. Many of the neighbors were up in arms over the proposal—too big, too much noise, traffic, etc. One of the dissenters came to my office asking for my advice. She knew I was on the commission. She said she felt the proposal really was detrimental to the character of the garden. I said it was not a landmark, so that would, in a way, tie the hands of the commission in dealing with the proposal. I said if she thought it was worthy of landmark status, she could nominate it. In fact, there is an entailed form to fill out to do that and I thought she wouldn't do it. But she decided to take my advice and nominated the garden. That changed the discussion at the commission hearings, and hundreds of people on both sides showed up. I was no longer on the commission when the issue was finally resolved, but the garden did agree to the historic designation with conditions. I think that it all turned out OK, but the meetings were not always friendly, and I had friends on both sides. I was glad I did not have to vote on that matter.

Another project that sparked public dissidence was a proposed restoration and rehabilitation of the Coral Casino, which is part of the Biltmore Santa Barbara hotel. The site included a dining room, cabanas, a beautiful pool, and locker rooms. Architect Gardner Dailey designed the Coral Casino in 1937 and it was one of his finest works. The major change, among others, that was being proposed was adding a second floor to the complex, and that seemed to me an unjustified alteration. There were three others on the commission who shared my view. However, members of the club turned out en masse in support of the proposal. As happens at such heated sessions, a lot of invective was spewed out against those of us opposed. The commission vote was in favor of the proposal, so the project went forward, and it reopened in 2008 after I had stepped down from the board. To be honest, upon visiting the club for special events and as the guest of a member after the reopening, I think it all turned out OK. But the nastiness that came out in the public hearings made this yet another unpleasant experience.

One other frustrating experience took place in June 2004 related to a bridge-replacement project brought to the commission for review. Unfortunately, the project came to us rather late in the game and a design for the new bridge, replacing the 1916 bridge, had already been created. The bridge ran across Nojoqui Creek on an early surviving section of the Old Highway 1 south of Buellton. The public works department was adamantly opposed to any reconsideration of saving the bridge, pleading to the supervisors that they would lose more than one million dollars of federal grant money and saying they would actually have to lay off a staff member working on the project if they lost the money.

The commission, however, felt this was a nice arched bridge that could be saved. I even contacted an engineer in Los Angeles who said he would design a retrofit to save the bridge, and I had someone to cover the cost of his engineering. Also, we proposed that a platform be created down a few steps where you could see the bridge with a plaque describing the history of the bridge. The commission then voted 9–0 to save the bridge, and the public works department appealed to the supervisors, where we got slaughtered in a 5–0 reversal of our decision. As a fond farewell to the bridge, commissioners and their spouses and friends, including the Jackmans, walked out to the bridge, which had been closed off to be demolished, and shared a few bottles of wine together. The bridge was then demolished and the new one has been completed.

Food for thought: My time on the commission was indeed a learning experience, but I did ask myself if it would have been more valuable to have devoted more of my time to the world of creative mudslinging.

CALPA—Learning to Love Parks and Parks People

I thought after this disappointment that I had better get back to my day job at the SBTHP—but during this same time period, I had committed to serving on the board of the California League of Park Associations (CALPA), which had a different name when I was elected in 2002. I asked myself what benefit the SBTHP received from my serving on the landmarks commission, and it was hard to say anything positive. In fact, some of my decisions may have irked members of the community and, as a result, impacted their image of the SBTHP negatively. In contrast, my service on the CALPA board had very positive impacts for the SBTHP and El Presidio de Santa Bárbara State Historic Park, which I will explain.

When asked to serve, I inquired with our local parks-district superintendent if he thought I should serve on the CALPA board. He got back to me that he thought they could use someone like me because California State Parks was having issues with CALPA. I wasn't sure how to take that, but I decided to go ahead and serve.

As with the county landmarks commission, I discussed serving with the SBTHP executive committee and they gave their support. I attended an annual conference of CALPA in Monterey, where SBTHP restoration-committee member Norman Caldwell received the Volunteer of the Year award—much deserved, for sure. I also attended a few sessions at the conference, and one of them had lawyers present talking about suing the Parks Department. That sounded a bit ominous. I honestly don't remember the issues, but the conflict had to do with nonprofits that were there supposedly to support the parks. The breakdowns usually had to do with authority—an intransigence on both sides. My point of view going in was that there was a "partnership" between the Parks Department and the nonprofit, but when push came to shove, the Parks Department was in almost all situations the final arbiter. You could complain to a legislator and that might cure a situation, but I saw over the years how it might make matters worse.

CALPA was a nonprofit formed to help other nonprofits in agreements with CSP department. In recent years, CALPA has expanded to include any nonprofit assisting parks, whether it has an agreement with the Parks Department or not. CALPA really serves as a liaison between the nonprofit and the Parks Department, not a legal mediator or arbitrator, but it is there to help both understand each other by explaining nonprofit best practices and the Parks Department's way of doing things, which often is bound by law and by the nature of bureaucracy. I was surprised to discover that some Parks Department employees did not have any understanding of nonprofit law that falls under the corporate codes, and conversely, how little some in the nonprofits knew about government operations, most of which are comprehensible if one gives government the benefit of the doubt regarding its rules and regulations.

The CALPA board met in Sacramento, and after just one year on the board, I was asked to serve as president. I agreed because it turned out these people were all park lovers, as it were, and just great to be around. The legal wrangling had calmed down and it seemed to me that there was nowhere to go but up with this organization. In addition, besides meetings with nonprofit people, we had meetings with senior staff at headquarters, including with the director. This contact was important because the SBTHP was frequently seeking acquisition funds for El Presidio de Santa Bárbara State Historic Park and, I hoped, for eventual state purchase of the Santa Inés Mission Mills site.

Part of my willingness to serve, I told CALPA board members, was because of their similar commitment to getting along with the Parks Department. We weren't going to be lapdogs, but we should make every effort to have a positive relationship with the Department. That would be one of the main themes of my presidency. Not sure where the idea came from but I said we should host the conference at one of my favorite places, Hearst San Simeon State Historical Monument. After a session at the conference, I got from a Department person in attendance the telephone number of Kirk Sturm, superintendent of Hearst Castle, who said he would be glad to host us. At the time, the local nonprofit supporting Hearst Castle was not a member of CALPA, but we were able to get its participation, plus the cooperation of the food concessionaires. I was able to announce this good news at the CALPA conference banquet in 2003. There, I also presented another goal I hoped to achieve—to make sure we had fun and remained as professional as possible at the same time.

One of the first things I thought CALPA should do was have a history researched on the twenty-five-year history of CALPA; not surprisingly, as you might have thought, this would be something important to a historian such as myself. I contacted the history department at California State University, Sacramento and asked if they might have a person doing a master's degree interested in writing a thesis on CALPA. We found a woman whose name escapes me willing to take on the task. She researched the minutes and other documents of CALPA and interviewed, she thought, key individuals in the organization's history—mostly CALPA people. Therein lay the rub: Two department people felt that the thesis did not fairly represent the squabbles that turned to disputes between the CSP department and the nonprofit from the department's perspective. I learned pretty quickly the sensitivity and hurt feelings regarding the disputes between the parties. The CALPA board members all saw the report, but we didn't circulate it among the membership in general even though some of the board members felt it provided an accurate narrative of the history of CALPA.

By fall 2003, after quite a bit of planning, we were ready to gather for our conference at Hearst Castle. The good news was we had the highest enrollment anyone could remember for the conference. That was a bit of a problem because sessions were going to meet at the hotel and the room was not large enough to accommodate our numbers. The CSP Department came to the rescue—setting up a video system in an adjoining room for the overflow. The opening-evening reception was in the foyer of the Hearst Castle theater—with more than 150 people present. At the opening, several of us spoke. This included a welcome by Donna Pozzi, chief of interpretation and education of the California State Parks Department, after which we were treated to a showing of *Hearst Castle: Building the Dream* on a giant screen. We were energized.

An interesting aside: The person who was in charge of California State Parks's overseeing construction of the theater and production of the film was none other than Don Kinney, who previously had been superintendent of our district at the Presidio. He had very positive memories of working with the SBTHP and invited my staff up for a tour and a special crab feast in one of the Castle casitas, and on another occasion invited my staff up to swim in the famous outdoor pool. Yes, there are some great memories of working with CSP Department.

The Hearst Castle conference was one of those great times as well. Food and potent potables were all taken care of by the park concessionaires, and all the sessions were held at the hotel, as mentioned. After the Friday sessions, we were bused up the hill thanks to Kirk Sturm for an outdoor session at the castle—which was all ours to walk around that evening.

The next day were tours to sites and parks in the vicinity of the castle as far south as Morro Bay (buses were provided by the CSP Department), ending that evening with a banquet at the hotel. Director of California State Parks Ruth Coleman was unable to attend but she sent her chief deputy. It was also at that meeting that I met for the first time dynamic parks people, including one of the most dynamic of them all, Laura Davick, who has been the major force behind the restoration of the cottages at Crystal Cove State Historic Park. The upshot of all this was the conference for the first time turned a profit—well over five thousand dollars. Since that time, all the CALPA conferences except one have turned a profit and have helped us build a financially stronger organization.

Instead of our meeting solely in Sacramento, I suggested the board meet at parks around the state. This included a strategic-planning session at Marconi Conference Center State Historic Park; some of our regular meetings took place at Calaveras Big Trees State Park, state parks at Lake Tahoe, and California Citrus State Historic Park in Riverside. I guess I had forgotten just how big our state is, as it became a burden to travel such long distances for some of the board members who lived in San Diego or up north in Red Bluff, so eventually we returned to Sacramento and then started conference-call meetings, and today, yes, CALPA is Zooming.

California League of Park Associations Board meeting in Sacramento, circa 2004. The author served on the board for twenty years with his fellow "park lovers." *Author's Collection*

The author completes visiting all 282 state parks at Point Sal in 2014. *Author's Collection*

After four years, I stepped down and handed the gavel to Randy Widera, at the time in the employ of Friends of Santa Cruz State Parks. Following him came Carolyn Christian of Pío Pico State Historic Park and, at present, George Loyer of the Valley of the Moon Observatory Association.

Michele and I really enjoyed our travels to our parks. At one point, I observed we had visited about two hundred of the 282, and then I decided to see them all. It took me about two and a half years to see the remaining eighty-two of them. Remember, these parks lie as much as one thousand miles apart—for example, Pelican State Park is on the Oregon border and Picacho State Recreation Area is located just north of Yuma, Arizona, on the California side of the Colorado River. There are very few people who have done such an adventure, and all it did for me was grow my appreciations for the natural and cultural wonders of this state. Also, in part for my work with CALPA, my sojourn to all the parks, and my thirty-five years at El Presidio de Santa Bárbara State Historic Park, the California State Park Rangers Association (CSPRA) named me honorary ranger in 2016j, an award I received at their annual conference in Morro Bay in fall 2016. At that event, I revealed my favorite state park, a secret that those at the luncheon were among the first to have heard of and to whom it gave a good laugh. For the general public it must remain a secret. Many people more influential and important than me have received the award of honorary ranger—including Walt Disney.

I mentioned earlier that my contacts with headquarters were really important in building a relationship with the senior staff there and especially with Ruth Coleman, who was director during some of the critical financial moments of the SBTHP that will be described in the upcoming chapters. I finally retired from the CALPA board at the end of 2021.

CHAPTER FOURTEEN

SURVIVING THE GREAT RECESSION

I AM WRITING this as we, my fellow Americans, are enduring one of the most trying times in recent memory—the COVID-19 pandemic. Who could have thought it would get worse than 9/11? Then came the Great Recession and we faced the greatest financial challenge since the Great Depression—now the pandemic, which at the time of this writing finally seems to be waning. I have to say I am glad to be retired and not to have to deal with all that nonprofits are facing in today's political and economic climate. In truth, the SBTHP actually, when all was said and done, came through the Great Recession in pretty good shape, although when we were in the midst of it, I wasn't sure how it was going to work out. It was real estate that was the source of potential financial crisis for us, and it was only California State Parks that could rescue us in continuing to purchase properties from SBTHP for the Presidio.

Quite often I have praised the SBTHP board for its business prowess. Another example of the board fortifying its financial position was creating an official endowment. The proceeds from the sale of El Paseo had been used as a quasi-endowment with the SBTHP finance committee investing the five million dollars between two investment managers. Over time, the committee changed managers who were underperforming but on the whole tended to stay the course with its managers. Use of the funds was restricted to the Presidio and Casa de la Guerra. Normally, the SBTHP drew out funds for operations at only a 5 percent rate. Depending on the state of the economy, the rate of the draw might be raised or lowered. It was not a pure endowment because while the California attorney general had restricted use of El Paseo sale proceeds to the Presidio and Casa de la Guerra, the SBTHP could spend the endowment down to nothing if it so desired—say, for example, spending it on reconstruction and restoration projects.

In order to create a pure endowment, the SBTHP hired a professional to develop the documents and materials for an endowment program. The endowment document turned out to be rather complex in its details, but a key is that spending out of the corpus should not normally exceed 5 percent, and amounts used above that 5 percent should be seen as a loan and paid back. The SBTHP wanted as much unrestricted money as possible to be available for operations. There also was a significant number of board members who wanted an education fund to be an option for donations to the endowment. At the time, I thought this was fine, but later I began to see this as the board shifting its emphasis away from reconstruction of the Presidio. Since its inception, the endowment has grown, and there are future planned gifts that could raise the amount two to three million dollars. If the SBTHP were to sell to the state a property it owns today adjoining Santa Inés Mission Mills, those proceeds likely would go into the endowment as unrestricted funds. Another piece of real estate the SBTHP owns in the Presidio might have to go into the quasi-endowment. Yes, the SBTHP finances are complex—two state budgets, separate budgets for the SBTHP itself, and a couple properties in Lompoc that are for legal reasons freestanding.

But even with the above financial planning and conservative management of its assets, the SBTHP was hit hard by the Great Recession beginning late 2008, and we did what most businesses do—cut expenses. That included salary cuts and reduction in travel to conferences. At first, what made it worse were real-estate purchases that came at the wrong moment, one might say.

Real-Estate Complaisance

One might also say that the SBTHP board and yours truly had been lured into complaisance by the organization's successes. Properties in the Presidio area that we had purchased in the preceding decade were one by one conveyed to the state in the first decade of the twenty-first century. These included the Phelan or Rochin Adobe property, sold in 2002, and the Presidio front-gate parking lot, sold in 2006. The last one sold during this time period was the second parcel of the Phelan property, conveyed also in 2006. The first two properties were sold to the state at market value, but the third was a special case that I will explain later. The SBTHP actually benefited from these sales financially as the properties were sold for more than we had purchased them for. However, this extra earned income was deposited in the quasi-endowment investment fund, to be used for operations and possible future acquisitions. All was well so far, but the yellow-brick road of real estate we were on was about to have some significant bumps.

Jimmy's Oriental Gardens Rolling the Dice

Early in the decade, in 2003, Lino Castagnola died. I went up and spoke at his funeral. Since his death, Michele and I have made annual stops at his gravesite in Ashland, Oregon, to pay our respects. Just a month or so after his death, the transfer of the parking lot that he was donating to us was quickly set in motion. We drew half a million dollars from our funds, which was half the appraised value of the property, and paid it to the Lutheran church, the other beneficiary in Lino's will. We then owned that property and received all the income from the parking rentals. Again, real estate was our pathway to financial success. I immediately contacted the state about purchasing the property, but that was taking a while to get programmed for acquisition. These were years Ruth Coleman was director of California State Parks, and she and her chief of acquisitions, Warren Westrup, were extremely supportive of the SBTHP. I was confident they would eventually find the funds for this acquisition. But it didn't happen as quickly as I had hoped.

Then in 2006, Tommy Chung, son of the original owner of the restaurant and bar, Jimmy Chung, announced he was going to close the Jimmy's Oriental Gardens after sixty years. The listed sale price was a cool three million dollars. Because it was inside the footprint of the Presidio, we had to buy it, but I suffered major trepidation that we couldn't handle this big chunk of money. But several on the board forced the issue and we made a bid on the property. Apparently there was a higher bid than ours, but Tommy wanted the SBTHP to have it because he knew the future of the

Jimmy's Oriental Gardens with Packard owned by longtime SBTHP volunteer Jeremy Hass. *Courtesy SBTHP*

Tommy Chung, owner of Jimmy's Oriental Gardens, made sure SBTHP was able to acquire the property. *Author's Collection*

site was in good hands if we owned it. After closing escrow, we went around to various foundations in Santa Barbara and were able to secure loans for the full amount. The interest rate was pretty good but nothing as good as today. The pressure was now on me—at least I felt that way.

The first thing we did was find a new tenant for the restaurant as we moved into 2008, and we finally found someone through a leasing agent. It was an unmitigated disaster. He was putting in a high-end deli, but it turned out he was not sufficiently capitalized. It reminded me of the El Paseo restaurant disaster of 1983. He barely got open and made only one payment, and we had to serve him a three-day notice. The owner went ballistic, locked himself in the restaurant, and began to tear out electrical wires from the walls and destroy anything new he had put in. By the time we got him out of the place, it was in worse condition than when he came in. Our lawyer tried to track down his finances to see if we could recoup our losses, but soon found out there were no funding sources to track down. He disappeared out of town. I had contacted the police because I thought his violent behavior was criminal, but the response was this was a tenant-landlord matter, a civil matter. Sorry, we can't help you.

Right next to Jimmy's was the Three Pickles sandwich shop in the Whittaker building. Its proprietor, Bob Lovejoy, approached me with an offer to take over the restaurant area while we would still keep the bar for our museum use.

For me, it was like an angel had just descended from the heavens. He was willing to take over the mess the previous tenant had left behind. We cut a lease that forgave rent as he restored the building into a sandwich shop. This was around 2009 when we were still climbing out of the Great Recession. Bob did a first-rate job in

SBTHP hero Bob Lovejoy, who made key tenant improvements at Jimmy's Oriental Gardens, installs a plaque commemorating the prince's visit to Santa Barbara in 2013. *Courtesy SBTHP*

his rehab work and never complained once about the mess that he had to deal with. I wondered if he would have even taken on the project had he known the damage the previous tenant had done to the property.

Then there was the slight problem of paying the loans on the property. Bob's lease did not cover the debt, even though he was paying market rates under a triple net lease.

Please, Governor Schwarzenegger, Show Pity

The financial hole the SBTHP dug itself into came at the same time as the national economy was tanking, and in my mind, the fact that the SBTHP came out of this stronger speaks to the sound financial underpinning of the organization that the board had laid over the years. In addition, there was a boldness to move ahead and take some risks, perhaps the Jimmy's purchase the riskiest of them all.

The Arnold Schwarzenegger administration came into office in 2003 and retained Ruth Coleman as director of California State Parks, which was good news for us. It is important to realize that property-acquisition funds at the state level were very limited due to the fact that the source of the money was mainly bond acts, and those funds had been nearly used up. That is why I believe the SBTHP owes a great debt to Ruth Coleman and her staff because they had to scrape around to find funds and sometimes we had to get creative to make acquisitions happen.

By 2008, with the national economy on the verge of collapse, the CSP Department, after years of prodding on our part, agreed to purchase the Santa Inés Mission Mills property, which included about thirty-five acres and was, with the mission itself, a designated national historic landmark. The state had programmed $1.7 million for the property with the appraisal coming in at $1.5 million. Because the state is allowed to pay up to 20 percent over an appraisal, we received the $1.7 million when the land was conveyed to the State of California in 2008. To this day, it is still a state historic property, awaiting the California State Park and Recreation Commission's designation as a state historic park. That is a story in itself: Until recently, the commission lacked a quorum due to the governor not appointing members. In any event, the SBTHP received an infusion of money from this sale just as the economy was failing and our investments were in steep decline.

In short, we were still in difficult straits not able to retire the debt on Jimmy's. I kept in communication with the state and asked Ruth and her staff to consider purchasing the Castagnola property from us. This went on for several years until around 2008, when some money for the acquisition was finally programmed. It was going along just fine. In many cases, I would go to Sacramento to be in attendance at the meetings of the public-works board that has to give approval for all state acquisitions. Normally our projects would be gaveled through without comments. A few times, I was called forward and asked some questions. The Castagnola acquisition was one of those no-brainers and it was approved without any dissent. Then the bureaucratic paperwork began and getting all the ducks in order, as they say, took several months. Come November 2008, we were closing in on the sale. I asked the staffer working on the project if we couldn't try to close in November, and he said there was a little more to do and we needn't rush things, and we would close in December. Of course everything was going to be OK, I said to myself.

Then December came and Governor Schwarzenegger shut down spending across the board as he attempted to deal with the state's fiscal crisis. That stopped cold the sale of the Castagnola lot and the $1.5 million programmed. So close, but no cigar.

Jim and Sue Higman: More Angels

I have made the point repeatedly that a smart board was vitally important in helping the SBTHP endure the stormy seas of unstable economic times. That was only one part of the organization's success. There also were the "angels" who have supported the SBTHP over the years: Charles Storke, Helen Pedotti, Lino Castagnola, Julie Forbes, and down the line to Jim and Sue Higman. Sue had served on the board through its years of crisis in 1978 and 1979 when the SBTHP board faced a packed election, which the court eventually reversed. After she left the board, she remained as a docent leading school and adult tours. Without a doubt, she was an SBTHP stalwart. We were pretty close and she would come in frequently to talk. One day she said, "Jerry, you saved the SBTHP," and I really appreciated her saying that, not because it was true but because it is nice to have someone say something

Jim and Sue Higman, major supporters of SBTHP in their younger years. *Author's Collection*

nice about the job you are doing. I am not complaining but only explaining when I say it is pretty lonely being a CEO in the sense that you have to maintain a professional distance from both the staff and the board. Being friends with individual staffers has the problem of being seen as showing favoritism—and relations with the board also have to be handled carefully. The CEO is the main vehicle of communication between the board and staff, not to mention being the public face of the organization.

All that said, I felt that Sue and I were friends. She made several trips to Sacramento with me to lobby for parks. On one of those trips, she said that she and Jim had reinstated putting her father's house in her will for the SBTHP. Then something sad occurred. She began to show signs of dementia and eventually had to give up being a docent, and after a while Jim had to have her placed in a home that cared for Alzheimer's patients. Several years went by and then one day Jim called me and said he was getting along in years—into his nineties—and wanted to make sure that Sue's wish of our receiving her dad's house happened, and he wanted to follow up with me.

We were now in 2008. Jim had his complete wits about him, went to his lawyer, had Sue declared incompetent, and then was able to have her father's property conveyed to the SBTHP. It was a small house, not a Montecito mansion. But in Santa Barbara, even the smallest residences at that time brought in medium-six figures. Jim said he knew that Sue admired Pearl Chase and wanted to make sure that the gift benefited the Presidio reconstruction. She had only one request, that we try to sell the property to the tenants, who had been in the house almost twenty years. Well, to find a price the tenants could afford, we had to sell it about 10 percent under market value. I felt that while we were not legally bound to abide by Jim and Sue's wishes, we should. One board member involved with the transaction felt we should get market value, but we sold it at the reduced price to the tenants, who were truly grateful and for a number of years came by my office to thank me for helping them buy the house. More importantly, we kept good relations with Jim, and every December for about three years he would come in and write a donation check of five figures. So, the SBTHP decided to use these funds to underwrite its volunteer program and name the program after Sue.

But wait a minute; Jim was not done. He wanted to donate parcels of real estate to us in Lompoc. There were some issues related to potential soil contamination in an adjoining property, but a board member of the SBTHP who was a CPA, another board member, and SBTHP's attorney came up with the legal legerdemain that required that the property be a freestanding asset of the SBTHP; this provided the legal protection we needed to allow the gift to happen. When all was said and done, the total gift from the Higmans totaled over one million dollars. This all was happening as the Great Recession was gripping the nation. Our better angels were saving us. Jim lived to be ninety-six and I spent time with him during his last days. On his sickbed, he kept asking me if he could write another donation check, and I said no, please, we are most happy with what you have done for us. I truly felt blessed to have known this extremely bright and unpresuming gentleman. And Sue as well. She was one of Pearl's girls who stayed committed to Chase's number-one project—reconstruction of the Santa Barbara Presidio.

Meanwhile, Back at the Castagnola Lot

I once heard a pundit say about Washington politics that delay is defeat. That certainly seemed the case with the Castagnola situation. The sale looked dead in the water, even as I tried to keep it alive with frequent calls and trips to Sacramento. I was on the board of CALPA and would stop by to talk to staff at headquarters after those meetings. Meanwhile, the sales of Santa Inés Mission Mills and the Higman property had taken the pressure off us financially. We were still not able to retire the Jimmy's debt because our sinking investments required us to dip into our cash reserves. Several months went by and nothing happened; then summer came and I was about to give up. One morning, Jean Liston, our longtime receptionist, got the mail and buzzed me: "Jerry, I just opened an envelope. Nothing in it but a check for $1.5 million from the State of California." "You're kidding?" Sure enough, it was a check signed by Governor Schwarzenegger. In recent years, all transfer of funds like this had been done electronically. I called local California State Parks offices to confirm that this was legit, as they say, which was confirmed.

Angels, miracles, smart businesspeople—take your pick. The SBTHP from that moment on was going to be fine financially and back on track. The Jimmy's mortgage was retired.

Jimmy's Becomes Three Pickles, Plus the Pickle Room

When we left Jimmy's, it had been Bob Lovejoy and his family to the rescue. Opened in 2010, Three Pickles was an immediate neighborhood success. We had kept the bar for the purpose of creating a museum in that space. After a while, the SBTHP property-management committee became impatient that nothing was happening on the museum front; Bob Lovejoy had his eye on the bar and said if we were interested, he had purchased a liquor license on another property and would be happy to reopen the bar. Most importantly, Bob said he would re-create the bar exactly to its 1950s appearance. Interesting thought: a bar museum. With pressure from the management committee, the SBTHP entered into negotiations with Lovejoy for the bar—resulting in a detailed agreement that outlined how the bar was to be restored. It included extending the bar to its original length and reupholstering the booths and bar seats to their original colors. Tommy Chung, who was still alive then, required that we not use the original name, so the bar was renamed the Pickle Room, and the original Jimmy's sign was allowed to be brought in and was installed above the large mirror facing the bar customers. The copies of the original Asian chandeliers were located and installed, and the original artwork that Jimmy had hung of Chinese women were also rehung. Bob had gone out and purchased these at his expense. The SBTHP has recently mounted a new museum exhibit on Jimmy's family history. In 2018, Bob died unexpectedly, and in 2019 the SBTHP honored him posthumously with the George and Vivian Obern Preservation Stewardship Award, which was presented to his family at the SBTHP's annual meeting that year. At one point, while the SBTHP was struggling to close various real-estate deals, I made a remark at an SBTHP board meeting that I felt in some ways Bob had saved us from a Jimmy's disaster by rehabilitating the restaurant and later the bar at his expense and then paying rent besides—always on time. One of the board members on the management committee, Don Sharpe, seconded that comment.

Jimmy's: Let's Finish the Job

Since we had Ruth Coleman's attention and support, I thought this might be the time to see if we could generate interest in state acquisition of Jimmy's Oriental Gardens. At about the same time, the SBTHP found itself in a real-estate quandary at Santa Inés Mission Mills, which put pressure on us to find funds for the Mills acquisition, which I will return to in the next section. The real-estate rollercoaster seemed never to have an end.

I suggested to the board that it might be time to take a group to Sacramento to pitch Jimmy's to Director Coleman. I put together a team that included volunteers, an SBTHP staffer, and Tommy Chung and had the SBTHP pay to send all of us to Sacramento. I can't remember who was there from the director's staff, but I did feel positive that our group made an impression, especially because Tommy had agreed to come along and urge the director to purchase the property. Afterward, before returning to Santa Barbara, I took everyone to Frank Fat's, the most famous Chinese restaurant in Sacramento. I suggested that Tommy select the meal, which he did. What a feast; what a wonderful moment.

Lot-Split to the Rescue

Back in Santa Barbara, some time went by before we heard anything from Sacramento about Jimmy's. I finally did hear from Ruth that indeed the department was willing to program $1.5 million to purchase Jimmy's. We were pleased to hear that Ruth and her staff were trying to help us. Ruth told me later that Chief of Acquisitions Warren Westrup was a big supporter of this acquisition. But I had to respond to Ruth that we couldn't sell at that price, especially because we had a commitment at Santa Inés Mission Mills. She said her staff recommended that we hold back and wait until the next year to find additional funds. In the back of my mind, of course, was the nearly failed Castagnola sale. Then came an idea that I broached with her, or it might have been with one of her staffers: a lot-split in which we would sell them an amount that equaled $1.5 million. She didn't say no, but I got the impression it was not a firm yes. We hired appraiser Michael Arnold, who carved out the area of the restaurant and the garage and an apartment above it. He left the Chung residence in the parcel to split off. It turned out just right—his appraisal came out at $1.5 million. I was starting to think we were living a charmed life as an organization. One of the advantages of the state drawing property lines is its authority supersedes that of the city and it can draw parcels as it sees fit. The city, however, did not voice opposition, and we proceeded with work to pull off this idea. Needless to say, our lawyer did his job proficiently helping with the documentation, and we hired a surveyor to draw the map. The deal was ready to close, but not before Ruth Coleman left the California State Parks Department in 2012 after ten years of service, the longest tenure of any director in the department's history.

The new director was Anthony Jackson, a retired two-star Marine general. I immediately made an appointment to see him, but he was new on the job and did not give me a firm assent that Jimmy's was going to happen. Later I spoke to our district superintendent, Rich Rozzelle, and he assured me that the wheels were still turning to acquire Jimmy's. I actually built a friendly relationship with Director Jackson, mostly seeing him at CALPA events, and we were on a first-name basis. Jackson stayed only two years in the job, but the Jimmy's sale to the state closed during his time, and the site is now part of the Presidio state park. Two park directors contributed to the Parks Department's acquisition of Jimmy's, and it was the capstone of Ruth Coleman's support of the SBTHP and El Presidio de Santa Bárbara State Historic Park.

CHAPTER FIFTEEN

Santa Inés Mission Mills Takes Center Stage

AT THE END of my SBTHP career, I would receive many accolades, but one of them I mention facetiously: Life Honorary Real Estate Agent. As we were midway into the second decade of the twenty-first century, I calculated that a third of my time was spent in the real-estate world. Around 2005, for example, Aaron Petersen, a local businessman and a descendant of an early Solvang family, approached me about building spec homes next to our Mills property. He proposed giving the SBTHP a significant payment in exchange for allowing access to the parcel next door, where the homes were to be built. The details of this transaction are too complex and probably overwhelming to the average person, but in essence he wanted access and was willing to pay for, and give us access through, an easement on High Meadow Road. One of the major issues with the Mills property for us was lack of good access to the Park—in short, we had access only across the creek, which meant that we would need a bridge for automobile access. There was not a lot of enthusiasm for this project on the board. In the backs of our minds, with this negotiation was eventual state ownership of the property, and visitor access is important at state parks. In a close vote, the board eventually approved the agreement, and the next step was for Petersen to take the project through the county. I told Petersen that I didn't think he had to take it through the county-review process, but he went ahead and submitted it to the county. In the meantime, he made his payment to the SBTHP, which helped us with some of our operations deficits due to our real-estate commitments. The Petersen project failed to get the vote of the supervisors, and that was the end of it.

I think there were a lot of people on the board relieved by this failure. I thought Petersen had made every effort to meet our demands, including screening the viewshed from the Mills. But what was done was done. Meanwhile, by 2008, the Parks Department had purchased the Mills property, and by 2010, Petersen, who had purchased the parcel of about fourteen acres adjoining the Mills state property, decided to sell his fourteen acres. No rest for the wicked.

I don't quite remember the price but it was slightly over market value. One of the negotiators of the SBTHP on the board felt we should not pay over market value. I and others pointed out that the agreement included our keeping the six-figure down payment from the failed deal. That latter point carried the day and we purchased the property. Believe it or not, we did yet another lot split—leaving the house on the west side of Alamo Pintado Creek on one parcel that we sold, and retaining the open space and creek area of twelve-plus acres that remains in SBTHP ownership today. During the first few years after 2012, the SBTHP wrote a letter to the county seeking a property-tax exemption without a response. Michele, who told me the county assessor had been a student of hers in a training course she did for the county, recommended that I call him directly—so I did. I don't think that made any difference in his decision other than to get his attention. The property is open field coterminous to the state-park land that is today planted with olive trees. Eventually the county assessor issued a letter saying that the SBTHP was exempt from paying tax on the property. That saves the SBTHP ten thousand dollars per year. I assume that sometime, I hope in the near future, the SBTHP will seek funds from the state to acquire this Petersen parcel.

Olive Trees: They Seemed So Right for the Site

SBTHP relations with Mission Santa Inés were from early on nothing but extraordinary. I have to confess a deep Christian faith, albeit I am a Lutheran, not a Catholic. That faith was deepened as I came to know Father Michael Mahoney, pastor at the time that we were in discussions with the church about our acquisition of the Mission Mills. Father Michael fully comprehended the importance of connecting the mills across the field from the church. Without hesitation, he was on board creating easements from the Mission itself, across Mission property, to SBTHP property that contained the mills. The mills complex, containing a grist mill for grinding wheat and corn and a fulling mill for processing wool, are a significant part of Mission history, interpreting agriculture and farming introduced to California during this early-California period. With the approval of the archdiocese in Los Angeles, the church granted pedestrian easements to the mills and even allowed for some motorized method for the disabled. In addition, an easement was granted for parking in the Mission lot for visitors going to the mills. The easement document was signed and sealed before the Mills property was sold to the state in 2008.

Before the sale, we had the grand idea of planting olive trees in the fields between the Mission and the mills with the help of SBTHP board member Craig Makela, who was the owner of the Santa Barbara Olive Company at the time. Together on the church's and SBTHP's acreage, we planted around thirty acres of olive trees. What could be more perfect—as olives were introduced to California through the

Author's grandchildren, Paloma and India Longo, with olives from Santa Inés Mission mills property. *Author's Collection*

Spanish Missions. Eventually we would have a crop, press the oil, and have a Mission label for sale. In flights of Don Quixote fancy, we envisioned a pathway down the middle of the field with appropriate stations interpreting the faith, and a statue with a bench. The easement document includes the pathway as described.

I became so enthused about olives that I read up on their history—the Mount of Olives, the olive branch in Greek mythology, then the olive industry in southern Europe from Spain to Greece and across to North Africa in Morocco to Tunisia. On a trip to Greece in 2011, Michele and I came across an olive museum in Sparta, on the Peloponnese peninsula. This is without question a world-class museum and I thought something like this on a more modest scale would be great at the mills. Other aspects of farming and crops could also be interpreted.

Then catastrophe struck. Things were going along well, the trees were growing nicely—when all of a sudden after about a year, the mission's trees almost overnight began to die and within a short time only a few were left alive. Ours, too, were affected and we lost about half of our trees. Where the field sloped slightly upward, the trees tended to survive. All of our trees on the other side of the creek were OK. Bringing in some agriculture specialists, we learned that there was a deadly fungus that had entered the soil and was about a foot below the surface. The culprit was probably a crop of tomatillos previously planted there introduced the fungus. As the trees had grown, the root system had eventually reached the fungus. How utterly depressing. We should have tested the soil but "should" was not the best word when the damage had been done. Father Michael was devastated; so were we. We were able to salvage about ten acres of trees, maybe a few more acres that still have some of the trees on them. The SBTHP is now picking every fall and in recent years has had some excellent crops and sells this extra-virgin olive oil by the bottle. The Jackman family buys its share, usually several cases per year. But the church removed the few trees left and has left the field unfarmed. Perhaps a different Mission-period crop should be considered, and I hope someday the SBTHP helps make that happen. I have some ideas for the Mission and Mills properties that through a partnership might still make Mission Santa Inés and the Mills a wonderful outdoor museum interpreting early-California history.

Lot 72

It is rather prosaic to have an important archaeological site called Lot 72. The open-space site was created when a housing development next to it deeded the land to the city of Solvang as part of the negotiation to gain approval for the Village Collection subdivision housing development. I don't remember the year when that happened, but from the day the open space became public, there were efforts to develop it, one of the main ideas being soccer fields. Needless to say, neighbors were not too keen on this idea, and year after year they resisted other attempts to develop the site. Its archaeological importance lies in the fact that it was the site of some of the residences of the neophyte Indians at the Mission. Apparently, it was the one mission where the Indians were allowed to live in their tule conical huts rather than in adobe barracks. Finally, after years of back and forth, the SBTHP entered the scene. I'm not sure whose idea it was that the SBTHP lease the land and preserve the open space, but it was overwhelmingly popular with the neighbors, especially one of the residents who was a prominent local lawyer.

Thus, in 2011, the SBTHP signed a fifty-five-year lease to manage the sixteen-acre parcel. It is possible that it might someday become part of the state-park system, but for now it remains open space under the current lease. The land is located directly east of the Mission and could easily be incorporated into a trail system with interpretive signage. It also would be interesting to do some cross-trenches on the site to see what might be uncovered archaeologically. Ground-penetrating radar has been tried. The site would have to be temporarily fenced to undertake such archaeology. Another feature of the site is that it provides access to the Mission and Mills parcels that someday might be of value for any needed ADA parking. Neighbors probably would not like that, but compromise is always needed to benefit the greatest good for the greatest number.

Nostalgia and Rabbit Holes

Looking back to the 1980s, I remember many visits to the ranch house on the Mills property when the Knills lived in it. Harry Knill is known for his commitment to making real-estate deals, some of significant magnitude. During the time Michele and I have known Harry and Ellen, they have lived in many different places—we remember three different homes in Hope Ranch, a house in Summerland, and another in Lompoc, and today they live in a ranchette in Paso Robles. Plus, as mentioned, the Mills ranch house, where they lived for maybe five years. It was a rather smallish place for the Knills with their three children, in contrast to some of their larger houses. I remember Harry had a garage built to house their books. In March 2021, Michele and I visited them at their ranchette and I noted the nice Ionic columns that surrounded the house. That pleased Harry as he had just had those built. Plus, the house is large enough for their art and book collections—a reminder that Harry liked to have artists re-create historical scenes. One of the best of these is a painting of Santa Barbara in 1793 with the three ships of George Vancouver anchored in the harbor, and a view of the Presidio and Mission onshore. The painting was made into a poster, and we sold hundreds of them at the Santa Barbara Presidio. An amazing couple, Harry and Ellen once had a printing business that covered many subjects, including one of my favorites—Shakespeare. We used to see their books for sale in the bookshop of the Oregon Shakespeare Festival and at the Utah Shakespeare Festival.

While it was a different time and place, I have to tell the story of a dinner we hosted at our place years ago with the Knills—the conversation was lively, and in the course of the evening we discovered that we all had interesting language backgrounds. At the table was then-SBTHP President Alice Rypins—she had majored in French in college; also there was famous art historian Norman Neuerburg, who had majored in classical Greek at UCLA; next to him was Ellen Knill, who had majored in Latin at UC Berkeley; and yours truly, a German major at UCLA, sat next to Harry. Michele's first language as a child was Italian, and in her college days, she did research on Machiavelli in Italian while a student at UC Davis. How different the world is today—where German and the other language majors mentioned barely exist on UC campuses, not to mention at other colleges. All of those people I mentioned contributed to the Presidio project and other projects, such as the Santa Inés Mission Mills.

I have grown to love the mills—especially sitting above them looking out at the open space. The mills sent me down many rabbit holes, one of which, olives, I have already talked about. Another was the fulling process. I guarantee you if you give a talk and ask what a grist mill is, the audience to a person will know the answer; but if you ask what a fulling mill is, maybe one person will know. Fulling is the process of removing the lanolin from wool using a water-powered hammer system, which dates back to at least the sixteenth century. This we know because Cervantes describes a jousting battle of Quixote not only with a windmill but also with a fulling mill. In some of the classical editions of *Don Quixote*, there is often an image of the knight riding up to a fulling mill. Fulling as a process dates back at least to Roman times—a fullery, for example, has been uncovered at Pompeii. But then the feet of slaves were used to full the lanolin out of the wool.

I remember an exhibit we did of paintings by local artists of the Mills that were put up for sale. One of the most fascinating was a woman's painting of the Santa Inés fulling mill showing the wool placed on racks drying. After the show, I found out that painting had been sold and felt it inappropriate to ask to buy it back. Someday a painter should take on that subject. There is so much else about the mills that fire the imagination—and I can hardly wait to tell you in the closing chapter, "Why the Presidio Project Succeeded."

Lastly, I remember a disaster that turned into nostalgia at the Mills. I should remember the year, but it is not relevant for this true story. After a driving rain in the Santa Ynez Valley, the Alamo Pintado Creek reached flood stage, and debris began flowing down the creek until the debris backed up at the bridge at Highway 246. When the debris finally broke loose, it flowed down and flooded the Mills acreage on both sides of the creek. When I arrived to see the damage, both sides of the creek were underwater. I couldn't cross the creek, so I drove to High Meadow Road and walked into the site. It was scary. Half the land between the creek and the house was covered in water, mud, and debris. I walked the hillside to get to the mills, but fortunately the flow was away from the mills out onto the field between the mills and the Mission. The entire field was covered with water, with boulders and hundreds of old tires that had come rushing down the creek. Nature had asserted herself. I said to myself: How are we going to deal with this?

For one thing, at that time we did not have an easement from High Meadow Road, but the owner of the adjoining property let us enter through his property because a quagmire of mud was impassable. In fact, it remained so for several months. Then I began asking around about how to deal with the damage to our land. I can't remember who told me, but I found out that the US Department of Agriculture had grants to repair damaged farmland. I contacted our local legislator and found a contact person. Eventually we filled out the forms and received grants that enabled us to pay to have the fields repaired and plowed, and as I remember, the grant also covered having the tires disposed of. I will never forget the feeling of seeing all that water everywhere, and then the end result of getting it back to normal. One of the main themes of this memoir is the positive power of the partnership between a non-profit and government. Here was another example of it at work. In this case, mud had *not* been our friend.

CHAPTER SIXTEEN

WHEN DOES AN INTEREST BECOME A DISTRACTION?

ONE COULD ARGUE that sponsored trips are a waste of time as fundraisers for smaller and medium-size nonprofits. Larger museums and institutions with large memberships stand to do better for an obvious reason—larger pools of people to draw from. Another option is to pool with another nonprofit, but that can both dilute your profit potential and reduce your opportunity to promote your organization—you have to share the stage. That didn't stop the SBTHP from doing trips, and there were three of them worth discussing, all of them programmed by Spectrum Tours of Santa Barbara and its CEO, Lynn Kirst. All of these raised very little money and probably barely offset my salary as I went on the three trips. Still, they were so interesting and educational that they were worth doing. We had some great times together, and the tours built camaraderie.

Mississippi

The first tour with Spectrum Tours was in 2001 just before 9/11 Kirst proposed a trip to Mississippi to experience the *Majesty of Spain* exhibition in Jackson. It turned out a person named Jack Kyle had been key in organizing world-class art events from Russia and France, and thus the *Majesty of Spain* was mounted at a cool $8.9 million and showcased six hundred royal objects, as well as sixty paintings (yes, Goyas) from the Museo Nacional del Prado in Madrid and from the Patrimonio Nacional in Spain, which comprises six of the royal palaces of Spain, including two of the most famous—the Royal Palace of Madrid and the Royal Palace of Aranjuez. The enormous difference in wealth is evident in this exhibit compared with the Presidio outpost in faraway California. I remember the simple dishware that Vancouver's men commented on in their dinner with Goicoechea in 1793 in the Presidio comandancia.

Most of the artwork in the show had never been displayed outside of Spain before this event. It was a rare opportunity to share this great show with our membership, and we had about twenty people sign up, including Michele's sisters and longtime SBTHP volunteers George and Vivian Obern. The tour, about a week in length, included more than the *Majesty of Spain* exhibition. We were also able to see *Mississippi: Outpost of Majestic Spain*, an exhibition at the Old Capitol Museum of Mississippi history tracing Spanish influence in the region from de Soto's explorations in the 1540s through Spain's imperial rule in the late 1700s. I made contact with the historian organizing this exhibition and obtained materials on the Spanish history along the Mississippi River that went all the way north of St. Louis, Missouri, at different periods of time.

On our bus tour after we left Jackson, we stayed at several plantation mansions with mint juleps waiting for us when we arrived. We were traveling in April and this was the time when many of the mansions were open for tours, and the sweltering summer heat had not yet arrived. We also spent a day in Natchez and went to a dance in the evening, a sort of debutante ball that definitely had a southern flavor.

The splendid week ended in Vicksburg, where we toured Vicksburg National Military Park. This had special meaning for me as my great-great-grandfather William Magden III was a lieutenant under Generals Grant and Sherman at this battle site and siege and was seriously wounded. The Battle of Vicksburg, along with the Battle of Gettysburg, ended with Union victory July 4, 1863, and was a turning point in the Civil War. I also had another relative serve but not at this battle—the son of William Magden III. He was a corporal wounded at different battles who happened to be born December 5, 1843. His great-grandson, yours truly, was born December 5, 1943.

One of the highlights of the trip was a dinner that evening at a local Vicksburg restaurant, celebrating, as I remember, George Obern's birthday. It was one of those fun evenings, and as we left the restaurant, we noticed a building next door with a National Historic Landmark marker. It turned out to be the residence and headquarters of the Southern general John Pemberton, who was defending Vicksburg against the onslaught of Grant. He eventually surrendered, as most historians of the Civil War know. It turned out the house was being restored as a bed and breakfast, and the owners happened to be present in the building planning the restoration. They invited us in and took us on a tour of the house—including the room that was Pemberton's office. One of the owners pointed to scratch marks on the floor where the general's desk used to be. He told us those were from Pemberton's spurs that he wore at all times.

This trip I thought was going to be hard to top. Little did I know that Lynn Kirst had an idea for a grand finale. She said to me she was about to close down her business but wanted to do one more grand tour—a trip to northern Spain.

I said I was game. But then came 9/11 and everything seemed up in the air. But somehow Lynn put it all together—a nearly three-week trip that made stops in some of the most historic sites in all of Europe, including the birthplace of one of Santa Barbara's most famous citizens, José de la Guerra.

Ramona

The next excursion with Spectrum Tours preceding the European trip was in May 2002 to see the *Ramona Pageant* play held annually in Hemet, California, and based on Helen Hunt Jackson's 1884 novel *Ramona*. It was a bestseller whose main purpose was to draw attention to the Native people's plight in California, but it had a different effect, instead providing what came to be a romanticized version of the Mission period of California. Jackson had previously written a book titled *A Century of Dishonor* (1881) that focused on injustices Native people had suffered in America. I think if one takes the *Ramona Pageant* as an interesting piece of theater and not a presentation of historical truth, then the show is rather amazing with people on horseback and live music that may not be the exact music performed during the Mexican period. Lynn set it up as a three-night trip—with our staying at the Mission Inn in Riverside, one of the most famous hotels in southern California re-creating a Spanish architectural setting that could just as well be in Seville. We stopped on the way down to Riverside at Rancho Camulos near Piru in Ventura County, the site where author Jackson set her novel. We also visited Mission San Fernando Rey de España and Mission San Gabriel, going and coming.

The *Ramona Pageant* play reminded me of our creating a Don Quixote event at the Presidio—just to have some fun. We also did a Zorro event. It is hard to think in terms of fun in the hyper-politicized world of today and its anti–Father Serra mood. Native people had to adapt to a forceful European civilization that also brought with it some dangerous pathogens. As a result, we are told that suffering and grievance supersede any attempts at just having fun. Putting those aside for an evening, our tour group enjoyed the Ramona play, and everyone should see it at least once.

Once in a Lifetime

I say without hesitation that Lynn Kirst's northern Spain trip was a once-in-a-lifetime experience. That may seem like an odd way to start out, but I want to describe first a trip about a week long that we took to Germany before we left for Madrid from Frankfurt. I have a purpose and will try to explain it at the end of this German adventure. In fact, Michele was with me on this trip from beginning to end, and it started after a long flight from Los Angeles to Frankfurt. We arrived to pick up a rental at the airport, both of us pretty exhausted, but I wanted to drive to Kassel that morning before continuing on to Lübeck. To my surprise, I was given a brand-new Audi Quattro with just 6 "clicks" on the odometer, as we Americans living in Germany used to call kilometers. Within five minutes on the Autobahn, Michele dropped off to sleep and it began to rain, while on the radio a German station was doing a history of the Beach Boys, playing all their music. Porsches were passing us as if we were standing still, even though I was cruising along at 130 clicks per hour. We arrived safely in Kassel, overnighted there, and got up to go to the Brothers Grimm museum. That was the main purpose of our stop in Kassel, but the museum was closed for restoration. There you go. Travel miles to see a museum but it is closed. This is one of my pet peeves: coming to a museum that is closed without advance notification. No matter what, I told my staff, we must always avoid this kind of situation at our Santa Barbara museum sites. We must always be open for the visitor that may never be able to see us again.

After Kassel, we drove to Lübeck to visit Thomas Mann's birthplace for a second time. Actually, it was the first time for Michele. We bought books and tapes at the Buddenbrookhaus and walked the streets where Mann spent many days and got his idea for his famous novel *Buddenbrooks*. Then we went on to the island of Rügen, where we spent the night, to cross over to an island called Hiddensee, where Mann and his family used to spend some summers. Interestingly, just down the block from their summer home was the summer residence of another Nobel Prize–winning author, the German dramatist Gerhart Hauptmann. Mann saw Hauptmann as literary competition and caricatured Hauptmann in his novel *Der Zauberberg* (in English, *The Magic Mountain*). We ended the day with a fantastic meal back at the hotel before we started the next day for Berlin and a hotel that Mann liked to stay in during his visits before the Nazis. On the way, we stopped at Peenemünde, where the famous missiles of Wernher von Braun were built—V-1s and the more deadly V-2s. I could find here a Thomas Mann connection, as the "V" stood for *Vergeltungswaffen*, or "revenge weapon." The weapon got its name as revenge for the allied bombing of Thomas Mann's former home, Lübeck.

Then we went on to Berlin to Hotel Adlon Kempinski, where Mann used to stay, but it was booked up, so we stayed at another hotel. Obviously I had built the trip around my Thomas Mann obsession. We did take a side trip, as it were, to my favorite museum in the world—the Pergamon, with its Greek treasures from the city of Pergamon, which is in present-day Turkey. Also, we did a day trip to Sanssouci in Potsdam to visit this famous palace of Frederick the Great. Then we rushed down the Autobahn to Weimar to the famous statue of Goethe and Schiller in the city *Platz*. There is a famous photo of Mann standing before this statue after the war that got him into trouble with American authorities; Weimar was in communist East Germany just as the Cold War was heating up in 1949. Afterward, we tried to see the Bauhaus Museum in Weimar, but it was just closing. I saw on a Weimar city map where the famous German philosopher Friedrich Nietzsche spent his last days, so I thought why not: at least drive by it. It turned out to be open and we saw the room where Nietzsche spent his last day. Of course Thomas Mann was under the influence of Nietzsche and wrote various essays on him.

So what did this German part of the trip have to do with the upcoming portion to northern Spain and the Spanish world of the Presidio? One response might be, Why would anyone want to travel with me and be dragged to see Thomas Mann sites? I was normally not that hectic in planning our trips, but for me Thomas Mann and German history were a way to put into perspective my day-job world. Today as I write this, we hear this nonsense about Father Serra being an Adolf Hitler and Spanish soldiers being Nazis. This reckless abuse of history is something I am more than willing to address. Thomas Mann and his family, and thousands of other intellectuals, suffered the Nazis' wrath (not to mention specifically the Holocaust itself) and would have found offensive comparing someone like Serra to Hitler. This is not the place to go into the absurdity of these comparisons, but I am ready to talk about them any other time.

Madrid

Before departing Frankfurt, where we had spent over four years in the 1970s, we visited with friends from those years, and the next day went to the airport to be off to Madrid. But this was 2002, less than a year after 9/11, and there was a bomb scare. We were frustrated as it looked as if we would not make our plane to Madrid; a United Airlines woman sensed our panic and took us over to the first-class check-in—we made it.

There was a fairly small group of us on the tour, around fifteen. We gathered the first night at a Madrid hotel. We spent a few nights in the city—one evening we enjoyed a dinner with flamenco dancing of high quality; during the day we visited the royal palace of the Bourbons. It was the residence of Charles III, the enlightened despot, who was king of Spain when Santa Barbara was founded April 21, 1782. Reports of the founding and work on the building of the Presidio were reviewed at meetings in the throne room of the royal palace. Faraway Santa Barbara was one of the last colonial expansions of Spain, and it had Charles's interest and attention. One of the coincidences was the fact Charles had his hand in archaeology overseeing excavations at Pompeii while monarch of the kingdom of Naples and Sicily prior to becoming king of Spain in 1759. These excavations included the Villa dei Papiri in Herculaneum, the latter of which was re-created as the Getty Villa in Pacific Palisades, California, in 1976. A few years later, in the 1980s, as I alluded to earlier, a statue of King Charles III was donated to Santa Barbara by Spanish Bourbon king Juan Carlos and it ended up located at the Presidio, where a major archaeological investigation has been going on for years—almost as if the king is overseeing it. By the way, the statue of King Charles III was a casting from an eighteenth-century mold; there are two other castings—one in the Botanic Garden in Madrid and one in the plaza in the city of Burgos.

The trip was designed for us to see the major sites of northern Spain, when possible connecting them to Santa Barbara, and to visit the birthplace of José de la Guerra. There was a de la Guerra descendant on the tour—more on that to come. On the pleasure side, we stayed at paradores, historic sites turned into first-class hotels, and at a few regular hotels with four- and five-star ratings. Meals were always special—by the end of the trip, we had been treated to three Michelin-starred restaurants: a one-star in Cantabria, a two-star outside of San Sebastian, and a three-star in San Sebastian itself.

One would expect that if there were Gaudí offerings you must be in Barcelona, but it turns out that the great Catalan architect did three works outside of Catalonia—and we would see all three: a commercial building in León, a restaurant that was near the coast and a former residence, and the bishop's castle in Astorga. I mention Gaudí because it is a stretch to relate his architectural work to Santa Barbara, but he was and still probably is the most famous Catalan, and from what I have previously written we know of the important California connections of Catalans then and now, especially at the Presidio thanks to SBTHP volunteer Carmen Farreras. I do not want this to become a travelogue, so I mention the food and hotels and some other historic moments but by no means all. Every parador, every meal had something special about it—the setting, the particular cuisine, the excellent *vinos tintos*. I will drop in a few experiences that particularly piqued my interest but do not necessarily add to the point of understanding this voyage from an SBTHP perspective. What it probably will do to some readers is make them wish they were on the trip.

A Brief Side Trip

We had a bus waiting for us early in the morning to leave Madrid, with an unusual first stop—the small town of Candelario, which is 130 miles west of Madrid, right on the border of Extremadura but still in the state of León, south of Salamanca. Why a stop here in the foothills of the region? Before we left Santa Barbara, an article in the local *News-Press* by a reporter captured our attention. She had a background in studying Spanish, spent some time in Spain, and ended up marrying a Spaniard. While in Spain, she became aware of the de la Guerras, proceeded to research the life of José de la Guerra, and visited his birthplace in Novales, in northern Spain. We naturally communicated with her, and she arranged a meeting with her Spanish father-in-law, who was from Candelario and was the retired police chief of Madrid. He was there to greet us, and we had a pleasant reception in the town.

Most memorable about the lovely town were the doors facing on the street that had these unusual Dutch-style doors in front of the double doors. We were told that in years past pigs ran through the streets at certain times of year and these half-doors kept the animals from entering houses. While the pigs no longer run through the streets, the half-door tradition survives and the doors are used throughout the town. I also noted channels of water running down streets, feeding fountains for which the town is known. The pig theme was continued the next day after we had traveled on to Ávila and Segovia. In Segovia, famous for the intact Roman aqueduct that dominates the center of town (it was used to carry water until the 1990s), we had an afternoon feast of a whole pig roast served to our group on a platter. Most people are unaware that it was Spain that introduced pork to the New World—Columbus had pigs on board, and Ponce de León introduced the pig to North America. Thus the side trip to Candelario became a way to connect historical dots—from Spain eventually to California. In Mexico, pork was added to the native diet of tomatoes and corn (hominy) to create a Spanish/Mexican staple called *pozole*. We have had several *pozole* feasts at the Santa Barbara Presidio, the last one about 2010 put on as a "friend-raiser" thanks to local businessman David Bolton, who personally prepared the *pozole* for our guests.

We did overnight in Ávila, one of the great walled cities of Europe. Famous as the home of one of the most influential religious figures of Spain, Saint Teresa, it was also the residence of a youthful George Santayana, whose Spanish mother married an American and took her young son to Boston, where he became one of the most important American philosophers at Harvard University, later moving to Rome, where he stayed for the rest of his life. I mention him because he was a favorite of my mentor at UCSB, Harold Kirker, and I read quite a bit of his writings, including his autobiography *Persons and Places*. We stayed in a parador next to the cathedral and were off the next day to Salamanca, home to one of the oldest universities in Europe.

Some feel the plaza of Salamanca is the finest in all of Spain and it is a powerful place to stand in. For us in Santa Barbara, we have had flights of fancy of having a true enclosed plaza, but parking has always been an obstacle; yet today as I write this Santa Barbara has closed its main road through town, State Street, to cars and maybe the time has come for Plaza De La Guerra to fulfill its destiny. Experiencing the Plaza Mayor de Salamanca might convert some of the naysayers in Santa Barbara. Plazas are powerful public spaces.

One of my major disappointments happened in Salamanca. Miguel de Unamuno was the author of one of my favorite books—*The Tragic Sense of Life* (published circa 1912). I read it twice over the years. The first time I hated it and may not have finished it; then the second time for reasons I can't remember I started to read it and it resonated. The title of the book says what it is about, and so it is not for everyone, but it is a beautiful book about the struggle to find meaning in life. Unamuno, of Basque origin, spent most of his years at the University of Salamanca, twice being rector and a couple times removed for political reasons. He died tragically as Franco came to power. In Salamanca, his house has been made into a museum. I looked forward to seeing it, and when I came to the museum door, it was locked. In the window was a handwritten note in Spanish—"Museum closed today due to illness."

My pet peeve again: six thousand miles from home—my only chance to see it as the tour had to continue. In some ways it was more than just missing a museum—I was there to pay my respects to a man who had influenced my life. I got over it, but I will say this one more time—a museum should always be open when it is supposed to be open.

To El Camino de Santiago

On this part of the trip, we were making our way to the famous pilgrimage route that dates from the Middle Ages, begins in France, traverses northern Spain, and ends up near the coast of northwest Spain in Santiago de Compostela at the church that has the putative remains of Saint James (a translation of *Santiago*). Thousands of *peregrinos* walk the famous route, some knocking off certain miles every year and returning until they can say they have walked all five hundred miles. First, we bused through Valladolid, where Columbus spent his last days, and we failed to arrive in time to see his house museum. We overnighted on the way to León and visited a town that was interesting with its wooden-plank "sidewalks." Then finally we arrived in León, where we stayed at the parador. We were now right on the St. James trail and we saw people with their backpacks and walking sticks pass us by outside the hotel. Downtown we saw the Gaudí commercial building—I believe it was now a bank—and had a walking tour of the historic district. The highlight of the city is the massive gothic cathedral in the French style designed by a French architect.

The next day, we were heading to Santiago—on the bus, not on foot, as we were still two hundred miles away. Then one of those overwhelming experiences lay in front of us as we passed through the city of Lugo—a giant walled area in the center of town. I mean huge walls, twenty feet high. I asked the driver to circle the walled area, which was completely enclosed and intact. This wall is as imposing as the Roman aqueduct in Segovia—and also was built by the Romans. I thought of Richard Lugo, one of the great descendants of the Santa Barbara Presidio, and wondered if he might be descended from a Roman soldier from the first century A.D. For sure, we know that he is descended from a Presidio soldier. One might say that this walled, fortified area was the origin of the presidios that would make their way to California. The Latin term for a fort is praesidium.

Late that afternoon, we arrived in Santiago de Compostela and checked into our hotel in the plaza located right next to the cathedral with its famous archway at the front doors dating from the late Romanesque period. We had another splendid meal in the hotel, and at night walked around the town. This area of Spain is much cooler and cloudier and the weather was very much like Santa Barbara. One odd experience—we were at a local museum and were upstairs when we heard chanting outdoors in a small plaza; a door was left open and I looked out and saw signs promoting gay rights. This was 2002, and an indication that the Spanish were no longer the Spanish of Franco's time.

The cathedral visit is an essential part of the experience where the bones of Saint James putatively lie—thousands of people pass through the portal of the church as the final experience of their trek. Many of the people are of the faith; at least an equal amount do it for their individual, nonreligious purposes. I am not sure that I can add much to the discussion of this experience. A Hollywood movie has been made on the subject, and numerous books have been written, including actress Shirley MacLaine's book *The Camino* (2001).

One idea that did spring out of my head was to have our El Camino Real in California become designated a UNESCO World Heritage Site. In fact, my friend Carmen Farreras and I drew up an initial proposal that compared El Camino de Santiago with our El Camino Real de California, the former already a designated site. So far this idea has not gained momentum, but our California site's similarity with El Camino de Santiago is that there are *peregrinos*, even an organization supporting them, who walk the length of California's Royal Highway—albeit many thousands fewer in number. Nominations for World Heritage designations have to go through the National Park Service, and are political. There are those who doubt UNESCO would be interested in our Camino, not to mention those here in California who are resistant to anything connected to the United Nations—so it remains an idea, if for no other reason than that it could serve as an organizing principle for understanding the political, economic, and cultural evolution of California. Even famed Apple CEO Steve Jobs noted the fact that his company had its location on California's El Camino Real.

Am I a Visionary?

One of my employees once called me a visionary. I apparently did not have enough Sancho Panza in me—instead too much dreaming, and not enough practical day-to-day commitment to the immediate world of the SBTHP. I interject this at this point because I confess to thinking about connecting ideas and how they might be applied to the long-term goals of the SBTHP. This trip engendered the Camino idea; that became a valuable symposium we held at the Presidio with Professor Julianne Burton-Carvajal, my co-organizer. As we left Santiago de Compostela and continued our journey toward José de la Guerra's birthplace, the wheels were still turning in my head. What would come of this visit in the long term for the SBTHP?

We were now off the Camino de Santiago and on a coastal road heading east to Oviedo in the principality of Asturias. The heir to the Spanish throne has the title of Prince of Asturias, as the heir to the British throne is the Prince of Wales. There is a special theater in Oviedo and an annual award is given out to a person of note in the name of the prince. The year we were there, 2002, the winner was none other than Woody Allen. Today there is a life-size statue of the filmmaker located in the town.

As a UCSB graduate student of Harold Kirker, most of whose scholarship was on architectural history, I naturally became interested in the subject. Not on the scheduled tour was a religious site north of the city in the mountains. I asked that we detour to see that site because the Church of Santa María del Naranco, built in the ninth century, was the precursor of Romanesque architecture that came to dominate not only Spanish churches but all those of Europe from the tenth through the twelfth centuries. For some of us, Romanesque architecture is perfection, and our side trip to the church was one of the most pleasant surprises of the entire tour. The site also has political resonance, as it was from Asturias that the *Reconquista*, or reconquest of Spain, began against the Moors. The simple, powerful Romanesque architecture came to symbolize that *Reconquista*. One might say that the birth of modern Spain began in Asturias, and it is the reason why the rulers of Spain chose it as the place to represent the future of the monarchy and their country.

On to Santander

Leaving the heady brew of the Spanish monarchy, we descended into the smaller world of our own José de la Guerra. After a day of driving, we checked into a hotel in Santander, the capital of the state of Cantabria, which lies between Asturias and the Basque region to the east. Twenty-five miles to the west, still in Cantabria, is the little town of Novales, where José de la Guerra was born March 6, 1779. We headed there to meet the mayor and to visit the house in which de la Guerra was born. This all took place July 4 and with us was Teresa Siebert, a direct descendant of José de la Guerra who just happened to be celebrating her birthday that day. We were received at the small city hall by the mayor, whose name has long faded from my memory, but he presented us with gifts including a plaque with the Novales insignia on it. We sang happy birthday to Teresa. We also were treated to a tapas feast at José's birthplace, which is still a residence occupied by a retired pilot and his wife. They were most hospitable. It is a small place with only a moderate-size living room and small bedrooms upstairs. It is indication that the de la Guerras were an ancient family but not very high up on the ladder of nobility. There also is a guard tower near town that we visited that supposedly belonged to the de la Guerra family. Seeing the modest size of his family home, we came to a better understanding why José gave up his birthright under primogeniture, i.e., being the firstborn. There doesn't appear to be very much to have inherited, while he had become one of the wealthiest men in Alta California, with land holdings all the way up to near modern-day Lompoc and to the south in the Simi Valley.

While we stayed in Santander, I made sure to collect names and addresses of research institutions, such as the Archivo Histórico Provincial de Cantabria and the Biblioteca de Menéndez Pelayo, for those wishing to pursue further research on the Spanish history of the de la Guerras. Nearby Novales is the famous cave of Altamira with its prehistoric paintings. To minimize damage from human breath, a replica of the cave has been created nearby and it is to scale with the original. I believe something like five thousand visitors per year are allowed into the original cave, but those numbers may have changed as nearly twenty years have passed since our visit. One last stop before we journeyed on was at Santillana del Mar, a pleasant Middle Ages town that is popular with tourists.

Last Stop: Saint Sebastian

We were now on the way to the last couple of nights of this overwhelming trip. I say overwhelming because there was so much to absorb—historical sites, meals, human encounters—and my head filled with ideas that today have become memories. We were now entering the Basque country, with a people who speak a unique language unrelated to the Spanish and French spoken in the countries in which they live. The Basque also have a unique culture and they transferred much of that culture to the New World, to northern Mexico, to Alta California, and in the person in charge of building the presidio of Santa Barbara and about whom I have written as the person in whose shadow I remain today. Of course, I am referring to Felipe Antonio de Goicoechea.

Our first stop in the Basque country was in Bilbao to visit the incredible Guggenheim museum designed by the influential architect Frank Gehry. This giant titanium structure is fantastic. It is something to look at from the exterior—it feels innovative; it is different from anything that has ever been created. Michele and I walked around the exterior along the water's edge. The interior is unique in its angularity—nary a straight line—creating a wonderful feeling of openness and interconnection. I don't remember looking at any of the artwork, and it made me think of the Getty Villa, where some critics felt the building overwhelmed the collection. What a difference, though, between the Getty Villa and this Guggenheim museum—the former based on classical forms from Roman times, the latter making the ultimate statement of modernism in its use of steel (and titanium), concrete, and glass. This experience had to add to the overwhelming feelings mounting from this once-in-a-lifetime tour of Spain. By the way, there is a full-size statue of US President John Adams in Bilbao in Doña Casilda Park, but that is a story for another time.

Later in the day, we arrived in San Sebastián, the major Basque city that is built around an enclosed bay that empties out to the Bay of Biscay. The comandante of the Santa Barbara Presidio traced his family roots on his father's side to somewhere in this Basque country. As I noted earlier, I have yet to determine the birthplace of his father, Juan, and the answer to this question probably can be found in Basque libraries and archives. After a nearly three-week trip, we arrived in San Sebastián, and the agenda was filled with Michelin-star meals. There is a major Basque museum in the city and it was closed when I was there. I should have made arrangements to talk to someone at the museum in advance, and that option is still there. I have a strong suspicion that Goicoechea's father was born in Spain, and there are people you can hire there to do the genealogical research for you.

Thinking about Goicoechea as I looked out from our hotel room at the bay below in its beautiful setting, I couldn't help thinking I was here at this moment because of Goicoechea and his fellow Spaniards settling in Santa Barbara. It reminded me of the diversity of people in general who settled California. The myth of the monolithic conquistador Spaniard coming to the New World is balanced by the historical truth that even in the early centuries of Spanish colonization, there were Basques, Catalans, and Galicians who were part of one of the major movements of peoples in the history of humanity. This group of colonizers was joined by indigenous people to form the Spanish frontier.

Then another thought crossed my mind as I looked at a diving platform offshore below. It brought to memory what many consider Ernest Hemingway's best novel, *The Sun Also Rises*. One of the late scenes in the novel takes place in San Sebastián, when the main character, Jake Barnes, swims out to that platform in the bay and dives off the board. Hemingway implies that Barnes, who has been part of the Lost Generation of Americans living in post–World War I Europe, emerges cleansed from that decadent world and ready to move on with his life. I thought about swimming out to the platform myself to see what feelings I might have after diving into the water. Well, we didn't have time for that swim, and instead I prepared to pack for the final trip home.

Less than a year after the fateful 9/11 tragedy, travel on this trip was very restrictive. We had that difficult incident in Frankfurt, and in Madrid we were made to take everything out of our luggage—most of it dirty laundry. We were by this time pretty travel-weary with considerable ground having been covered in Germany and Spain in slightly over a month. It was good to be on the way home, but this indeed had been a trip of a lifetime—one made possible by Lynn Kirst and one that helped me and others on the trip realize more deeply that Santa Barbara, its Presidio, and its original leaders were inextricably bound together with Spain and its many cultures. Our Santa Barbara founding fathers and mothers were connected to Spain, not England, and that heritage was ours to interpret and convey to our children and the general public at El Presidio de Santa Bárbara State Historic Park.

CHAPTER SEVENTEEN

Casa de la Guerra: Profit Versus Interpretation

Wedding Redux

Michele and I came home to prepare for a major Jackman family event—the marriage of our daughter, Renée, to local attorney and dedicated surfer Dana Longo. Dana had taken over the law practice of his father, who had recently died. Across the street from his office on Brinkerhoff Avenue in Santa Barbara was a landscape architect for whom Renée was working, and they saw each other and reconnected—both were San Marcos High School graduates and attended Dana's senior prom together. Dana graduated a year before Renée.

The stars were aligning. Dana as a boy had become an Eagle Scout writing his final report on the history of adobes in California—that put him in good stead with me. Plus, one of his mother's first encounters relocating to Santa Barbara from Los Angeles with her husband, Phil, was to volunteer at the Presidio—this was around 1969. One of her friends told her the Presidio project was one of the most interesting projects to volunteer on in Santa Barbara.

Eventually Dana and Renée announced their engagement and we planned their wedding for September 21, 2002. That date was fast approaching as we arrived back at the end of June from our Spanish trip that had centered around a visit to José de la Guerra's birthplace. The Longo-Jackman wedding was to take place in the Presidio Chapel and the reception to be held at Casa de la Guerra. Perhaps suffering from a bit of delusions of grandeur, we hoped to put on an affair that matched the famous wedding of January 24, 1836, between the American Alfred Robinson and Anita de la Guerra, the daughter of José. That wedding had taken place at Mission Santa Barbara with a reception following that went on for days at Casa de la Guerra. Richard Henry Dana Jr. immortalized the wedding in his famous book *Two Years Before the Mast*.

For one thing, we were going to have only a one-day celebration—the wedding at the Chapel and the party at the Casa. The first problem we encountered was the Chapel was not large enough for all the people we wanted to invite—350. The chapel held only 190. We had to limit those who would be invited to the actual wedding. Of course, family took priority, and both sides had relatives coming from out of town—as far away as the Middle West. It all worked out, but I was sorry that some had to miss the wedding, because it turned out to be a phenomenal event.

The wedding in the Chapel took place in the afternoon with Rev. Jerry Bellamy officiating. I can't remember the order of things because I was a little nervous myself. First of all, I brought Renée down the aisle in my eighteenth-century Spanish officer's uniform. After words of introduction, we had poetry readings from Michele and Perie Longo, Dana's mother, who was at the time the official Poet Laureate of Santa Barbara. Then, Dana's friend, Julian Hallmark, a professional violinist, came down the aisle playing a Mozart concerto, and you could feel the audience oohing and aahing; above in the choir loft, Francisco Gonzalez of *pastorela* fame played his Mexican harp, and it was capped with my cousin Eileen Squillo, an opera singer, singing several Schubert lieder. Except for a moment when I accidentally pulled off Renée's veil, it all came off perfectly. Goose-bump time.

Then to the Casa to celebrate—a sit-down dinner for 350. It helped that the city let us close down the street in front of the adobe, and we put up a fence enclosure that steered cars around the plaza. The band was in the street and the dancing also took place there. I couldn't help thinking that this event matched the famous wedding of 1836 and was really living history. We did have the museum open to give a full sense of the site to our guests. Afterward, I heard nothing but wows; one board member said it was without question the best wedding he had ever been to; another said it was like a stage setting with the moon casting its light from above city hall. My only disappointment was that my parents, who had spent so many years volunteering at the SBTHP, were not able to be at the wedding as they had relocated to Florida. They were there in spirit.

I felt very fortunate indeed to have been able to experience such a wonderful family event—it was surely one of the benefits of the job of being CEO of the SBTHP, and I will always be grateful to the board for allowing this to happen and to the staff who volunteered their time to all phases of the event. There is more family fare to talk about, but first let me discuss other events that were in some ways spurred by the Longo-Jackman wedding.

The author presents his daughter for marriage to Dana Longo on September 21, 2002, in the Presidio Chapel with a reception to follow at Casa de la Guerra. *Author's Collection*

Events and the World of Earned Income

The SBTHP had its annual events that included Founding Day ceremonies April 21 and a Veterans Day celebration November 11. We had also begun to rent the Chapel for weddings, with Renée coordinating these. As the Casa restoration neared completion in 2006, we also started to rent out the Casa courtyard for receptions, with the porch area usable space but the interior usually closed.

Over the years, I was amazed at the breadth of financial means available to the SBTHP. Commercial and residential rentals, investments available from the sale of El Paseo, membership dues, donations, grants, museum- and online-shop sales, eventually an official endowment program, and finally earned income from events at our historic sites.

Weddings are a no-brainer in the sense that they are short term—they require a short rehearsal, and the wedding itself usually lasts only two to three hours followed by after-the-event photography. Also, if you keep the flower petals off the floor, the impact on the church is minimal.

Wedding receptions are another matter—they usually start late in the day, and while you set a time limit, they can go on for six-plus hours, not to mention they usually involve some fairly heavy alcohol consumption. I used to peek in on some of these events and wondered if we should be doing them. They do bring in considerable income but carry risks. I give all the credit in the world to my daughter Renée Longo for overseeing these receptions. Over a twenty-year period at both sites, there were hardly any incidents. One time I observed a rehearsal at the Chapel with a drunk priest who was flown in from out of town; very rude, and controlling. I would have thrown him out, but Renée worked through it. A couple times, I saw people jumping off the porch at the Casa who were inebriated, and that made me nervous. In the long run, however, these events produced six figures in annual income and became a top rental venue.

Casa Cantina: Profit Versus Mission

It didn't take me long at the SBTHP to come to the conclusion that while being a nonprofit, the organization was just as much a business. In the free-enterprise world, a business goal is to make a profit, and at worse break even. For nonprofits, the goal is to zero out so that there isn't a profit or loss. That's why when you do something like Casa Cantina and it is separated from any particular project, then profit seems to come to control the situation. Casa Cantina started in the 1990s, a four-day event timed with Santa Barbara's annual Old Spanish Days held in August. Plaza De La Guerra becomes a food court with various nonprofits serving Mexican food; plus, there is a stage for music and dance activities that draw big crowds. I don't know whose idea it was to jump on this bandwagon and begin to serve food and beverages at our site during these four days. It could have been yours truly, but it doesn't really matter.

The first couple years, the emphasis was on serving food and alcohol and having music, not all of which had a Mexican or Spanish flavor. That became a problem for the SBTHP as the rock music was blasting away one evening when board member Charles Storke stopped by to check on the goings-on. I remember his taking me in the house and insisting this was wrong and shouldn't be happening at the Casa. The other thing that happened was we were not making a lot of money serving food. So we canceled the Cantina and kept the adobe off limits during Fiesta.

After Charles's death sometime in the first decade of the twenty-first century, we discussed reviving the Cantina. But with a different approach: Emphasis would be on serving beer, wine, and margaritas with some limited food fare, and in turn we would allow those who bought entrance tickets and a drink to bring in food they purchased at the Plaza booths. Music also was programmed every night. There was an attempt to explain the history of the site with some printed materials and opening the museum during the daytime. People only interested in seeing the museum were allowed to go to the museum—the entrance fee was waived. The result of this new approach was a financial success. We started netting thousands of dollars over four days, and the net kept rising year after year as we approached the second decade of the century. Truthfully, visitors came to drink and dance and did not really care to learn much about history. Having fun was their goal. Over time, we had very few incidents with drunks, and to keep things in order we hired a security company every year. It was easy money and some volunteers loved to pour beer and margaritas. One mistake I made was hosting a margarita party in the bodega and another room for staff, some volunteers, and friends. In days past, these types of parties were common during Fiesta, and businesses and even some banks had parties for their clientele and employees. But some of the people drank too much at these parties, and I eventually decided enough was enough.

One of the volunteers, in fact, had too much to drink and served a minor. The Department of Alcoholic Beverage Control cited the volunteer and we were closed down for the rest of that Fiesta, and we had our liquor permit revoked and then limited the next few years for this mistake. Eventually I went to see the city manager and told him that we had been in error—big time—and that we would adhere closely to the police training regarding alcohol sale and consumption. The city manager said he would talk to the police chief, who in turn contacted the state Department of Alcoholic Beverage Control and recommended that the SBTHP again be issued a permit, eventually a full permit that included serving margaritas. On top of all this, the SBTHP received very bad publicity in the *Santa Barbara News-Press* over this incident. The question arose, Should we be doing this—dispensing keg after keg of beer? The answer from the board was that we should, but training and strict rules would be applied to volunteers—particularly that they would not be allowed to drink during the time they were working. Also, a company was hired to assist with the event, and the SBTHP tried to use Fiesta for private events for its members.

All said: It still is a drinking event and raises the question of how it fits with the mission of the SBTHP. It does net over thirty thousand dollars per year, not counting staff time spent working on the event, which is substantial. One of the benefits is it raises unrestricted funds, and those can be used on discretionary projects that the board may choose to program. Ultimately, I don't think that the Cantina does damage to the SBTHP image. I remember seeing a lot of older SBTHP members enjoying themselves at the Casa during Fiesta.

Renée also arranged wine-festival events at the Casa—I believe these took place in spring, maybe fall, and brought people who paid the producers of the Festival an entrance fee, and these came off without a hitch. These events used the space under our normal rental rates. Oftentimes I would volunteer in the Casa museum and greet any of those who cared to learn about the Casa's history—the numbers of these were pretty low.

The Bard at the Casa

Anyone who knows me soon becomes aware of my deep interest in Shakespeare. Michele and I own a house about five hundred meters from the Oregon Shakespeare Festival in Ashland, Oregon. I have seen every play of the Bard performed live at various theaters around the world—but mostly in Ashland. We have in recent years enjoyed the productions at the Utah Shakespeare Festival. Could I justify Shakespeare at the Casa, other than for it being a personal obsession?

Research on Shakespeare indicates that his plays had been performed in Santa Barbara as early as around 1850. One history even speculated that the first play was performed in the courtyard of Casa de la Guerra. I believe it was *Hamlet*. That was all the justification I needed to support Shakespeare at the Casa. The first play we did was *The Merchant of Venice*. I can't remember the year, but it had to be in the 1990s. I don't remember either who put on the play either but I remember a scene with Shylock delivering a soliloquy just as the Casa pigeons landed on the dirt near him, a reminder of the famous pigeons in the great St. Mark's Square in Venice.

After this initial effort, I was approached by Jennifer Casey of the Santa Barbara Shakespeare Company, and we began running plays in September after Old Spanish Days was over. Most of the actors were graduates of the UCSB drama program, but occasionally an equity actor was brought in to play a lead. I remember one equity actor who was brilliant as Malvolio in *Twelfth Night*. They did *Much Ado About Nothing*, *As You Like It*, *The Comedy of Errors*, and *The Merry Wives of Windsor*. Erwin Appel—the son of Libby Appel, former artistic director of the Oregon Shakespeare Festival—played Falstaff in *Merry Wives* and gave a hilariously funny performance. Each play ran about ten performances and drew on average 150 to 200 people per performance. They also paid at the sponsorship rate, which made

A staple at Casa de la Guerra, Shakespeare was performed for many years during the author's tenure at SBTHP. *Author's Collection*

the events affordable for them and enabled us to cover our costs. In addition, the theatergoers had a tendency to be more interested in the museum, which we opened before the performances. A definite win-win—especially for a Shakespeare lover like myself. I hoped to see the backyard defense wall rebuilt at the Presidio in time to produce plays there such as *Coriolanus*, *Julius Caesar*, or *Antony and Cleopatra*, but that was a dream never realized. The Don Quixote in me refuses to die.

CHAPTER EIGHTEEN

More Museum Space: More Exhibitions

I HAD THE PRIVILEGE to be at the SBTHP at just the right time to help it grow from being a "sleepy little park," as one ranger described the Presidio, into a site with multiple rooms available for display—all totaled at the Casa and the Presidio, there are nearly thirty rooms usable for exhibitions and permanent displays.

The problem at Casa de la Guerra is the rooms are not large and do not lend themselves to changing exhibitions, especially those that are on loan from other sites and museums. Temperature and humidity controls are usually required by lenders, and the SBTHP determined that it was too intrusive on the adobe structures to install HVAC and similar systems. Then the decision was made that at least a third of the house, the north wing, would be interpreted as a house museum, but to date only two of the three rooms have been furnished to the period. The dining room awaits its turn. In the west wing, the bodega, or wine room, has been re-created, as well as the store in room one. In the east wing, two rooms were left for changing or rotating exhibitions. Two other rooms in the east wing were to be used to interpret the history of the house and include a model of it during its heyday in the nineteenth century. Thus there was limited space to do changing exhibitions, which I will return to in a moment. The lighting system was created with the various uses of the rooms in mind. It has worked reasonably well. Treatment of the floors was also based on how the rooms were to be used. These decisions were made with input from the Casa de la Guerra restoration committee. Perhaps it would have been better to hire a company to design a master plan, but I have my doubts because we did this at a later time and I am not sure the SBTHP got anything out of it that would eventuate in a world-class museum. I will return to this opinion in my closing chapter.

At the Presidio, again the problem, with the exception of the Chapel, is that the rooms are relatively small and some of them have yet to be furnished. Metaphor Communications, a London-based company of some renown, was hired in 2010 to develop a first-phase plan to interpret the multiple communities that occupied the Presidio area over time and tell their stories. This was the beginning of the fort becoming a neighborhood park. There were some interesting ideas in the plan, but so much more could have come from focusing on the fort instead of trying to capture the layers and flow of history after the original Presidio had gone into decline. Later, in 2012, the Parks Department decided to do a follow-up interpretation master plan. Both documents, that of Metaphor and that of the Department, have value, but I have less enthusiasm for them today seeing what has resulted from them. On the good side, the Department eventually gave the Presidio a large grant to put up interpretive panels outdoors all around the Park, and these have been a big plus. On the down side, these plans, in my opinion, could have done more to interpret the Spanish-period fort.

This leads me to discuss three exhibitions that were installed during the first decade or so of this century that typify how each site—the Casa and the Presidio—was used. First at the Casa: Rotating exhibits at this site have tended to deal with subjects not necessarily related to Casa history but history in general and were perceived in our minds as a way to draw in the public with a variety of subjects. Among these were an exhibit of photographs from the Mexican Revolution, an exhibit put on by the Gaviota Coast Conservancy, and a traveling exhibition done in cooperation with the California Historical Society. There were many more done by the staff and one made possible in 2001 by board member Carol Storke called *Bits and Spurs* that actually spilled over into the Casa dining room. But I thought I would focus on three exhibitions from the 2000s that I particularly liked and I believe raised the level of our museum presentations, and in two instances extended beyond the walls of the museum. I also would like to add that I personally had very little involvement in these shows but let the staff and volunteers do their thing.

Vanishing Landscapes: Homeland

This exhibition was installed in 2005 in the museum of Casa de la Guerra. What made it special to me was that it was interactive. Teachers, students, parents, and artists came together to define "homeland"; to do this, they went to various sites to see homelands firsthand, and that included visiting the Rancho Paloma on the Gaviota Coast that dated from the Mexican period of California history and was still owned by a member of the original family that had started the rancho. Her name was Elizabeth Hvolboll and she was also at the time a member of the board of the SBTHP. There were many distinguished artists who participated in *Vanishing Landscapes*, including one of my favorite artists, Ray Strong. Besides visiting sites, participants were treated to a concert in the Presidio Chapel with Elizabeth, a trained opera singer, singing songs from early California accompanied on guitar by Luis Moreno, also one of my favorite Santa Barbara musicians. What resulted were some of the works of the artists on display, but what made this show special was that the artwork the students created and their personal journals were a major part of the exhibition. What a great idea to treat young people with the thrill of seeing their own work on display for the first time in their lives. Also, the show was carrying out the mission of the SBTHP to teach our upcoming generations the importance of identifying and preserving their homeland. We were turning them into historic preservationists! Karen Anderson, curator of the SBTHP, worked with Charlene Piticher-Huston and Robin Bisio, who coordinated the project. I provided little input on this project and didn't raise any money for it but in this instance just let it happen. I loved it.

Forged in Iron: The Expressive Art of the Roof Cross Tradition in Chiapas, Mexico

By its title, one can see this is off on a different direction from *Vanishing Landscapes*. What captured my attention was its subject: Whereas *Vanishing Landscapes* had a local focus, this exhibition brought the wider world into our midst. Not to forget also that the de la Guerras were extremely religious, with their own altar niche in the sala and prayer taking place several times per day. The exhibition was the brainchild of Virginia Ann Guess, who also published a book on the subject titled *Spirit of Chiapas: The Expressive Art of the Roof Cross Tradition*. She also wrote an article for *La Campana* on the exhibition. She did what I like best, tracing the ironworking and iron-cross tradition to its sources in Spain and explaining how the tradition evolved in one town in particular by the name of San Cristóbal de las Casas, where she and her husband own a house and split their time with Santa Barbara. She also traced the history of the iron-cross tradition in Mexico, how it faded during the period of the Mexican Revolution with its anti-religious proclivity only to be revived in the twentieth century due to San Cristóbal becoming a tourist destination. However, because roofs of residences had become flat, the crosses had started to be made more as decorative art for interior wall display. In her article, she points out that one of these crosses traveled from Chiapas to Santa Cruz Island off Santa Barbara and was most likely a gift to Carey Stanton, who then owned the island. What struck me most about the exhibition was its strong aesthetics, proof to me that folk art can reach the level of high art in the hands of creative craftsmen. What also appealed to me was the exhibition's strong religious content. I am sure José de la Guerra would have also approved.

Instrumental Neutron Activation Analysis (INAA): Oh My God!

How could something so scientifically obscure end up the finest semi-permanent exhibition during my years at the SBTHP? First, calling something semi-permanent has to be explained. The exhibition in question, *Ceramics Rediscovered: Science Reshapes Understanding of Hispanic Life in Early California*, became the opening show in the first two rooms of the Presidio's northwest corner. We never said in the beginning how long we would keep it, but fortunately it stayed up for five years, from 2009 to 2014. In a way, I wish we left it up, because what followed it was a promotion of the next Presidio reconstruction project that was canceled when I left in 2016. INAA is a scientific method of measuring and determining chemical makeup and it was applied to try to better understand the history of ceramics in Spanish California. There's no need to explain here the actual scientific process but rather to say it could and did provide accurate chemical makeup of all the ceramics from the eighteenth century that the principals of this project could get their hands on. There were many others involved but this exhibition was the brainchild of primarily five people: Russell K. Skowronek, anthropologist; Ronald L. Bishop, Smithsonian anthropologist; M. James Blackman, Smithsonian research chemist; Mike Imwalle, SBTHP archaeologist; and Ruben Reyes, master potter. Their primary goal was to identify the sources and types of Spanish California ceramics. Before they ever got to this exhibition, they spent years researching and publishing on the subject.

Anyone who has spent time with archaeologists and is not one, rolls his or her eyes at meetings and conferences with them, as for sure you can count on numerous presentations on potsherds. I remember at the Gran Quivira conferences I wrote on earlier that there were multiple presentations on ceramic potsherds. Be that as it may, I have become a potsherd enthusiast based on my experience with this unbelievable project and exhibition. Perhaps the Smithsonian involvement and support was a contributor to raising this interpretive event to the level of world class; maybe it was the variety and the talent of people leading this; maybe it was the excitement of our first show in our newly reconstructed adobe rooms. The exhibition was done bilingually in English and Spanish (absolutely important at a Spanish site); there were photos, panels with text, and museum cases with artifacts and replica pieces. Part of the exhibition was potter Ruben Reyes, with Mike Imwalle, building a replica kiln in which the process of making ceramics was interpreted. School kids over the course of several years learned how ceramics were molded and fired; they learned about glazing, with lead and tin. One of the great outcomes was many of the replica pieces fired in the kiln ended up as part of the permanent display in the comandancia. Basically, one of the fundamental points made was that pottery manufacturing was widespread through all of Spanish California. Glazed and unglazed ceramics were made at almost every mission and presidio—a self-sufficiency was at play. In short, while majolica pottery, that is, tin-glazed ceramics, came from Mexico

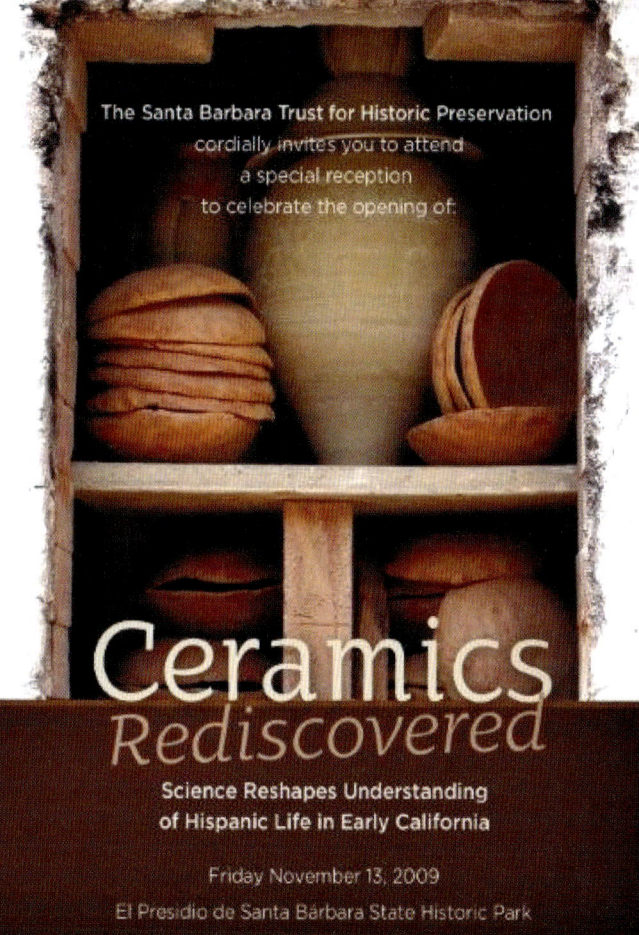

We acknowledge the generous contributions of many individuals and our partner organizations who provided knowledge, time and resources to create this exhibit.

Smithsonian Museum of Natural History,

Smithsonian Latino Center

Santa Clara University

National Institute of Standards and Technology

Ruben Reyes, Master Potter

Santa Barbara Trust for Historic Preservation

California State Parks

University of Texas-Pan American

The Santa Barbara Trust for Historic Preservation cordially invites you to attend a special reception to celebrate the opening of:

Ceramics Rediscovered

Science Reshapes Understanding of Hispanic Life in Early California

Friday November 13, 2009
El Presidio de Santa Bárbara State Historic Park

Please join members of the project team for a first look at this exhibit on the manufacture, trade, and use of ceramics in early California.

We look forward to sharing this surprising glimpse into daily life in Alta California.

6:00 – 8:00 pm
Presidio Chapel
El Presidio de Santa Bárbara State Historic Park
123 East Canon Perdido Street
Santa Barbara, CA 93101
(light refreshments will be served)

Reservations are required.
Please respond by October 31.
(805) 965-0093

A flyer for the ceramics exhibit acknowledging contributors. *Courtesy SBTHP* by trade, most of the other earthenware was made by local Spanish craftsmen and Indians.

What is left of the exhibition is the kiln, which is still used today in presenting living history, but the kiln also can be used to test different fuels and the amount of heat needed to fire ceramics. In one of the publications on the exhibit, the authors mention that the fabrication of replicas provided researchers and the general public a clearer picture of the sophistication of California's colonial potters. In fact, that statement is a microcosm of the whole idea of the Presidio reconstruction—i.e., providing the public with a physical representation of a Spanish fort on the eighteenth-century California frontier. The Santa Barbara Presidio is the only presidio being rebuilt and its importance grows with each new section that we construct. I had a personal experience in coediting a volume of papers from a Smithsonian Institution colloquium titled *The Muses Flee Hitler*, and it was a thrill to be a small part of the dynamic ceramic event that was given an extra boost thanks to the involvement of the Smithsonian. Instrumental neutron activation analysis has opened doors to the past, and *Ceramics Rediscovered* ended up the finest exhibition at the Presidio during my time at the SBTHP.

Ruben Reyes at the Kiln built for the Ceramics Exhibit. *Courtesy SBTHP*

CHAPTER NINETEEN

Building a New Research Center

THE SBTHP during my time was never reluctant to put a lot of balls in the air: property acquisition, restoration of Casa de la Guerra, Presidio adobe conservation work on the oldest building in the state-park system (El Cuartel), repairing the roof of the Rochin Adobe, and yes, a new, bigger research center at the Old City College site. We selected the one permanent Spanish Colonial–style building that dated to the 1920s to house the new research center. The other buildings at the site, including the Alhecama Theatre, were wood-frame structures meant to be temporary and replaced with more permanent buildings in the Spanish architectural character of the town that Pearl Chase and others had promoted after the destruction of the 1925 earthquake. But the Great Depression intervened and the School of the Arts at the site never went through that transformation, instead becoming part of the Santa Barbara City College , then being sold to the SBTHP, and finally being conveyed to the State of California. One of the problems already discussed is that artists occupied many of the spaces in the complex, and even though they were in the state park and were told their tenancy was temporary, they came to think that they should be allowed to stay in their studios indefinitely. It wasn't always easy politically to ask them to vacate. Sometimes there was some back channeling with the city council and we got some bad press. I remember a reporter quoting my saying something about the artists I didn't say, but in the fullness of time, maybe I was at least thinking it as he read my body language? I did get frustrated sometimes, but on the whole I kept my cool, as they say. Eventually we were able to vacate the two-story building and begin planning the new, expanded research center.

Beginning in 2000, many of our longtime employees began to retire and with them some of the board members who were key Presidio enthusiasts who pushed the Presidio project forward—these were the diehards whose loss I will talk about later. Among the losses on the staff level was Research Center Director Cathy Rudolph. She had been working on developing the new research center. Following the typical SBTHP and required state-park process, Mike Imwalle, with other SBTHP staffers, undertook in 1999 preparation of the report "Phase 1 Archaeological Resource Evaluation for Proposed Improvements at 215 East Canon Perdido Street" for the building to house the new research center. Architect Milford Wayne Donaldson was retained to create the plans for the building. Fortunately, we were able to hire Lee Goodwin, from Santa Fe, New Mexico, to replace Cathy Rudolph, and she brought to the position experience in working in archives and was able to contribute to the final plans for the new research center. The renovation of the building included exterior and interior finishes and removing and repairing the tile roof. One of the main challenges was the north-facing window that had served the artist-studio function of the building well but was letting in too much light and would have damaged the books and documents. A filtering system was designed to remedy this problem. The first two floors were to accommodate public spaces and offices, and the basement to house the small artifact collection of the SBTHP and the state park. Normally, it is not advised to put collections in basements because of potential flooding, but the architects designed a system that required removing the floors and peeling

The new research center during renovation. Note the large artist studio window that had to be filtered to reduce sunlight. *Courtesy SBTHP*

230 SANTA BARBARA'S ROYAL PRESIDIO

The completed interior of the new research center. *Courtesy SBTHP*

back the walls to install waterproofing materials. It required permanently closing up windows and one outside doorway. Around 2000, we put the project out to bid. As with any restoration, we were not naïve to think there would not eventually be change orders as the project advanced. It was hard to know exactly what would be found behind the walls.

The exterior of the new presidio research center. *Courtesy SBTHP*

The SBTHP received two bids for the project, with the low bid coming from Channel Coast Corporation. They would eventually be involved with the rebuilding of the Presidio northwest-corner project. I would sum up the work of Channel Coast in two words: "high quality." They restored perfectly the hardware of the windows and doors, did a first-rate job restoring the beautiful 1920s hardwood floors, and right on down the line. But of course the problem of change orders reared its head. Funding from various sources, including from the City of Santa Barbara, California State Parks, private gifts, and grants, proved not enough to finish the project. That was when the board stepped into the breach and offered to sell an SBTHP property that was within the Presidio footprint at 828 Santa Barbara Street, and in turn invest the proceeds of the sale into the Research Center. I talked to California State Parks Acquisitions Chief Warren Westrup, and he in turn said the department had an emergency fund not to exceed five hundred thousand dollars to buy purchases of opportunity. Again the stars were aligning for the SBTHP: The appraisal of the property came in at five hundred thousand dollars. This took a while to get through the state bureaucracy, but I believe it happened within six months.

At the same time as the sale of 828 Santa Barbara Street, I was following up with the California Cultural and Historical Endowment (CCHE), which had been created under the leadership of State Librarian Dr. Kevin Starr in 2003. I had known Dr. Starr during my days as a grad student at UCSB, where in 1974 he delivered the Corle Lecture on campus on the first of his California Dream series books, which would grow into multiple volumes. He was then fresh out of Harvard University, where he earned his PhD. I stayed in contact with him over the years and Michele and I went to hear him give a talk in Los Angeles in 2016 that had an interesting title: "Postmodern California: A Pat Brown Perspective." I used to visit him on trips to Sacramento and he told me CCHE was coming and be ready to apply.

Strange Encounter with Then-Oakland Mayor Jerry Brown

When the time came to apply, I made sure we had our grant proposal in among the first round of applicants from around the state. This voter-funded endowment had millions of dollars to give away. Applicants were required to make five-minute presentations to a grant-review board in the auditorium of the California State Library. These presentations took place over several days, which is an indication of how many applicants there were. When I got my number, we all had to stand in line while individuals went forward to the microphone to speak, with the grant reviewers on the stage. Of all things, I noticed the person directly in front of me in line was Jerry Brown, former governor and at that time mayor of Oakland. He was there to pitch funding for a historic theater in downtown Oakland. Of course there was a buzz all around him, people coming to talk to him, one after another. I also noticed up on the stage that the reviewers looked rather bored with being there—some of them walking off the stage during the presentations, and many of them barely paying attention. Then came Jerry Brown's turn. Everyone looked up in rapt attention as he spoke—even by then, 2004, Brown was already one of the most famous California politicians of all time. Once he finished, it was my turn. I thought about comedian George Gobel's line on *The Tonight Show Starring Johnny Carson* when he was there with a star-studded cast that included Bob Hope: He felt like the world was a tuxedo and he was a brown pair of shoes. In that instant I felt like a brown pair of shoes. When I rose to speak, one person onstage walked off and I didn't use the Gobel line—maybe I should have. Not surprisingly, our six-figure grant proposal was not funded in the first round: Oakland's historic theater was.

Never say die; there was a second round of grants to be awarded. I asked Research Center Director Lee Goodwin to replace me this time. She put together a first-rate proposal asking for a six-figure grant. She also went to Sacramento well rehearsed, and voilà, we were funded. The five hundred thousand from the sale of the property matched the grant from CCHE. We were home free. The Research Center was unveiled in 2007 at an SBTHP fundraiser. It was a stunning renovation. After the opening, Lee decided to return to Santa Fe. She had begun a PhD in history, and her topic was focused on New Mexico. She could continue her research there. She remains for me one of the staff's unsung heroes. But let's not forget too that the SBTHP's partnership with California State Parks sealed the deal creating the finest research center at any state park in California.

Unfulfilled Potential—Still Time

During the decade after the turn of the century, our research was not as vibrant as it had been earlier. The UCSB public-history program became exclusively a PhD program and the public-history MA program was transferred to California State University, Sacramento. The MA class projects we had benefited from were no longer available, and PhDs were not as available to work with us. In fact, the one person who wrote his PhD on the Presidio wrote a negative history of the presidio project. We did have a faculty member on the SBTHP board who worked with the history department to create a borderlands-history chair that would be connected directly to the SBTHP and our research program. That chair came to fruition as the twentieth century neared its end and it became promising for the SBTHP as UCSB professor James Brooks organized with Lee Goodwin and others a symposium that drew scholars to the Presidio. Many SBTHP docents and other volunteers showed up for the talks. I remember a scholar who came from the University of Charleston commenting that she got more feedback from SBTHP people on her talk than she ever got in the classroom. We were a really lively group—I could have explained to her that many of these people, while so-called amateurs, were immersed in Spanish-colonial history and had strong opinions. I had personally experienced that myself over the years. To my disappointment, James Brooks took a position in Santa Fe and was gone by 2002. Much time passed before a replacement, Pekka Hämäläinen, was hired. Like Brooks, he wrote a book that won the Bancroft Prize. Both were respected scholars. I had Pekka come down and give a talk and asked how we might involve him more. I remember his response: It had to be connected to Native Americans. I felt his head was elsewhere and it turned out that he was recruited away to the University of Oxford, where he recently finished a book titled *Lakota America*. He is all the rage in the academic world.

Interestingly, after years away in Santa Fe, where he rose to be president of the prestigious School for Advanced Research, James Brooks left that position and returned to UCSB under a joint appointment in history and anthropology. After I left the SBTHP, he served for a term or two on the SBTHP board. The potential of connecting the Research Center to scholars and specifically UCSB has remained a potential unfulfilled, but there is still time—the Research Center isn't going anywhere. As far as the public-history program goes, the generation of PhDs now entering the academy probably haven't even heard of former giants in the field of borderlands history: Herbert Eugene Bolton and John Francis Bannon. If they have, they would see them as old fashioned and out of date. That raises the question of whether the Presidio project itself is out of date. I will eventually explain why I disagree with that latter possible assertion.

Research Still Central

As the SBTHP hurtled toward its fiftieth anniversary, perhaps the main result of research was not in book form but a film titled *My Friends Call Me Miss Chase*. An SBTHP committee was formed to raise the funds for the project and then public historian Dr. Shelley Bookspan was hired to write and direct the film. I mention she was a product of the public-history program at UCSB, where she earned her doctorate. Truthfully, Shelley was not a big fan of the Presidio project, and early versions of the script brought a brisk response from the SBTHP. Eventually she came up with a version that reflected less her personal opinion about the Presidio project. Was it really the role of the SBTHP to produce a movie that takes exception to a project that was a lifelong commitment of Pearl Chase and of many in the organization that she had founded in 1963? When I first arrived at the SBTHP in 1981, Pearl Chase had already died and her entire estate benefited the SBTHP.

The one major SBTHP publication after the turn of the century was Marie Christine Duggan's *The Chumash and the Presidio of Santa Barbara: Evolution of a Relationship, 1782-1823* (2004). We paid Marie a stipend to research and write this important monograph. An economic historian, she recorded the political and economic relations that evolved over time, how Indians came from the missions to work at the Santa Barbara Presidio, and how the Indians used competition between the Mission and Presidio to their economic and political advantage. In my foreword to her monograph, I wrote: "Is the story that Dr. Duggan tells unique to Santa Barbara, or is it typical of soldier/Indian relations at other sites? This is an important question whose answer will help place the Santa Barbara frontier experience into a broader historical context." That's me over and over again, and why I found the Presidio project so interesting: It was a window into a world beyond. This perspective is in contrast to the public-history approach that focuses on the local. This is a salient issue that I will return to several more times.

While there were not any other major publications that came out in print during the period leading up to 2013, Mike Imwalle's huge unpublished archaeological report on his work on Casa de la Guerra should, in a more condensed narrative version, be published. It is an invaluable document that captures the research that went into the restoration of one of California's most important surviving adobes. As a research tool, archaeology has continued almost every summer even up to today thanks to field schools—that is, until the pandemic hit. These field schools have been run through California Polytechnic State University San Luis Obispo under the guidance of Dr. Robert Hoover, a longtime SBTHP board member. In some ways, these excavations reflected a scaled-down version of earlier archaeology that had undertaken exposing large sections of the foundations of the northeast and northwest corners of the Presidio. It was good to keep alive the SBTHP's sixty-year tradition of archaeology at the site.

Lastly on the subject of research, the SBTHP's quarterly publication, *La Campana*, continued to provide researched articles across the board on subjects related to the Presidio, Casa de la Guerra, and Santa Inés Mission Mills.

The Value of Conferences Revisited

Previously, I have written how information I learned at a conference alerted me to a grant program that eventually helped fund the northwest corner of the Presidio. Also of importance was the general knowledge acquired regarding adobe technology and conservation at various conferences and workshops I and other staffers attended. I found National Trust for Historic Preservation conferences particularly interesting, two of which I attended in the middle of the decade, one in Louisville and another in Pittsburgh. I also attended an American Association of Museums annual conference in St. Louis, where, among doing other fascinating tours, I went to see the famous Indian mounds at Cahokia across the Mississippi River in southern Illinois. An impressive site, the main mound soars above its surroundings; across from the museum is a state Indian museum interpreting the Indians of that region—it is world class, including re-created archaeological sites explaining stratigraphy and other aspects of excavating prehistoric sites. I photographed the exhibits, and these images are available in the Presidio Research Center.

I really wanted to return to this subject because the last National Trust for Historic Preservation conference I attended was in 2011, in Buffalo, New York, with a team of SBTHP people. But at this conference, the SBTHP was to receive a top award from the National Trust on October 21. The SBTHP received the 2011 Trustees Emeritus Award for Excellence for the Stewardship of Historic Sites. The award acknowledged the nearly fifty years of achievement of the SBTHP in its restoration and preservation projects and its concomitant research projects and education programs. We received the award onstage from the president of the National Trust.

Ending with a Sidebar: Restoration Leads to Family Reunion

Certainly the main purpose of historic preservation is to preserve memory of the past. In spite of the fact that we have been a forward-directed people, Americans have grown to appreciate their history. I loved one event that proves the point—the restoration of Casa de la Guerra resulted in a great family reunion at the site organized by Victoria de la Guerra Seaman, now a resident of Las Vegas, Nevada. It began as a Facebook page and eventuated in a reunion attended by more than 150 people in July 2010. I also hosted descendants of the Whittakers at the Presidio, and there is an annual luncheon honoring Presidio descendants. Imagination is wonderful, but having the physical reminder of the past around you has its particular charm and added meaning to remind us of connections to the past.

CHAPTER TWENTY

STILL MUCH TO CELEBRATE

AS MY THIRTIETH YEAR at the SBTHP approached in 2011, a lot of good things were still happening, including the National Trust award previously mentioned. The economy was only gradually recovering from the Great Recession and that made the board's financial decisions fall on the conservative side. Also, until the state purchased Jimmy's Oriental Gardens in 2013, the SBTHP's financial position was still not what it had been before the Great Recession. In addition, the board's focus was evolving into more concern over maintaining existing buildings in the Park. That meant an eventual slowdown in "creative mudslinging" (i.e., adobe reconstruction), but that did not mean the SBTHP was not very busy—quite the contrary.

Greening a Historic Building

To turn back the clock for a moment: Since the Alhecama artist studios had become part of the Park in the 1980s, no improvements had been made to them. Archaeologist Mike Imwalle and I had a similar idea in 2008—the Santa Barbara Contractors Association (SBCA) was looking for new space, and certain vacated studios might be the right fit. The SBCA eventually signed an agreement with the SBTHP and the California State Parks Department to create the Built Green Resource Center. Our contract property manager drafted an agreement that gave rent concessions for tenant improvements. Built in the 1920s, these historic buildings would be the first we knew of in any state park to be "greened." The most difficult task was to get the city and the state to agree to allow solar panels on the building. Eventually, both agencies—the California State Parks Department and the city landmarks commission—relented. Double glazed windows were installed; wood siding was removed, restored,

Artist Studios, the first greened historic building in the state park system. *Courtesy SBTHP*

and insulated; beautiful wood floors were restored and in one instance had to be replaced. A sophisticated temperature-control system was installed with shutters that opened and closed as the outside temperature changed. One room was converted into a classroom with all the high-tech equipment. All told, the building was about 2,500 square feet with three large spaces. It was beautifully done and finished around 2009. I remember the grand opening with Mayor Blum in attendance. As mentioned, in exchange for its greening work on the building, the SBCA was given rent forgiveness for a defined period of time.

There arose two problems, however: The first one was there was inadequate parking for the training programs, and this made it difficult to schedule classes at the site. The second issue was cost overruns, and these had to be renegotiated with the SBTHP. The SBCA came to the SBTHP property-management committee and asked for a several-year extension of their lease with further rent concessions. The SBTHP and the SBCA eventually agreed to a one-year extra rent concession.

After this, the SBCA decided that the site did not work for them and subleased the studios with the approval of the state. In a way, this was another example of the SBTHP's fundraising successes: In this instance, the SBTHP and the Park benefited from a tenant's improvements in exchange for rent offsets, not to mention we provided a model for environmentally sensitive renovations of historic buildings. The question remains of what is the best long-term use of these buildings to benefit the Park.

Now for a moment, let's turn the clock forward to the future: This site could become the new home of a Presidio Archaeology and Green Resource Center, where artifacts found during archaeology could be stored and studied; the public could come to learn about the "green world" that is being promoted by the State of California. The buildings already have a classroom and other facilities appropriate for such use. This is more than just an impossible Don Quixote dream; it is very much achievable.

2013: It Was a Very Good Year

Many good things happened in 2013. Many of them related to the SBTHP getting back to normal in its financial situation. One of the pluses was the work of property manager Rob Ramirez, who took over direct management of the Park rentals. He did an outstanding job over the course of the next several years—with an end result that the SBTHP's net rental income increased by 10 percent. Another SBTHP/Park fundraising success.

Another piece of good news in 2013 was escrow closing on the sale to the state of Jimmy's Oriental Gardens. We had friends in Sacramento who supported this complicated transaction, with its easements and a lot split. I give all the credit to Director Ruth Coleman and Chief of Acquisitions Warren Westrup. Plus, there were other people in Sacramento who made it happen.

I have already related the story of Bob Lovejoy re-creating the original interior of the Jimmy's bar under a new name, the Pickle Room. The name was derived from the Three Pickles sandwich shop located next door in the old Jimmy's restaurant location. The restored bar was opened to the public in 2013 and was a perfect example of tenant historic preservation improvements. What a great outcome: As with the SBCA, the SBTHP took advantage of a tenant's desire to do something special in the Park. Bob and his family made a sizable donation to the SBTHP to fund a permanent Chinese neighborhood museum exhibit. Also returning as part of the "historic restoration" was Willy Gilbert, bartender at Jimmy's for more than twenty-five years. During this time, Bob had a tile business and actually installed the tile plaque commemorating the second visit of Prince Felipe of Spain in 2013. Sadly, Bob died suddenly and unexpectedly July 7, 2018, in the prime of his life. He loved sports but he also had talent that he developed while earning a master's degree in design from California State University, Northridge. His family collected antiques, developing a keen interest in history, and he became a master woodworker and later started his tile-trade business. This was the type of person drawn to the SBTHP and of whom we took full advantage to the benefit of our town and the Park.

The SBTHP's Fiftieth Anniversary

A third major positive of 2013 was the celebration of the organization's fiftieth anniversary with a big banquet at El Paseo set for May 18 and titled "Un Paseo en Oro." The event had some great moments, with a special greeting from the prince of Spain delivered by Spanish Consul General Enrique Ruiz Molero. There were some Hollywood theatrics to open the event with a rider on horseback in a parade saddle provided by board member Dr. Art Najera greeting guests as they entered El Paseo through the historic Street in Spain. By the way, actor and state-park enthusiast Leo Carrillo used to ride his horse during Fiesta into the courtyard of El Paseo. History repeats itself.

Larger-than-life images of historic figures who visited El Paseo in years past lined the Street in Spain, including one of President Herbert Hoover. Awaiting the guests in the main courtyard were refreshments and music. Doorways were open to offices and studios, including the former studio of famed cowboy artist Edward Borein. Upstairs, guests visited the Ranchero Room—complete with artwork of some of the best Western artists of the 1920s era. Also, one of the apartments was open for viewing, as well as some of the rooms of the restored Casa de la Guerra.

Once seated in the main restaurant, guests were treated to a stirring performance by flamenco dancer Timo Nuñez. Board members gave interesting talks, and the featured speaker was the honorary chair of the event, Milford Wayne Donaldson, chairman of the Advisory Council on Historic Preservation. Yes, that is the same person who was architect of numerous SBTHP restoration projects. Wayne challenged us to look ahead to the next fifty years—and envision an inclusive community built around the historic heritage of Santa Barbara. This was a perfect parallel thought that Consul General Ruiz shared in a personal letter from the prince of Spain reminiscing about his visit to Santa Barbara in 1995 and his appreciation of the fact that Santa Barbara had embraced its Spanish history, and that in doing so, it would benefit the future of our society in embracing its diverse past.

My contribution to the event was narrating a twelve-minute video on the history of the SBTHP, with emphasis on the accomplishments of the organization over the past fifty years. Videographer David Bolton donated his time creating the video, which the audience that evening seemed very pleased with as they gave it rousing applause. David had donated many services over the years, and this was yet another example of his generous support of the SBTHP.

As I look back at that event, it is satisfying to realize that in 1981 El Paseo was in major disrepair and the SBTHP in financial stress over it: Now in 2013, here we were at a completely renovated El Paseo, plus we had the murals in the Ranchero Room, and the St. Francis Room had been restored by the new owners. So much of what the SBTHP did came through leveraging its real-estate position to have tenants make the improvements at their costs but to our preservation standards.

We also printed a booklet on the SBTHP's fifty-year history—it provided a nice timeline and summarized our achievements. We put our goals on the back cover, but perhaps we should have promoted those a lot more. The booklet was sent to all members and foundations and to public officials. A memory project asked for people with any documents or photos related to the SBTHP to please consider donating them to be archived in the Presidio Research Center. In addition, the SBTHP asked members and others to draw memory maps, some of which were displayed at the Presidio throughout the year 2013.

Spanish Crown Prince Felipe of Asturias Returns

At the May 24 banquet, I heard from Spanish Consul General Ruiz that there was going to be another visit from Prince Felipe to Santa Barbara in November for a meeting of the US Spain Council, a group of businessmen and government officials promoting commercial, cultural, and leadership programs between the two nations.

A moment of levity at the reception as soldado and descendant Jim Martinez reads a proclamation honoring the prince. (Left to right): the author, Mike Hardwick as Governor Felipe de Neve, Mayor Helen Schneider, SBTHP board member Craig Makela, SBTHP board member Giorgio Perissinotto, Foreign Affairs Minister José Manuel Garcia-Margallo, the prince, and Spanish Ambassador to the United States Ramon Gil Casares. *Courtesy SBTHP*

Group photo with the prince, his entourage, and SBTHP members at the Biltmore reception, November 2013. *Courtesy SBTHP*

I briefly alluded to this visit earlier in describing his visit to the Presidio in 1995. The major event was to be a seminar at the Bacara Resort west of Goleta. But there was time for activities in Santa Barbara. Officials from Spain came ahead of time and I urged them to consider a dinner outdoors at Casa de la Guerra. The enticement was that José de la Guerra had been born in northern Spain in the state of Santander, which was right next to the principality of Asturias. The idea was unique, but it was getting late into the fall season with the threat of rain a possibility. Eventually, a series of events including a bus tour with Spanish dignitaries and businesspeople would include a drive by the Presidio and Casa de la Guerra. Prince Felipe and Princess Letizia would stay at the Biltmore and a Saturday banquet would be held at the Montecito Club. Recognizing the important role the SBTHP played in interpreting Spanish history in California, Consul General Ruiz arranged a special reception

with the prince at the Biltmore in the Loggia Ballroom for selected SBTHP members and guests the evening of November 15, 2013.

It turned out to be a wonderful event, the capstone for me of the many great achievements of the SBTHP being able to have a future Spanish king greet the more than seventy-five people present. In attendance besides the prince were the Spanish ambassador to the United States and the foreign minister, Spain's equivalent of our secretary of state, and a whole entourage of others, including a person carrying a briefcase that I assumed was full of something important in case of a national emergency that might require the prince's attention.

The ceremony was perfect—on our side we had our soldados out in force, as it were. Soldado Jim Martinez did a presentation; then Michael Hardwick impersonated Governor Felipe de Neve, who was at the founding of the Presidio in 1782, and

The prince with the Presidio soldados at the Biltmore reception. *Courtesy SBTH*

made some humorous remarks about coming back from the past. Presidio descendant Craig Makela also made some remarks, followed by board member Giorgio Perissinotto, who presented the prince with publications that he had edited related to Santa Barbara's Hispanic history. Mayor Helene Schneider also made a presentation and had a city staffer show the prince the decoration of the Order of Charles III that Santa Barbara Mayor Norris Montgomery had received in 1952 from the Spanish Council of Ministers for perpetuating Spanish traditions and culture. Santa Barbara is the only city in the United States to have received this prestigious award from the Spanish government. The prince then made a few remarks, again thanking the SBTHP for all it had done to preserve and interpret its early Spanish history. I was the emcee of this event, certainly one of the highlights of my career as CEO of the SBTHP. I could hardly have imagined years ago that I would ever be so fortunate as to be part of such a ceremony. It was a truly amazing personal experience.

The next day, I met many of the Spanish dignitaries at Mission Santa Barbara, where we had a brief tour of the church. All told, it couldn't get any better than this. And for a while it didn't come close, as entropy was definitely beginning to set in, but I just kept thinking about what was next for us at the SBTHP. My last couple years at the SBTHP would be challenging, but I always stayed true to the cause of rebuilding the Santa Barbara Presidio.

CHAPTER TWENTY-ONE

FINAL PROJECTS AND PRAISES

IN THE LIFE OF A NONPROFIT, there are phases the organization goes through, and the SBTHP had its version of these. In thirty-five years, I had personally experienced various cycles of growth, and the trajectory, with some setbacks, had been in the ascendant. The SBTHP's setbacks were, up to 2014, almost entirely related to forces outside itself. The 9/11 attack and the Great Recession slowed the SBTHP, but it weathered these political and economic cyclones in good shape in the end. I came in 1981, when many of the original founders and volunteers were still active. Even though I never met Pearl Chase—she had died in 1979, two years before I arrived—I certainly knew of this force of nature.

Several of my fellow history grad students at UCSB had been hired to deal with her papers in the 1970s, including photos and materials she collected over the years; she had donated them to the UCSB Department of Special Research Collections. I actually researched in those papers and used some of the photos in the book I published with the *Santa Barbara News-Press*, then owned by the *New York Times*, under the title *Santa Barbara: Historical Themes and Images* (1988). That book gave me fifteen minutes of local fame as the *News-Press* ran full-page ads several times to promote and sell the book. In the event, Chase was deservedly a local legend involved with so many different projects, but the Presidio became her final project, to which she devoted thousands of hours, usually behind the scenes as she had others to serve as president and vice president of the SBTHP.

The early success of the Presidio project was built on a foundation of volunteerism and I picked up on that right away. I met most of the key early volunteers—Bill Luton, Jeremy Hass, Russell Antonio Ruiz, Richard Whitehead—in my early years at the SBTHP. They were unbelievably dedicated to the project and inspired me through their efforts to carry on what they had started. Of those who continued on the board into the 1990s and beyond, the most committed to the Presidio reconstruction were Dr. Garvan Kuskey, a dentist, and Dr. James Mills, a pharmacist. Once they stepped down from the board, the mudslinging world did not have the same passion driving the Presidio reconstruction.

It also is worth mentioning how changes in intellectual attitude had an impact on the Presidio project. The *Zeitgeist*, or climate of opinion, was changing in the history profession: 1960s politics seeped into the heads of historians; the march of civilization began to look more to an incoming generation like colonialism and conquest, dispossessing Indigenous peoples. Today that *Zeitgeist* is pervasive in the academy. The Vietnam War and the civil rights movement influenced the way people viewed history in general, and that spilled over to how some in the public viewed the Presidio project. Probably the worst thing said about the Presidio was when one mayor compared the site to a blob taking over a neighborhood, but thousands of visitors drawn from all over the world came to visit and would disagree.

Another movement that emerged in the 1960s came from historic preservationists. A specific project that set a new preservation direction was the Rockefeller reconstruction of eighteenth-century Williamsburg. It was noted by some that historic nineteenth-century buildings had been removed (real history) to be replaced with eighteenth-century remakes. This mentality reared its head as the Presidio project was reviewed in public meetings that I wrote about earlier. From this came the flow-of-history approach that tended to identify all the layers of history of a site as important and worth saving. Then in the 1970s, there emerged public-history programs at various universities. These programs had more impact in the 1980s as local history organizations all across the nation began to see a decline in attendance at their sites. One of the outcomes of this was the notion that it might be better to rebuild museums based on local needs and interests—the idea that all history is local. One of the best public-history programs emerged at UCSB, and I have recounted how it helped the Presidio project treat the diverse layers of history of the site by researching and writing the histories of those various layers.

In the early days of UCSB and the Presidio project, the history department, one might say by today's standards, was old school. For example, Professor Philip Wayne Powell was a Latin Americanist who published books on Presidio soldiers and sixteenth-century New Spain's frontier, and who also served on the board of the SBTHP. Another Latin Americanist at UCSB served on the SBTHP board also. Both of these men supported the idea of Spanish colonial history being not necessarily a 100-percent-positive event but at least doing more good than bad, to state it in simple terms. By the 1980s, a new generation of historians had arrived at UCSB under the influence of 1960s politics. I was trained under the tutelage of professors from the earlier generation—Harold Kirker and Joachim Remak.

So while great progress had been made, the writing was on the wall that future reconstructions after 2013 would face significant headwinds. I don't want to say that there was not support for the Presidio project, but those left on the board who believed in the project just didn't have the same zealousness of the founders. During this time period, there were those who wanted to pay more attention to museum design and implementation, and in truth that made sense given all the museum space that the creative mudslingers had created.

The 4x4x4 Campaign

The last big project proposed during my time at the SBTHP was called the "4x4x4 Campaign," which included funding for museum interpretation. The four components contained the following: ongoing archaeological excavation of the backyard area, completion of the defense wall behind the Chapel and creation of a paseo outside the wall connecting Santa Barbara and Canon Perdido streets, relocation of the Bonilla House as part of a new education complex and a new visitor center with exhibits. It would have taken about four million dollars and four years to complete.

One of the staff members put together a nice brochure for the campaign that I unveiled at a CALPA conference, and a fundraising committee started the process of trying to raise money for the project. Then SBTHP board member Tony Spann and the firm he worked for, Harrison Design, did some preliminary layouts of a restored Alhecama and Old City College site that involved relocation of a building and an enclosed plaza. Related to the 4x4x4 campaign, his office did some marvelous renderings of the relocated Bonilla House next to the Pico Adobe. These were all donated services and gave a visual picture of the site after completion of the project. The board eventually designated Tony and his Santa Barbara staff SBTHP volunteers of the year and handed out this award at an annual meeting. The staff also created an exhibit in the new visitor center promoting the campaign.

There was a big problem—funding sources that had been available for years dried up. Governor Brown was not happy with the redevelopment agencies' use of state funds and he dissolved these agencies statewide—that included the Redevelopment Agency of Santa Barbara, which had provided so many grants in support of the Presidio and Casa de la Guerra. A second loss came when the Santa Barbara Foundation shifted its emphasis away from supporting cultural institutions to underwriting more of the needy specifically. The Foundation had been over the years during my tenure a key supporter, often providing the key grant that got a project underway. The last one I remember the Foundation supporting was the renovation of the building to house the new research center. The 4x4x4 Campaign never really got off the ground despite the efforts of the fundraising committee. This project has been temporarily set aside by the current board, which has changed the emphasis to restoring and upgrading existing buildings in the Park.

The Alhecama Theatre: My Last Hurrah

Over the years, more than twenty-five in all, the SBTHP and the Ensemble Theatre Company (ETC) had gone back and forth on their use of the Alhecama Theatre. Turned into a black box with 140 seats, it was really a challenging place to make a go of it financially. At one point, the ETC was unable to pay its rent, and the SBTHP forgave it for one year. We had been encouraging the ETC to relocate so that the theater could be returned for state-park uses. Finally around 2009, under the ETC leadership of Derrick Westen, a local lawyer and president of the ETC board, we began to make some progress. The city Redevelopment Agency had programmed $1.5 million for a new theater at a site next to the Granada Theatre on State Street. But that project fell through when the owner of the property in question would not sell. Next, ETC began looking at the Victoria Street Theatre site, but there were some legal issues that had to be resolved before they could advance restoring that building. I had been in discussion with Derrick about all of the preceding. Around 2010, a lot of this came to a head—with the Victoria Street Theatre site still up in the air, it looked as if the $1.5 million from the Redevelopment Agency might be lost, especially since the Granada Theatre was being restored and the money might go to that project. I came up with one of my better ideas. I suggested to Derrick that we go to the City and propose that the funds be reprogrammed as follows: five hundred thousand dollars be used to upgrade the Alhecama Theatre and one million be kept in reserve for use at the new site, and if that failed the one million be kept for the Alhecama for its use there with ETC retaining its tenancy at the Alhecama Theatre. Derrick was on board. He was considered one of the better fundraisers in Santa Barbara.

I remember a board member asking me if all the time I had been spending on the Alhecama had been worth it. My response was: If we got the five hundred thousand dollars, yes, it would be worth it. In any event, Derrick and I went to the Redevelopment Agency staff, who really liked the idea, and proposed it to the Redevelopment Agency board, which in turn voted unanimously for the proposal. Thus we proceeded with making repairs to the building, most on the exterior, while ETC was still in the building. In addition, we had earlier received funds from the state to sprinkler the building and we also upgraded the electrical.

Things were looking up, especially when ETC worked out its legal issues related to the Victoria Street Theatre and vacated the Alhecama. Amazing how persistence had finally borne fruit. ETC proceeded with restoration of its site, and finally opened its new theater in 2013 after millions of dollars of donations to their project. One problem they faced was Governor Brown's decision to dissolve redevelopment agencies, which put the $1.5 million at risk from our agreement. Eventually a legal decision ruled that those funds were programmed in advance of the governor's decision. I like to think that the SBTHP turned out to be a million-dollar donor for their Victoria Street Theatre project.

In 2011, the SBTHP began the slow process of restoring the Alhecama Theatre. There were a lot of negotiations behind the scenes as we began to look at the building. There was no plan to begin with, but we just gradually started working on the building. One of the first moves was to remove the very old seats; Michele and I spent a few Saturdays carefully scraping black paint from windows, as did others. Next, the stage extension that ETC had constructed was removed. Pretty soon it became obvious that returning the theater to its early configuration was warranted. There were beautiful wood floors that had been preserved under the raked seating; the double-hung windows and French doors gave the building an open feeling that had been lost when it was turned into a black box. Most importantly, the beautiful mural on the wall above the entrance from the foyer now stood out. Most theatergoers had not seen the mural because it was on the back wall facing away from the stage.

The interior of the restored Alhecama Theatre. *Courtesy SBTHP*

The exterior of the restored Alhecama Theatre. *Courtesy SBTHP*

Now there was the question of how to fund this next phase of the renovation. We had an engineering firm involved, and one of the SBTHP's board members was an architect who worked with me on the renovation. We more or less proceeded with the work piecemealing the permitting process. Most of the project was funded in the following manner: First, a few years before, I met with Helen Pedotti, a former board member of the SBTHP. The name of the theater, Alhecama, came from using the initials of her and her sisters—"Al" for Alice, "He" for Helen, "Ca" for Catherine, etc. As a member of the Schott family, Helen had connections to the site. After our meeting, she set up an annuity, which upon her demise turned into a gift for our theater project. Next, I came up with the idea of seeking a large grant from the Hind Foundation, which had funded much of the northwest-corner defense wall. They had declined further support of that project, but I thought Alhecama would be right up their alley. I asked the architect working with me to have his son, a contractor, come up with a cost estimate to finish our project. This was not a bid but an estimate—a big difference. He came up with a number, something like $238,451.38. We submitted our grant proposal to Hind and they funded it down to the penny.

Not to my surprise, as with all restorations, when you open up an old building you find new issues that cost extra money. Channel Coast Corporation was doing the work and Harrison Design was providing plans again pro bono. As time went by, we were coming up short on funds. I had met several times with Ed Birch, CEO of the Mosher Foundation, seeking grants for the 4x4x4 Campaign, but eventually Ed came through with a grant for the Alhecama restoration; then I realized that the Santa Barbara Foundation might do a grant for this project because the theater had many possibilities of serving the public at large, which was a key element in programs and projects the Foundation wanted to support. I personally wrote the grant and submitted it. By the time I left the SBTHP in 2016, the theater had been 90 percent completed.

I consider Alhecama my last hurrah at the SBTHP. Yes, all the effort that I put into that project was worth it—since its completion, the theater has been designated a city landmark! This was an example of a project that was not foreseen by the founders of the SBTHP, but it was certainly an excellent byproduct of the Presidio project itself.

Knighted

Just prior to the end of my tenure as CEO in 2015, I received a letter from Ambassador Javier Vallaure at the Consulate of Spain in Los Angeles that I had been named a knight of the Order of Isabel la Católica, a decree signed by King Felipe VI of Spain. Yes, this was the same person who as prince of Asturias had twice visited Santa Barbara. His father, Juan Carlos, had abdicated, and Felipe became king in May 2015. This decoration honored me for my efforts to preserve the Spanish history and culture in California and the United States. I learned that only two other people had received the award in Santa Barbara—Professor Philip Wayne Powell being one, and the other Father Maynard Geiger, the priest-scholar who had developed the Santa Bárbara Mission Archive-Library and written a definitive biography of Saint Junípero Serra. August company to be in. I learned of others around the US who had received this honor as well. The official signed document was dated December 5, 2015, my birthday, and also the birthday of Walt Disney. Why mention Disney? You will understand in what follows.

Walt and Me

In January 2016, I learned that I had been named the year's Honorary California State Park Ranger by the California State Park Rangers Association (CSPRA). I was in the old Presidio research center when CSPRA Secretary Jeff Price arrived to deliver a letter from then-CSPRA President Victor Bjelajac making the announcement. This was a great award honoring my work at El Presidio de Santa Bárbara State Historic Park and efforts in support of the California League of Park

Joining luminaries such as Walt Disney and Clint Eastwood, the author receives one of California's most prestigious awards—Honorary State Park Ranger for 2016. Then CSPRA president Victor Bjelejac presents the hat at the Morro Bay State Park ceremony. *Author's Collection*

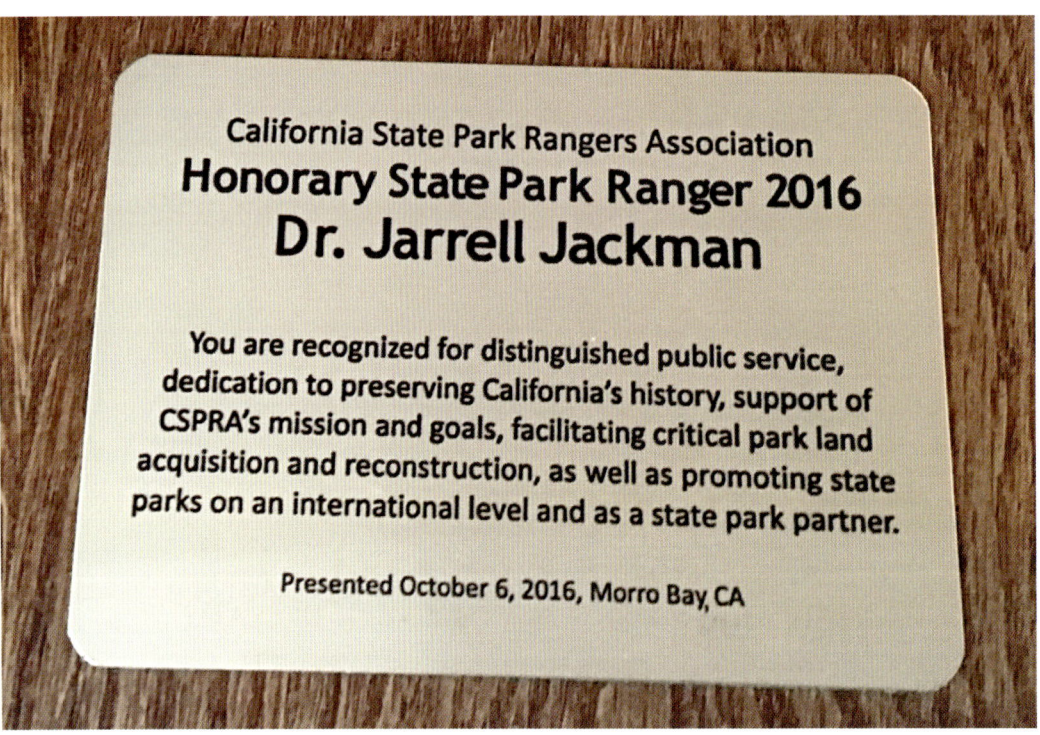

The legend on plaque honoring author as Honorary Ranger. *Author's Collection*

Associations (CALPA). In addition, I was one of the few to have visited all 280 California state parks.

When I looked at the list of past winners, I saw that some of the great park leaders and environmentalists were on it. Locally, only one person had received the award—yes, our own Pearl Chase. Also, there were celebrities on the list: Clint Eastwood and Walt Disney, the latter with whom I share a birthdate. Disney had been given the award for his support of a parks bond, promoting it in film shorts on TV and in theaters; his nature documentaries also promoted environmentalism. He actually received his hat in person in 1965. Again, I was in august company. The ceremonies for the knighting and honorary ranger award were memorable. First, I received my honorary ranger Stetson at the CSPRA annual meeting in Morro Bay in November 2016. The director of the California State Parks Department, Lisa Mengot, was in attendance. In my acceptance speech, I said for the first time I was going to reveal my favorite park as I was one of the few people who had visited all 280. I did just that on that occasion, but discretion requires that I not reveal the reason but only the name of the park—Jedediah Smith Redwoods State Park. The rangers in attendance gave rousing applause. Also in attendance at that event were my wife Michele; daughter Renée; our son-in-law, Dana Longo; and our three grandchildren, India, Paloma, and Zane.

Grand Ceremony at the Santa Barbara Courthouse

In February 2016, I received the Chairman's Award from the California Missions Foundation at its annual meeting in San Juan Bautista. This was followed by a setback as an MRI showed that I had damaged, worn-out vertebrae in my neck that required surgery. Although he did not take Medicare, I chose Dr. Tom Jones to do the surgery because he was the best. Incidentally, he had performed surgery on one of my employees who suffered from an aneurysm back in the 1980s and on another person who had been a mainstay musician in our *pastorela* Christmas play. The outcome was positive, although I was laid up at home through the month of March. I was back in the Research Center working in April and we began planning the decoration event. We decided to do the event at the county courthouse with its famous murals that portray the Spanish history of Santa Barbara and the area's famous islands and channel.

The date chosen was May 26, and Michele and Renée began arranging the event. I asked videographer and David Bolton to emcee and help produce the event as he had professional skills that could add drama, which he did in fact do. He arranged for the national anthems of Spain and the United States to be played and helped coordinate our grand entry with the soldiers and Ambassador Vallaure into the room, which was adorned with the US and Spanish flags. I am grateful to David, who is now CEO of the California Missions Foundation, for his efforts that included videotaping the entire event. I am grateful also to Bill Dewey, who worked for the

The author receives decoration from Spanish Ambassador Javier Vallaure, inducting him as a knight in the Order of Isabél La Católica in recognition for his efforts preserving and interpreting the Spanish history of Early California. *Courtesy Bill Dewey*

The tile given to all who attended the decoration ceremony, created by Jeannie Davis, a direct descendant of Don José de la Guerra. *Author's Collection*

Guests at the decoration ceremony in the famous mural room of the county courthouse, May 26, 2016. *Courtesy Bill Dewey*

Among the many friends and supporters at the decoration event were Cindy Makela, Presidio descendant Ignacio Cota, his partner Veronica Llosa, and descendant and past SBTHP board president Craig Makela. My cousin Nancy Gifford is on the far right. *Courtesy Bill Dewey*

SBTHP for years as its on-call photographer, eventually donated thousands of his images to the SBTHP, and photographed that day pro bono. He gave me hundreds of magnificent images.

For the event, we arranged to have Jeannie Davis, a de la Guerra descendant, make individual fired and decorated tiles for each person who attended, thanking them for making possible my receiving the high honor. My son-in-law Dana read the text from the king in Spanish; Renée then read it in English. Next, the ambassador spoke, explained why I was receiving the award, called me forward, and fastened the decoration around my neck. My speech explained this award was for all those who had contributed to the Presidio project over the years, and I named a lot of people who have been written about in the foregoing pages. I meant it: I was riding on the wave they had created. In the audience of about one hundred were my family, friends from in and out of town, many SBTHP board members and staffers, and others who did not fit into any category except they, in my opinion, contributed to the many successes of the organization and the development of the state park. Some people came from out of state.

For the end, Michele had arranged for well-known local opera singer Eduardo Villa to sing a cappella (in the manner of the Chapel!) "The Impossible Dream." The audience was spellbound, and it was perfect for me as I love Don Quixote, the man who jousted not only with a windmill but also with a fulling mill. Afterward, Michele and Renée had arranged a feast of hors d'oeuvres and wine. I thought about all the trials and tribulations that had to be endured as CEO and during my last days at the SBTHP, and at that moment they all faded away permanently as I realized that I was, to quote Lou Gehrig, the "luckiest man on the face of this earth" to have been at the helm of the Presidio project for so many years. But unlike Gehrig, whose life was shortened by a disease named after him, I lived on to appreciate the good fortune I had had at the SBTHP helping build a presidio and an organization. There were so many great learning experiences along the way—so many different types of projects and interesting people to work with. I certainly didn't foresee that this was how my study of history would turn out, but it really was quite something to stand on the shoulders of the giants who came before me and carry forth what they had started.

CHAPTER TWENTY-TWO

Why the Presidio Project Succeeded

WHEN I THINK ABOUT the SBTHP's success, what comes to mind is a line from a Burt Bacharach and Hal David song: "Without true love we just exist, Alfie." That has motivated me for as long as I can remember—a romantic view of the world. I brought that passion to the SBTHP from the beginning, and it didn't take long for me to fall in love with the Presidio project. The people who made this project happen were also passionate—and inspired and intelligent. When I first started, I had no idea I would be around as long as I was—for some it was too long. How does one account for the fact that a Spanish fort that represented the founding of the town of Santa Barbara could make a comeback, so to speak, and reemerge out of its original mud? I believe that the people I just mentioned made the difference, for starters, and that a major strategic decision was made—that is, to build a partnership between the private sector (the SBTHP) and government, which was mostly with the State of California but also involved positive relations with the city and county governments of Santa Barbara, not to mention federal support through recognition (e.g., a Take Pride in America Award) and funding through an ISTEA grant.

The Presidio could not have had a better advocate than Pearl Chase, who never took no for an answer. Another key moment was the gift of El Paseo donated in Chase's honor, and then the smart move to sell it but make sure that it was renovated. It put significant money in the SBTHP coffers. I don't want to get into false modesty, so I mention that it didn't hurt to have the continuity of a director who was a total supporter of the SBTHP's noble goals. There also was a very smart board over the years making positive business decisions. Plus, several of the board members were nearly fanatical in their commitment to building the Presidio. It was something bold of Garvan Kuskey to push ahead demolishing the Shalhoob building. You almost had to be at the meetings to appreciate the way Restoration Committee Chair James Mills was determined to build the bell tower of the Chapel. There was a singlemindedness of female board members like Pearl Chase, Amelia Acres, Heather Bryden, Julia Forbes, and Alice Rypins in supporting the SBTHP.

After thinking about how to sum up all that happened, I decided to put things in categories and list the top ten in each category in an appendix that is available online. There is no way I can capture all that happened, and I know that years from now I will realize I have overlooked something or someone important. I can't help that, and I know omissions will be noted and I hope forgiven. This is the story of how a state park was born, created, and maintained. It is the story of a nonprofit business involved in the complicated world of real estate. It is the story of preserving something that is very important—an international site whose history is intertwined with Spain, Mexico, and the United States. It is the story of a variety of restoration projects that center around adobe technology but involve renovating buildings of different types of construction. It is an interesting story of renovating a major commercial complex called El Paseo—and having someone else pay for it, and do the work meeting the preservation standards of the SBTHP. Lastly, it is a human story—whose success was a vital combination of volunteerism and paid professional work. I was pleased to have been a part of this world, as was my family. My father did the electrical work pro bono in the Chapel, my mother volunteered in various ways, my daughter was married in the Chapel, and my three grandchildren were baptized in it—one by the venerable priest Father Virgil Cordano of the Old Mission and another by Father John Yanek.

I was mostly an administrator, but I was allowed to do research that contributed to the history of the Presidio, not to mention coedit in the 1980s a Smithsonian volume titled *The Muses Flee Hitler* (1983). Later, the *Santa Barbara News-Press*, then owned by the *New York Times*, offered to underwrite my writing a local history of Santa Barbara—which I did under the title *Santa Barbara: Historical Themes and Images* (1988). I had the opportunity to do research in Spain and Mexico, and in my free time even did some work in German archives on the novelist Thomas Mann. I got to learn about the real world of business while at the same time using my professional training as a historian to make sure that what we did at the SBTHP was based on an in-depth commitment to historical research. In addition, since retiring I have created an organization called the Presidio Alliance, whose goal is to interpret and integrate the history of presidios in North America. "Always important to think big" is my motto. Thus I am still here, still promoting the Hispanic history of Santa Barbara, California, and the United States.

Finishing the Job

One never knows how things will ultimately turn out in history. Contingency is what makes it interesting. Cause and effect don't always seem to tell us why things turn out the way they do. At the time, around 1989, not many people had a clue that the communist Iron Curtain was about to fall and that the Berlin Wall was going to collapse with it. Afterward historians had explanations, but at the moment it happened with such totality hardly anyone saw it coming. Down in the small world, comparatively, of the Santa Barbara Presidio, I am not sure how many of the Presidio dreamers thought the project would actually happen to the degree that it has. I have tried to document this success as much as I could. I am sure there are other facts and factors that I haven't addressed that can explain how a mud fort could make such a comeback and at the same time the SBTHP universe could expand to a full restoration of Casa de la Guerra and creation of a new state park at Santa Inés Mission Mills.

There is, however, work still to be done. Thus my last words are to lay out a plan for the future fulfillment of the Presidio project dream—to achieve its potential for interpreting the Spanish history that provided the underpinning of this region. If the following is realized someday, the Presidio will not only be a national historic district but also become a UNESCO World Heritage Site.

1. The first step is to complete the defense wall behind the Chapel to Santa Barbara Street. To do this, the Bonilla House needs to be relocated. It can go, as the Presidio general plan suggested, into the area next to the Pico Adobe. Or it could be relocated somewhere across the street on the Old City College site. That small change will have a dramatic effect on the Presidio site—creating a fantastic *paseo* (passageway) for pedestrians. Along the outside, a wall of native plants should be planted to interpret those that the Chumash used medicinally and in other ways. Inside the walls, all the plants and vegetables the Spanish introduced should be interpreted. To date, this has been done largely thanks to the green thumb of SBTHP archaeologist Mike Imwalle, but a main garden needs to be planted where the old research center building stands after it has been removed. The neighbor problem of the small piece of land needed to complete the wall has to be vigorously pursued. A small section of the back of the Cañedo Adobe needs to be removed. The entire backyard should be redesigned as a public space. It also will become a place where kids can come and overnight as they do at Fort Ross State Historic Park.
2. A section of the front gate should be rebuilt that includes projection of the foundations out into the street as has been done connecting the comandancia with the buildings across the street. The current owner of the easement over the parking lot where the front gate will be located is amenable to this idea.

A rendering of the Presidio showing the rebuilt back defense wall and stonework in the street connecting with El Cuartel in a similar fashion as was done connecting the Presidio Comandancia and northwest corner. *Courtesy Heritage Architecture*

3. Keeping the creative mudslinging alive: A long-term, five- to ten-year program should be commenced to build the defense wall whose foundation is across the street from the site of the front gate. The long duration of this is to create an archaeology and adobe-technology program that brings people to the site on a regular, year-round basis to learn the hands-on aspects of archaeology and adobe-making. This program could be run out of the metal garage on 828 Santa Barbara Street.
4. The SBTHP should ask permission from the state to rebuild the Asakura Hotel on Canon Perdido Street, outside the westerly defense wall. This site would be dedicated to interpreting the history of the Japanese presence on the site for fifty years.
5. A program should be commenced to relocate the parking from lot from the front gate site; this can be achieved by following some of the recommendations for relocating parking in the general plan. Then the soldiers' barracks and the jail should be rebuilt, and most importantly the corral next to the front gate should be created to bring in horses for Presidio events such as Founding Day.
6. Shifting to the Santa Inés Mission Mills state property, the SBTHP should create a barn to house up to a half dozen horses. These horses could be stabled at the Mills and brought down to the Presidio for various events. In this way, the

Members of the historic Japanese [Nihonmachi] community enjoyed gathering at the lost Asakaura Hotel, which, in the opinion of the author, itself deserves reconstruction as another founding landmark of Santa Barbara's history. *Courtesy of SBTHP*

Mills and the Park become connected, and the argument can be made that since the two parks are connected, Presidio-restricted funds can be used to develop this equine program. The Mills also can be a place to have sheep and process wool. But the horse world is essential to interpreting the history of the Presidio. Each soldier had up to six horses of his own.

7. Speaking of soldiers—the soldier program should be regenerated, starting with a program for younger children, probably at the age of ten and up and including girls. This program could be developed in cooperation with the Police Activities League and would be an interesting way to introduce Santa Barbara's large Latino population to the Hispanic heritage of Santa Barbara.

8. The artist studios that the Santa Barbara Contractors Association greened should be turned into an archaeology and green-resource education center. The model for this can be the archaeology center that the National Park Service has

Janet Blair rendering of the Presidio when the city- and state-approved third phase of the presidio is rebuilt. Unfortunately a large apartment complex has appeared where the tree stands on the right. *Author's Collection*

created at the San Francisco Presidio. The collection of the site can be curated and knowledge shared with other presidios and colonial sites.

9. The Presidio Research Center lives up to its name by encouraging research into the Spanish history of Santa Barbara by offering stipends to students in high school and up. Also, an ongoing cooperative program with the Bancroft Library can be set up to copy to CDs microfilmed documents from Spanish and Mexican archives that pertain to presidio history. These CDs would be made available to students and scholars researching the Spanish presidio history of the Southwest.

10. The SBTHP has a museum plan in place, but the following should be added—at least one room should interpret the history of soldiers and their families and their diverse social and ethnic backgrounds; other rooms should be dedicated to interpreting the arms and armaments of the Presidio. It was a fort, after all, and weaponry is important in interpreting it. Also, something on shipping is needed as this was how the Presidio was supplied and how it communicated with the outside world.

These are ten steps to fulfill the goals of Pearl Chase and the generation of fellow volunteers who during and after her time drove the Presidio project forward. As I write this, the downtown area of Santa Barbara needs something to revitalize it. These ten steps outline how the Presidio can become a major downtown attraction while preserving its earliest history. Forget the small ball: Let's think big like the SBTHP founders. Let's finish the job, fellow mudslingers. It seems fitting to end with a quotation from Dr. Garvan Kuskey, one of the Presidio project's greatest advocates: "Someday the entire Presidio is going to be rebuilt. Visitors from near and far will stand in awe of this oasis of history right in the midst of our bustling city. *Will you* be able to say, 'I helped build this place'?"

Acknowledgments

In its early years, the Presidio project was volunteer driven. An amazing amount of talent was found among these volunteers—without them the Park and the reconstruction would never have happened. I have created an appendix online to provide the opportunity to identify many of the achievements of volunteers and staffers. This appendix will be fluid—readers are encouraged to contact me with corrections and additions.

Over the years, I received various awards—and I want to thank Spanish Ambassador Javier Vallaure for nominating as a commander in the Royal Order of Isabel la Católica; state park district superintendents Rich Rozzelle and Steve Treanor for nominating me for the CSPRA Honorary Ranger award; Carolyn Christian for presenting me with the legacy award of the California League of Park Associations; and Wayne Donaldson, who nominated me for the California Missions Foundation's Norman Neuerburg Award and made the presentation to me at the organization's conference in Monterey, California, in 2001. He also agreed to write a foreword for this book, and I truly appreciate his doing this.

With regard to the book itself, I am grateful to Rick Rinehart of Lyons Press and his fellow staffers Kristen Mellitt, Meredith Dias, Alyssa Griffin, and Erica Tape. The copy-editing was first-rate, and I love the book design by Mary Ballachino. I am also totally indebted to Lou Thompson for creating my Presidio Alliance website, and for attaching the appendix of this book to it with such great ease. She and husband Bob are dear friends.

At the Santa Barbara Trust for Historic Preservation, I thank the following for their help and cooperation: Anthony Grumbine, Michael Arnold, Mike Imwalle, and Dez Alariz.

For several decades, photographer Bill Dewey provided yeoman service recording the growth and progress of the Presidio project, and he donated his time to photographing the event of my being knighted at the Santa Barbara County Courthouse Mural room. Lou Thompson, a dear friend, was amazing in helping set up the appendix online.

While my mentor Professor Harold C. Kirker died shortly before I began writing this book, he has been a major inspiration behind it—he was always so supportive and I was indeed fortunate to serve as his teaching assistant at the University of California, Santa Barbara. Thus, I dedicate this book to him, a truly fine man and scholar.

My entire family was involved in so many positive ways during my SBTHP tenure, especially my daughter, Renée Longo, who volunteered as a child at many events. As part of the staff for over twenty years, she brought character and reputation working as our wedding and events onsite coordinator, resulting in the Presidio being acknowledged as one of the best wedding and historic reception venues in Santa Barbara, California. She also connected this project with the art and music communities while generating revenue at public events to preserve and protect this site. Her husband, Dana Longo, and her children, India, Paloma, and Zane, carry on that tradition of volunteering and community service today. I must mention also my parents, Ruth and Steve Jackman, who not only volunteered at the site over the course of many years, but also passed on to me the skills and temperament that enabled me to help advance the Presidio project.

Lastly, there are two people who said I had to do this book, my longtime friend and fellow historian Al Runte and my wife, Michele. As the author of the definitive work on the history of national parks that is now in its fifth edition, Al said that I had an important story to tell about how a park was created, and he kept encouraging me to do it until I finally said, "OK, I will." He also oversaw so much of what has ended up in this book. He is a true friend. Michele, who was at my side for the thirty-five years I dedicated to the Presidio project, seconded Al's encouragement. I would never have survived as long as I did at the Santa Barbara Trust for Historic Preservation without her devotion and sage business advice over the years. She not only cared about me but also came to love the Presidio as much as I do. We made a great team.

APPENDIX

AS I WAS WRITING this history of the Presidio and its rebirth, it became apparent that I couldn't come close to capturing all that transpired in my thirty-five years at the Santa Barbara Presidio. I felt intimidated when I first started at the SBTHP, and even today I feel a little bit that way because I know that the story has many details that I have not recorded in the preceding pages. What came to mind was that I should allow the Presidio story to continue evolving by putting more of the history online, which will allow employees, volunteers, and the general public to add to and correct what they consider omissions as they have read this account.

I have decided to create categories that identify key elements and people that may have been mentioned in the text, and others that I may have omitted but want to give recognition. While it is indeed a subjective way to go about identifying projects, I have listed the categories in order of importance. Among these categories are the following:

Top Restoration Projects
Top Tenant Improvement Projects
Top Archaeological Discoveries
Top Research Projects, Publications
Top Permanent Museum Displays and Room Furnishing
Top Changing Exhibitions
Top Ten Real Estate Transactions
Top Fundraising Successes
Top Ten Board Members
Top Volunteers
Top Ten SBTHP Employees
Top Ten Contractors
Top Ten State Employees and Some State and City Elected Officials
Top Ten Unique People
Friends
Top Events

All are invited to visit the website where this information is posted (so far more than twenty thousand words are included) and point out facts that need to be corrected or added at:

https://www.thepresidioalliance.org/santabarbararoyalpresidio.html#book

or using the following QR code:

The author can be contacted at: jarrell.jackman@icloud.com.

BIBLIOGRAPHY

"Acquisition and Development Plan for El Presidio de Santa Barbara State Historic Park." Prepared by the Santa Barbara Trust for Historic Preservation for California State Department of Parks and Recreation, 1979.

Anderson, M. Kat. *Tending the Wild: Native American Knowledge and the Management of California's Natural Resources*. Berkeley: University of California Press, 2005.

Bancroft, Hubert Howe. *The History of California*. Volume XVIII, *1542-1800*. Volume XIX, *1801-1824*. San Francisco: The History Company, 1886.

Bannon, John Francis. *The Spanish Borderlands Frontier 1513-1821*. Albuquerque: University of New Mexico Press, 1974.

Beilharz, Edwin A. *Felipe de Neve: First Governor of California*. San Francisco: California Historical Society, 1971.

Benté, Vance G., J. D. Tordoff, M. Hilderman-Smith. *Phase VIII Archaeological Excavations of the Chapel Site CA-SBA-133*. Santa Barbara: Santa Barbara Trust for Historic Preservation, 1982.

Blackburn, Thomas. "The Chumash Revolt of 1824: A Native Account." *The Journal of California Anthropology* 2, no. 2. https://escholarship.org/uc/item/1vb2c533.

Bolton, Herbert E. *The Spanish Borderlands: A Chronical of Old Florida and the Southwest*. New Haven: Yale University Press, 1921.

Chartrand, René. *The Spanish Army in North America 1700–1793*. Illustrated by David Rickman. Oxford: Osprey Press, 2011

Dana, Richard Henry Jr. *The Complete Two Years Before the Mast: Illustrated Classic*. Orinda: SeaWolf Press, 2020.

Duggan, Marie Christine. *The Chumash and the Presidio of Santa Barbara: Evolution of a Relationship, 1782-1823*. Santa Barbara: Santa Barbara Trust for Historic Preservation, 2004.

"El Presidio de Santa Barbara Archaeological Research Series." Seven Volumes. Prepared by the Santa Barbara Trust for Historic Preservation for California State Department of Parks and Recreation, 1990–2003.

El Presidio de Santa Barbara State Historic Park General Plan. Sacramento: California Department of Parks and Recreation, 1988.

Gamble, Lynn H. *The Chumash World at European Contact: Power, Trade, and Feasting Among Complex Hunter-Gatherers.* Berkeley: University of California Press, 2008.

Gebhard, David. *The Creation of a New Spain in America: An Exhibition Organized for the University Art Museum.* Santa Barbara: University of California, Santa Barbara, 1982.

González, Rafael. *A Spanish Soldier in the Royal Presidio of Santa Barbara: Experiences of a California Soldier.* As related to Thomas Savage in 1878. Edited by Richard S. Whitehead. Translated by Jarrell C. Jackman. Santa Barbara: Bellerophon Books, 1987.

Hardwick, Michael R. "Arms and Armament: Presidios of California." Unpublished.

———. *Changes in Landscape: The Beginnings of Horticulture in the California Missions.* Orange: Paragon Agency, 2005.

———. *La Purísima Concepción: The Enduring History of a California Mission.* Charleston: History Press, 2015.

Imwalle, Michael. *Final Report on the Archaeological/Architectural Investigation of the Casa de la Guerra Adobe.* Santa Barbara: Santa Barbara Trust for Historic Preservation, 2004.

Jackman, Jarrell C. "Felipe Antonio de Goicoechea (1747-1814)." *Boletín* 32, no. 1 (2016): 182–190

———. *Felipe de Goicoechea: Santa Barbara Presidio Comandante.* Santa Barbara: Anson Luman Press, 1993.

———. "Goicoechea Redux," *La Campana*, Vol. 36, no. 2 (Spring 2010) 14-16

———. "Introduction." In *Adobe Houses: Homes of Sun and Earth*, 14–34. New York: Rizzoli, 2017.

———. "Letter Exchange between Norman Neuerburg and Edith Webb, 1944-1946." *Boletín* 31, no. 1 (2015): 159–168.

———. *Santa Barbara: Historical Themes and Images.* Norfolk: The Donning Company, 1988.

———. "The Spanish Expedition to Bodega Bay in 1793: A Reconsideration of the 'Historical Facts.'" *Boletín* 30, no. 1 (2014): 106–116.

La Campana. Santa Barbara Trust for Historic Preservation, 1970–2021.

López Urrutia, Carlos. *The Spanish Royal Army of California.* Translated by author Unpublished. Originally published as *El Real Ejército de California* (Madrid: Grupo Medusa, 2001).

Miller, Robert Ryal. *A Yankee Smuggler on the Spanish California Coast: George Washington Eayrs and the Ship* Mercury. Santa Barbara: Santa Barbara Trust for Historic Preservation, 2001.

Neuerburg, Norman. *18th Century Santa Barbara Presidio Chapel: Secrets Uncovered by 20th Century Research.* Santa Barbara: Bellerophon Books, 1985.

———. *The Decoration of the California Missions*. Santa Barbara: Bellerophon Books, 1987.

Perissinotto, Giorgio, ed. *Documenting Everyday Life in Early Spanish California: The Santa Barbara Presidio Memorias y Facturas, 1779-1810*. Santa Barbara: Santa Barbara Trust for Historic Preservation, 1998.

Peterson, Anne, Jarrell C. Jackman, and Mary Louise Days, eds. *Plaza de la Guerra Reconsidered: Exhibition and Symposium*. Santa Barbara: Santa Barbara Trust for Historic Preservation, 2002.

Phillips, William D. Jr. and Carla Rahn Phillips. *A Concise History of Spain*. 2nd ed. Cambridge: Cambridge University Press, 2016.

Powell, Philip Wayne. "Genesis of the Frontier Presidio in North America." *Western Historical Quarterly* 13, no. 2 (April 1982): 125–141.

———. *Mexico's Miguel Caldera: The Taming of America's First Frontier, 1548-1597*. Tucson: University of Arizona Press, 1977.

———. *Tree of Hate: Propaganda and Prejudices Affecting United States Relations with the Hispanic World*. Albuquerque: University of New Mexico Press, 2008.

Price, Glenn. "The Santa Barbara Presidio: A Report on the Presidio of Santa Barbara." Prepared for the California Division of Beaches and Parks, 1959.

Pubols, Louise. *The Father of All: The de la Guerra Family, Power, and Patriarchy in Mexican California*. Berkeley: University of California Press, 2009.

Rae, Cheri. *Pearl Chase: First Lady of Santa Barbara*. Seattle: Olympus Press, 2013.

Rahn Phillips, Carla and William D. Phillips Jr. *Spain's Golden Fleece: Wool Production and the Wool Trade from the Middle Ages to the Nineteenth Century*. Baltimore: Johns Hopkins University Press, 1997.

Robinson, Alfred. *Life in California: During a Residence of Several Years in that Territory*. New York: Wiley and Putnam, 1846.

Sands, Janet Dowling. *On a Mission: The Real Story of the California Missions*. Flagstaff: Alta Loma Press, 2019.

Skowronik, Russell K., Ronald L. Bishop, M. James Blackman, Michael Imwalle, and Ruben Reyes. "Rediscovering the Ceramic History of the California Frontier." In *Ceramics in America*, edited by Robert Hunter. Milwaukee: Chipstone Foundation, 2015.

Terra 2000 Postprints: 8th International Conference on the Study and Conservation of Earthen Architecture, Torquay, Devon, UK, May 2000. Oxford: Routledge, 2002.

Weber, David J. *The Spanish Frontier in North America*. New Haven: Yale University Press, 1992.

Whitehead, Richard. "Alta California's Four Fortresses." *Southern California Quarterly* 65, no. 1 (Spring 1983): 67–94.

———. *Citadel on the Channel: The Royal Presidio of Santa Barbara, Its Founding and Construction, 1782-1798*. Santa Barbara: Santa Barbara Trust for Historic Preservation, 1996.

———, ed. *California's Mission La Purísima Concepción: The Hageman and Ewing Reports*. Santa Barbara: Santa Barbara Trust for Historic Preservation, 1980.

———, ed. *The Voyage of the Frigate Princesa to Southern California in 1782, As Recorded in the Logs of Juan Pantoja y Arriaga and Esteban José Martínez*. Translated by Geraldine V. Sahyun. Santa Barbara: Santa Barbara Mission Archive-Library, 1982.

Williams, Jack S. "Los Presidios: Guardians of Alta California's Mission Frontier." Four Volumes. Prepared for the California Mission Studies Association. Unpublished, 2004.

INDEX

Acres, Amelia, 260
Adams, John, 213
Adobe,
    Brickmaking/adobe technology, xi–xiii,
        4–5, 7, 56–57, 64, 93
        Roof construction for 116, 119, 121, 144,
           162
        Creative mudslinging, ix–xii, 4, 177
        Mixture, xi, 56
Aguiiar, Tim, xii, 94, 96, 119, 170, 172
Alfie, the song, 259
Ahmanson Foundation, 119, 171, 173
Alcibar, José de, Basque Mexican Painter, *54,*
    56
Alexandria Archaeology Research Center, 52
Alhecama Theatre, 6, 80, 104, 106, 129, 149,
    229, 239, 249–251, *251–252,* 253
Allen, Daryl, 163
Allen, Woody, 211
Altamira Cave 212
Anacapa School, 144
Anderson, Karen, 225
Antony and Cleopatra, 221
Anza, Juan Bautista de, 71
Appel, Ewin, 220
Appel, Libby, 220
Aragon, Maria, *105*
Archaeology at the Presidio, 3, 39–40, 42,
    51–52, *57,* 92, 94, 235–236, 262–263
        chapel, 49, 54, 56, 57

    aqueduct, 3, 92, 94, 95
    comandancia, 92
    northwest corner, 114–117, *116*
    corthwest corner, 165–166
    Casa de la Guerra, 123–131
Archivo General de la Nación (Mexico City),
    19
Archivo General de Indias (Seville), 19, 159
Archivo General de Simancas, 158
Archivo Histórico Provinicial de Cantabria, 212
ARCO, 64
Argüello, José Darío, 18
Arneson, Debbie, 171
Arnold, Mike, 85
Arundo Reeds, 120–121
Asakura Hotel, 112, 262
Asian history Presidio Neighborhood, xiv,
    103–105
    Nihonmachi Revisited, 107–112
As You Like It, 220,
Asturias, 152
Altamira Cave, 212
Ávila, 209

Bacharach, Burt, 259
Baja California, 4, 9, 11, 18, 72
Bad Homburg Germany, xi
Bancroft, Hubert Howe, 28
Bancroft Library, 10, 93, 158, 264
Bancroft Prize, 234

Bannon, John Frances, 234
Barnes, Jake, 214
Basque, 4, 13, 54, 63, 78, 152–153, 209, 213–214
Basque Country, 30, 213
Bauhaus Museum, 206
Bellamy, Rev. Jerry, 216
Bellerophon Books, 27
Benté, Vance, 114, 139
Berlin, 206
Berti, Richard, 46, 156
Biblioteca de Menéndez Pelayo, 212
Biltmore Santa Barbara, 156, 176
Bilbao, 213
Binford, Lewis, 39
Birch, Ed, 253
Bisio, Robin, 225
Bishop, Ronald, 225
Bits and Spurs Exhibit, 224
Bjelejac, Victor, 254
Blackman, M. James, 226
Blair, Janet, 264
Bodega Bay, 15, 272
Bolton, David, 209, 242, 255
Bolton, Herbert Eugene, 234
Bonilla House, 38, 249, 261
Bookspan, Shelley, 235
Borein, Ed, 171
Borg, Carl Oscar, 171
Bormes-les-Mimosas (France), 26
Botanic Garden, Madrid, 208
Botanic Garden, Santa Barbara, 176
Bouchard, Hippolyte, 7, 134, 151
Bouchard Raid, 24, 26–27, 81
Bourbon Reforms, 19
Borden, Carla, 160,
Braun, Wernher von, 206
Brinkerhoff Avenue, 215
British Museum, 163
Brooks Institute, 156
Brooks, James, 234
Brothers Grimm Museum (Kassel Germany), 206

Brown, Governor Jerry, 56, 233, 250
Brown, Governor Pat, 39, 46, 233
Broyles-Gonzalez, Yolanda, 67
Bryden, Heather, 53, 90, 260
Buddenbrooks, 163, 206
Buddhist Church, 109, 112
Buenos Aires, 26, 134
Burgos, 208
Burton-Carvajal, Dr. Julianne, 22, 211

Cádiz, 13, 160
Caldwell, Norman, 57, 92–93, 164, 178
California Census of 1790, 10, 13
California Citrus State Historic Park, 180
California Conservation Corps, 56, *57*, 60–61, 139–140
California Cultural and Historical Endowment, 233
California Historical Society, 224
California League of Park Associations, ix, xii, 177–181, 253
California Missions Foundation, 255
California Polytechnic State University, San Luis Obispo, 166, 235
California State Parks and Recreation Commission, 81, 188
California State Parks and Recreation Department, 22, 35, 73–74, 78, 144, 177, 224
California State Parks Ranger Association, 79, 181, 253
California State University, Los Angeles, 49
California State University, Northridge, 241
California State University, Sacramento, 179, 234
Calaveras Big Trees State Park, 180
CALPA see California League of Park Associations
Camacho, Art, 74
Camino, The, 211
Candelario, 297
Cañedo Adobe, 33, 38. 47, 51, 86, 141–142, 261

276 INDEX

Cantabria (Spain), 208, 212
Cardero, Manuel José Antonio, 7
Carlos III *see Charles III*
Carrillo, José Raimundo, 4, 11, 18
Carrillo, Leo, 242
Casa Cantina, 218–219
Casa de la Guerra, 31, 84, 89, 90, 139, 151, 156, 215–216, 220–221, 229, 244
    Original construction, 31–33
    Restoration, 114, 120–133, 160
    Exhibits, 223–228
Casey, Jennifer, 220
Castagnola, Lino, 147–148, *148*, 185, 189
Casals dels Catalans 152
Catalan, 13, 30, 81, 152, 154, 208, 214
Catholicism 67
Celabracíon de las Cuatro Apariciones de la Virgen del Tepeyac 66–67
Cella, Edward, 135
Century of Dishonor, 20
Ceramics Rediscovered, Exhibition, 226
Cervantes, 160
Chalfant, Cathy, 150
Channel Coast Construction, *169*, 170, 172, 232, 253
Charles III, King of Spain, xii, 23, 56, 207
    statue of, *2*, 140, 153, 207–208
Charles IV, 23
Chase, Pearl, x, xiii, 34, *33*, 35, 45, 73, 89, 113, 141, 146, 171, 190–191, 235, 247, 255, 259–260, 264
Chevron, 64
China, 162
Christian, Carolyn, 181, 267
Chumash, 74, 235
    as soldier auxiliaries, 27
    involvement with Presidio Construction, xii, 5–6
    relations with Soldiers, 15, 17, 26
    impact of colonization, 14, 30
    evangelization in villages, 7, 9
    migration missions, 19

Chumash and the Presidio of Santa Barbara, 235
Chumash Revolt of 1824, 26
Chung, Tommy, 185, *186*, 191–192
Civilian Conservation Corps, 23, 49
Cleveland, Bob, 50, 53, 65
Clinton, Bill, 99
Cob construction, 162
Coleman, Ruth, 49, 180, 182, 185, 188, 192–193, 241
Colorado Indian Uprising, 1
Columbus, Christopher, 95, 97–98, 15–160, 209
Comedy of Errors, 220
Conklin, Hal, 114–115
Coral Casino,176
Corle Lecture, 233
Cortés, Hernando, 15
Coriolanus, 221
Cosalá, Birthplace of Goicoechea, 13. 19, 98
Costello, Dr. Julia, 140
Cota, Ignacio, *258*
Cota, Pablo, 4, 11
Cota-Knox House, 38
Creative Mudslinging *see adobe*
Crouch, Dr. Dora, 135
Crystal Cove State Historic Park, 180
Cutter, Dr. Donald, 105

Dailey, Gardner, 176
Dana, Richard Henry, 103, 216
DaRos, Ozzie, 57
Davick, Laura, 180
David, Hal, 259
Davidson, George, 116, 172
Davis, Dave, 135
Davis, Jeannie, *256*, 258
Davis, Patrick, 75
Decker, Bud, 42, 101
Deetz, Dr. James, 40
De la Guerra, Anita, 216
De la Guerra, José, 4, 25–26 31, 114–115,152, 208, 211–213, 225, 244

De la Guerra, Maria, 18
De la Guerra, Pablo, 26, 67, 70, 114
De la Guerra Seaman, Victoria, 237
Der Zauberberg, 205
Deukmejian, Governor George, 88
Dewey, Bill, 255
De Yong, Joe, 171
Discovery, Vancouver's ship, 16, *16*
Disneyland, 73, 79
Disney, Walt, 79, 182, 253, 255
Documenting Everyday Life in Spanish California, 14, 24, 104, 122, 273
Donaldson, Milford Wayne, 115, 117, 130, 133, 166–167, 242
Don Quixote, 160, 200, 220, 241, 258
Dozer, Don, 95
Duggan, Dr. Marie, 18, 235
Durango (Mexico), 4, 19, 105

Earthquakes (1925 et.al.), x, xiii, 22–23, 32, 35, 116, 229
Eastwood, Clint 255
Eayrs, George Washington, 24
Egeberg, Donna, 102
El Baile, 7
El Camino de Santiago, 209–210
El Camino Real de California, 1, 20, 211
El Cuartel, 32, *37, 38, 261*
    History, 141
    Conservation efforts, 141–142, *142,* 229
Elderhostel, 157
El Paseo, 34, 64, 73–74, 89, 130, 171, 183, 242
    gifted to SBTHP, 44–46, 47, 50, 259
    sale, 73–74, 82–87, 143
    historic easement, 86, 171,
    renovation, 46, 84, 89
El Presidio de Santa Bárbara State Historic Park, xiii, 32, 36, 177–178, 214
    park general plan, 5, 36, 63, 79–82
    operating agreement, 46–47, 149
    genealogical charts in museum, 14

El Real Presidio de Santa Bárbara,
    founding, April 21, 1782, xii, 1, 3
    original construction, xii, 3, 4–5
    fourth military district, 1
    soldiers, 10–14, *13*
    arms and armament, 11, 42, 264
El Teatro de Campesino, 67
Endowments, 99, 150, 183–184
Ensemble Theatre Company, 149
Erburu, Lois, 119, 173
Erburu, Robert, 119, 171, 173
Extremadura, 208
Exxon, 64

Fagan, Dr. Brian, 40
Fages, Pedro, 92, 152–153
Fages Ground Plan, *168*
Farreras, Carmen, 152–154, 208
Felipe, Prince of Asturias (later King Felipe VI), 102, 119, 253
    1995 Visit. 151–156, *153–154, 156,*
    2013 Visit, 173, 243–246,
Fendon, Ron, 44–45
Ferdinand VII, 23
Firestone, Brooks, 152
Firestone Winery, 152
Flanders, Jeff, 105
Fontana, Dr. Bernard "Bunny," 71
Forbes Julia, 64, 113, 189, 260
Forged in Iron Exhibit, 225
Fort Ross State Historic Park, 24, 261
Fort Tejon Earthquake, 32, 56
Fort Tejon State Historic Park, 158
Fort Vancouver, xiv
Four by Four Campaign, 249
Frank Fat's Restaurant, 192
Frankfurt, 214
Frederick the Great, 206
Friends of Santa Cruz State Parks, 181
Fuji Cook, Roberta, 109

Galvéz, José, 27
Garcia-Margallo, José Manual Gil, *243*
Garrigues, Eduardo, 97–98
Garrigues, Pilar, 97–98
Gaudi, Antoni, 208, 210
Gaviota Coast Conservancy, 224
Gebhard, Dr. David, x, 32, 80, 86, 272
Gehry, Frank, 213
Geiger, Maynard, 253
Germany after World War, 162
Getty Villa, 213
Gilbert Willy, 241
Glassow, Dr. Michael, 40
Gobel, George, 233
Goethe and Schiller Statue, 206
Goicoechea, Felipe Antonio de, 18–19, 33, 72, 78, 92, 98, 101–102, 117, 158, 272
    Basque heritage, 4, 10, 13, 63, 105, 160, 213–214
    career in Santa Barbara, 4, 6–7, 9–11, 14–16, *16*, 17–18, 26, 97, 158–159, 166, 204
    Post Santa Barbara, 4, 9, 26, 72
Goicoechea, Juan, 105
Goicoechea/Fages Plans, 117
González, Francisco, 43, 66–69, *68*, 216
González, Rafael, 27
Goodwin, Lee, 230, 234
Goya, Francisco, 203
Gran Quivira Conferences, 71–72
Grant, U. S., 204
Grass, Günter, 163
Great Recession, 53, 161, 172, 183–184, 187, 190, 239, 247
Guess, Virginia Ann, 225
Guggenheim Museum, 213

Hallmark, Julian, 216
Horse breeding, 15
Hamlet, 220
Hämäläinen, Pekka, 234
Hardwick, Michael, 11, 42, 89, 99, 101, *243*, 244

Hardwick, Paula, 42
Harpham, Josephine, 64
Harris, Dr. Carl, 104
Harrison Design, 249, 253
Hart, Gary, 88, 90
Harvard University, 209
Hass, Jeremy, 38–39, 40, *43*, 44–47, 84, 144, 146, *185*, 247
Hass, John, 38, *39*, 44, 48
Hauptman, Gerhart, 206
Hemet, California, *205*
Hearst Castle: Building the Dream, 179
Hearst San Simeon State Historical Monument, 178–180
Hemingway, Earnest, 214
Herculaneum, 207
Heritage Architecture and Planning, 167
Higman, Jim and Sue, 189
Hind Foundation, 172, 252
Hirashima, George, 109
Historic El Camino Real see El Camino Real
Hitler, Adolph, 207
Horton, Roger, 170
Hoover, Herbert, 242
Hoover, Dr. Robert, *138*, 166, 235
Hvolboll, Eric, 42
Hvolvoll, Elizabeth, 42, 70, 119, 224

Ibáñez-Martin Mellado, Victor, 152
If These Walls Could Speak, 70
Imwalle, Mike, 11, 119–120, 123, *123*, 125, 133, 137, 139, 140, 142, 163–166, 172. 225, 230, 261
India, *162*
Inouye, Dave, 109
Inouye, Jan, 109
International Conference on the Conservation of Earthen Architecture, 162
International Significance of SBTHP sites, 151
Isabel, Queen, 22
ISTEA Grant, 167, 170, 259

Jackman, Jarrell ("Jerry"), 74–75, 78, 84–85, 96, *118*, 121, 154, 200, 217
    research and publications, xi, 43, 51, 98, 105, 158, 260
    administrative duties, 48–49, 65–66, 149, 150, 157, 195
    fundraising, 64, 114, 118–119, 129, 140, 147–148, 169–171, 201, 233–234, 247, 249–253
    involvement with CALPA, 177–181
    awards, 181–182, 236, 253, *254*, 255–58, *256–257*
Jackman, Michele, 48, 72, 78, 121, 147–148, 158, 160, 172, 196, 198, 200, 215–216, 255
Jackman Longo, Renée, 72, 255, 258, 260
    Wedding, 215–216, *217*
    Park facilities coordinator, 218–219
Jackman, Steve and Ruth, 260
Jackson, Anthony, 193
Jackson Family Foundation, 64, 171
Jackson, Helen Hunt, 205
Jackson Mississippi, 203
James, Will, 171
Japanese Buddhist Church, xiii, 109, 106, 112
Japanese Congregational Church, 112
Japantown (Santa Barbara), 108–109, 111
Jedediah Smith Redwoods State Park, 255
Jimmy's Oriental Gardens, 99, 184–186, 239, 241
Jobs, Steve, 211
Johnson, Frank Tenney, 171
Johnson, Dr. John, 19
Jones, Dr. Tom, 255
Joint Powers Agreement, 47, 113
Juan Bautista, Son of Chumash Chieftain Yanolani, 9, 8–9
Juan Carlos, King of Spain, *2*, 152, 207, 253
Juan Dieg, 67
Julius Caesar, 221

Kai, Karen, 112
Kaufman, Peter, 74, 83–86

KEYT-TV, 38
Kimbro, Edna, 122
Kinney, Don, 179
Kino, Father Eusebio, 71
Kirker, Harold, 134, 209, 212, 248
Kiromiya, Susan, 109
Kirst, Lynn, 203, 205, 214
Korematsu, Fred, 111–112
Knill, Harry and Ellen, 144–146, 199–200
Krakower, Michael, 117
Kumeyaay Revolt, 18
Kuskey, Dr. Garvan, 51, 75, 76, 86, 89, 92, 165, 247, 260, 265
Kyle, Jack, 203

La Campana, SBTHP newsletter, 53, 156
Lagomarsino, Robert, 47
Lake Tahoe, 180
Lakota America, 234
Lasuén, Padre Fermín, 3, 7
Laws of the Indies, 27, 22
Lenny, Henry, 86, 93
León, city and state of, 208–210
Librado, Fernando, 12
Letizia, Queen of Spain, 156
Liston, Jean, 157
Litschel, Dave, 156
Livestock, introduction to New World, 209
Living history, 101–103
LLosa, Veronica, *257*
Lobero Theatre, 85
Lodge, Mayor Sheila, 82
Loggia Room, 245
Lompoc, 3, 9–10, 190, 199, 212
Longo, Dana, 215, 258
Longo, Perie, 215
Longo, Phil, 215
Loreto, Baja California, 72
Los Alamos (Mexico), 98
Los Gatos Jesuit Retreat Center, 164
Los Lobos, 67
Los Rancheros Visitadores, 171

Los Soldados del Real Presidio de Santa Bárbara, 99, 101, 156, *246*
Lot 72 (Solvang), 198–199
Lovejoy, Bob, 187–188, *187*, 191–192, 241
Lovelace Jon and Lillian, 171
Loyer, George, 181
Lübeck, 163, 206
Lugo, City of, 210
Lugo, Richard, 89, 158, 210
Luton, William (Bill), 38, 40, 64, 73, 247

MacLaine, Shirley, 211
MacLennan, Eunice, 171
Madrid, 158, 207–208
Magden William III, 204
Magic Mountain, 206
Majesty of Spain Exhibition, 203
Makela, Craig, 197, *243*, *257*
Makela, Cindy, *257*
Malaspina Expedition, 7
Maldonado the Magician, 114
Malis, Hideko, 109 Mann, Thomas, 163, 206–207
Marconi Conference Center State historic Park, 180
Marre Fire, 119, 172
Martinez, Jim, 101–102, *143*, 144, 154, 158
Martinez, Marc, 101
McCargo, Les, 81
Mengot, Lisa, 255
Merchant of Venice, 220
Mercury (American Ship), 24
Merry Wives of Windsor, 220
Metaphor Communications, 224
Mexican Independence, 24
Miller, Dr. Robert Ryal, 23, 24
Mills, Dr. James, 51, 89, 90, 164–165, 247, 260
Mills, Paul, 140, 152, *153*
Milton Academy, 164
Mission Abó, 72
Mission Creek, 92
Mission Gran Quivira, 72

Mission Inn (Riverside), 205
Mission La Purísima, 3, 9, 10, 20, 23, 28, 49, 102, 127, 158 273
Mission Quarai, 72
Mission San Buenaventura, 1, 10, 20, 26
Mission San Fernando Rey de España, 10, 20, 69
Mission San Gabriel, 5, 20, 122, 205
Mission San Luis Obispo, 20
Mission Santa Bárbara, x, 3, 7, 9, 20, 23, 28, 125, 154, 216, 246
Mission Santa Inés, 10, 20, 22, 27–28, 144, 156, 160, 196
Mississippi: Outpost of Majestic Spain, 203
Monasterio de Santa María de la Rábida, 159
Monterey, x, 1, 6, 82 132, 136, 178, 267
   presidio, 7, 11, 18, 20, 26, 33, 144
Moore, Phyllis, 113, 149
Moreno, Luis, 43, 70, 225
Mori, Frank, 112
Morocco, 162
Morro Bay, 180–181
Morro Bay State Park, *254*
Mosher Foundation, 253
Mott, William Penn, 47, 49
Moullet Property, 38
Much Ado About Nothing, 220
Muneo, Ted, 109
Murakami, Grace, 109
The Muses Flee Hitler, 228, 260
My Friends Call Me Miss Chase (video), 235

Nagagawa, Cressey, 111
Najera, Arthur, 242
Napoleon, 19, 22, 24, 26, 27 134
Nasif, Bill, 85
Natchez, 204
Nazism, 207
National Park Service, 23, 49, 211, 263
National Trust for Historic Preservation, 163
Neve, Felipe, 1, 7, 42, 101, *243*, *244*
New Mexico State University, Las Cruces, 19, 160

Nietzsche, Friedrich, 207
Nihonmachi Revisited, 106
Nobis, Coram, 212
Noé, Nicholás, 24
Nojoqui Creek, 177
Noriega, Pedro González, 18
Northern Trust Bank, 151
Novales, Spain (De la Guerra birthplace), 208, 212
Neuerburg, Norman, 54, 56, 66, 95, 133, 200
Nuñez, Timo, 242

Obama, Barry (Barack), 49, 167
Obern, George, 97, 113 204
Obern, Vivian, 89, 97, 113, 152, 204
Occidental College, 49
O'Connell, Jack, 88, 90
O'Dowd, Patrick, 26, 99, 105, 122, 128, 132–134, 136
Old City College, 249, 261
Old Spanish Days, 53, 102, 158, 218
Old Town San Diego, 33
Order of Charles III, 42, 156
Order of Isabel la Católica, x, 253
Oregon Shakespeare Festival, 220
Ortega, José Francisco, 3, 4, 7, 38
Our Lady of Guadalupe, 66
Outhwaite Foundation, 173
Oviedo, 211

Peake, Channing, 171
Pearl Chase Award, 70, 16
Pedotti, Helen, 188, 252
Pedregoza Creek, 3, 92
Peenemünde, 206
Pelican Beach State Park, 181
Pemberton, John, 204
Peninsular War, 24
Pergamon Museum, 206
Perissinotto, Professor Giorgio, 14, 24, 104, 159, *243*, 246
Persons and Places, 209

Peru, 162
Phelan, Leontine, 144
Picacho State Recreation Area, 181
Pickle Room, 241
Pico Adobe, 32, 37, 249, 261
Piña, Ignacio, 56
Pio Pío Pico State Historic Park, 180
Pitcher-Huston, Charlene, 225
Plaza de España, 159
Plaza de la Guerra, 140, 218
Plaza de la Guerra Reconsidered, 135–136
Polzer, Charles, S.J., 71
Pompeii, 207
Ponce de León, 209
Police Activities League, 263
Pope Francis, 1
Population of Alta California and Santa Barbara, 30
Portolá, Gaspar de, 1, 3, 13, 22
Potter, Robert, 68
Powell, Phillip Wayne, 248, 253
Pownall, Mike, 60, 94
Pownall, Vince, 52, 64, 94
Pozzi, Donna, 179
Prado Museum, 203
Preece, Dan, 82
Presidio Alliance, 260
Presidio *Castillos* (gun emplacements), 11
Presidio descendants, 158, 237
Presidio ground plans, 92–93
Presidio military districts, 21–22
Presidio soldiers, 30, 33, 42, 159, 248
Presidio Volunteers (of SBTHP), 38, 40, 42, 47, 49, 51, 89, 166
Presidio Weaponry, 102
Presidios *see El Real Presidio de Santa Bárbara, Monterey, San Diego and San Francisco presidios*
Price, Dr. Glenn, 36
Prince of Asturias, 211
Prince of Wales, 212

Property transactions
    Santa Barbara Presidio, 38, 47–48, 65, 143–144, 184–193, 233, 241
    Santa Inés Mission Mills, 144–147, 188, 195–196, 229
Pueblo de Los Angeles, 3, 28, 30
Public History programs, 248
    At UCSB, 65
Puget, Peter, 16

Ramirez, Rob, 241
Ramona Pageant, 205
Ranchero Room, 171, 242
Rajoy, Mariano 156 Reagan, Governor, 39,39, 47, 49
Republic of Mexico, 27
Red Bluff, 189
Redevelopment Agency of Santa Barbara, 119, 140, 249–251
Redgrave, Vanessa, 163
Refugio Beach, 20
Refugio Pass, 20, 22
Remak, Dr. Joachim, 248
Reyes, Ruben, 225, *228*
Rhodes, Kendra, 172
Rickard, John, 37
Riverside, 180
Robinson, Alfred, 67, 216
Rochin Adobe, 31, 38, 144, 184, 229
Rodriguez. Moises, 9
Rogers, Tom, 109
Romanesque architecture, 212
Rose, Susan, 170–171, 175
Royal Highway *see El Camino Real*
Royal Palaces of Madrid and Aranjuez, 203
Royal Presidio of Santa Barbara *see El Real Presidio de Santa Bárbara*
Rozzelle, Rick, 193
Rudolph, Cathy, 14, 24, 85, 104, 157, 230
Ruiz, Alice Ruth, *43*, 44
Ruiz, Diane, 102
Ruiz, Kenny, 9, 94, *118*, 133

Ruiz Molero, Enrique, 242–244
Ruiz, Russell Antonio, *2*, 23, 35, 41–42, *43*, 44, 73, 89, 247
Ruiz, Russell Clay, *43*, 44, 102, *138*
Rusky, Bob, 112
Russian Incursion, 3, 15, 24
Rypins, Alice, 9, 200, 260

Saalburg, Roman fort, xi
Sacred Expedition of 1769, 1, 3
Saint Barbara Painting, *54*, 56
Saint Francis Room, 242
Saint James, 210–211
Saint Teresa, 209
Salamanca, 208–209
Salinas Pueblo Missions National Monument, 71–72
Sanchez, Gil, 50, 54
Sanchez, Dr. Joseph, 22, 159, 163
San Cristóbal de las Casas, 225
San Diego, 7, 180
San Diego Presidio 33
Sands, Janet Dowling, 22
San Francisco Presidio, 7, 33, 264
San Marcos High School, 216
San Sebastian, 208
Sanssouci Palace, 206
Santa Barbara Biltmore, *244, 246*, 244–246
Santa Barbara City College, 229
Santa Barbara Contractors Association, 239–240
Santa Barbara County Historic Landmarks Commission, 175–177
Santa Barbara Foundation, 64, 171, 249, 253
Santa Barbra: Historical Themes and Images, 260
Santa Barbara Mission Archive-Library, 253
Santa Barbara *News-Press*, 108
Santa Barbara Presidio Chapel, xiii, 215–216, 218
Santa Barbara Presidio Reconstruction projects
    Padres Quarters, 44, 49, 51, 53–54, 58
    chapel, 49, 53–54, 56–61, 63–64

INDEX   283

comandancia, 93, 97, *262*
   north east corner, 114–120
   bell tower, 164
   north west corner, 165–173
Santa Barbara Presidio Research Center, 14, 19, 22, 40–41, 71, 85, 89, 103–06, 157,159, 166, 229–234, 243, 249, 253, 255, 261, 264
Santa Barbara School of the Arts, 229
Santa Barbara Shakespeare Company, 220
Santa Barbara Trust for Historic Preservation, 34, 46, 47–49, 52–53, 64, 73–75, 81–82
   Board of Directors, 36, 53
   Santa Cruz Island, 6, 225
   Santa Inés Mission Mills, 89, 143–147, 151, 178, 184
   SBTHP acquisition, 89, 144–146
   Sale to CA State Parks, 188
Santa María del Naranco, Church of, 212
Santander, 212
Santa Monica College, 49
Santa Rosa Island, 6
Santillana del Mar, 213
Santa Ynez River, 20, 23
Santiago de Compostela, 210–211
Sardana, ancient Catalan folkloric dance, 152
Stauffer Foundation, 20
Saudi Arabia, 162
Sawasaki, Stuart, 167
SBCAG, 170
SBTHP *see* Santa Barbara Trust for Historic Preservation
Schneider, Helene, *243*, 246
Schwarzenegger, Arnold, 167, 188–189, 191
Scott, Virginia, 42, 70
Segovia, 158, 209
Serra, Saint Junípero, 1, 3, 7, 41, 63, 103, 160, 207
Seville, 159
Shalhoob Building, 75, *76*, 94
Shakespeare's *The Tempest*, 163
Sharpe, Don, 192
Shay, Bill, 112

Sheep Industry, 14, 17, 28, 30, 263
Sheets, Bob, 141, 164, 166
Sherman, William T., 204
Shimoda, Mas, 106, 109, *111*
Siebert, Teresa, 212
Slater Judge James, 87
Southwestern Mission Research Center, 71
Skowronek, Russell, 226
Smithsonian Institution, 226–228
Soldado de Cuera, 11, *13*
Spanish Barn (Torquay), 163
Spanish Colonial Research Center, 159
Spanish legal system, 17
Spanish Ministry of Culture, 158
Spann, Tony, 249
Spectrum Tours, 203
Soldado de Cuera See Also Presidio Soldiers
Spear, Lynn and Mary, *138*
Spirit of Chiapas, 225
Squillo, Eileen, 216
Stanton, Carey, 225
Starr, Kevin, 233
Stonehenge, 163
Storke, Charles, 87, 89, 97–99, 127–129, 133, 158, 189, 219
Storke, Carol, 224
Storke, Elizabeth, 96
Storke, Thomas, 37
Strategic Planning, 150
Strong, Ray, 224
Sturm, Kirk, 179–180
Sun Also Rises, The, 214
Suski Fendon, Irene, 44, 74, 83

Take Pride in America Award, 259
Tafoya, Elvira, 70
Terra 2000 Postprints, 163
Theimer, Jack, 89, 98–99, 102
Three Pickles Sandwich Shop, 187, 241
Torquay (Devon, England), 162
Tragic Sense of Life, 209
Trump, Donald, 167

Tubac presidio, 102
Turkey, 206
Twelfth Night, 220
Two Years before the Mast, 103, 216

Unamuno, Miguel, 209
Una Pastorela, 66–67, 68
UNESCO World Heritage Site, xi–xii, 20, 211, 261
University of California, Santa Barbara, 234
Un Paseo en Oro, 242
US Spain Consul, 243

Vallaure, Javier, 253, 255, *256*, 267
Valenzuela Adobe, 32
Valladolid, 158
Valley of the Moon Observatory Association, 181
Vancouver, Captain George, 6, 15–17, *16*, 151, 199, 204
Vancouver Expedition, 52
Vandenberg Air Force Base, 176
Vanishing Landscape exhibit, 224–225
Veterans Day, 218
Vicksburg, 204
Vicksburg National Military Park, 204
Victoria and Albert Museum, 163
Victoria Street Theatre, 250
Villa dei Papiri, 207

Villa, Eduardo, x, 258
Vischer plan, 93, 115, 164

Washington, George, 138
Weber, Dr. David, 98
Weimar, 206
Weldon and Hass Law Firm, 46
Westfall, Carroll William, 135
Weston, Derek, 129, 250
Westrup, Warren, 185, 192, 232, 241
Whidbey, Joseph, 16
Whitehead, Richard, 19, 40–41, 56, 73, 92–93, 103–105, *138*, 164, 247
Whittaker Building, 187
Whittaker, Elmer, 40, 141
Widera, Randy, 181
Williams, Dr. Jack, 7, 29–30
Williamsburg, 89, 248
Wilson, Guy, 60
Wine Cask, 152, 171
Winter, Dr. Robert, 135
Woodward-Clyde, 139

Yamada Brown, Kay, 109
Yamada Weisman, Linda, 109
Yanolani, 7–9, 8–9
Yoshimura, Valerie, 106–110, *108*
Yuma, 181